Jim d. Jordan

The Queen's Merchant

SIR THOMAS GRESHAM
HIS LIFE AND TIMES

The Queen's Merchant
Sir Thomas Gresham His Life and Times

Sir Thomas Gresham 1519-1579, born in London, descended from an ancient Norfolk family. His father, Sir Richard Gresham, a leading city merchant and Lord Mayor of London, was knighted by King Henry VIII for negotiating favorable loans with foreign merchants.

Like his father, Sir Thomas Gresham was an English Merchant and Financier who acted on behalf of King Edward VI (1547 - 1553) and Edward's half-sisters, Queens Mary I (1553 - 1558) and Elizabeth I (1558 - 1603).

After the accession of Elizabeth I to the throne, he spent most of his time in London when he wasn't traveling on diplomatic and financial missions for the Queen. He accumulated a great private fortune as a banker, mercer, and merchant.

Sir Thomas Gresham was the founder of the *Royal Exchange,* and he endowed *Gresham College* in London, both of which still exist today.

By applying his knowledge and principals to England's financial empire, he restored the debased currency of England and thereby reduced or in some cases eliminated the Crown's debts. The now well-known financial principal called "Gresham's Law" gets its name from him, which states: "Bad money drives out good".

BOOKS BY JIM D. JORDAN

Novels

Savage Lust ~ a Johnny Zen Novel
Bone Digger ~ a Johnny Zen Novel

Poetry
Chasing Emily
Dance of the Divine

Children's Poetry
I Found a Spider in My Shoe

Audio Book
Dracula's Journal

The Fall River Murders
and the Trial of Lizzie Borden

The Queen's Merchant ~
Sir Thomas Gresham His Life and Times

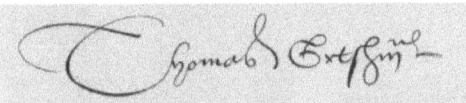

© 2017 by Jim d. Jordan

All rights reserved. No portion of this book may be reproduced without the express written permission from the author.

ISBN: 978-1-365-70961-6

Publisher Jim d. Jordan

Printed by Lulu.com U.S.A.

1st Edition: The Queen's Merchant
              Sir Thomas Gresham His Life and Times

Book Design by Jim d. Jordan

jimdjordan.com@gmail.com

Acknowledgment

This book is dedicated to my wife Jan Jordan, as always, for her love and support and for her guidance in all of my writing projects. This book carries a special purpose, as Sir Thomas Gresham is the 1st cousin 13 x removed of my wife, Jan.

Sir Thomas Gresham's father Sir Richard Gresham is her 12th great-uncle. The brother of Sir Richard - Sir John Gresham was her 12th great-grandfather, and is mentioned early in this book as well as *his* parents, John and Alice (Blyth) Gresham, Jan's 13th great-grandparents.

I also dedicate this book to my children and grand-children. This is a small piece of your history, I hope one day you'll treasure it. This book would not have been possible without the research of John William Burgon and his work entitled "The Life and Times of Sir Thomas Gresham" published in 1839, now in public domain. A full bibliography appears at the end of this book.

Certainly a huge thank you to all of my readers. Without you, all of this would be for nothing. Thank you!

~ Jim d. Jordan

PREFACE

The name Sir Thomas Gresham is prominent among those whom adorn the annals of England's past. His legacy is a tribute to the age in which he lived. His life was such that little time had he to leave any sort of written memorial of himself. Yet due to his contributions to the Crown he served, he deserves much more than a footnote in history.

He lived during the reigns of Henry VIII, Edward VI, Mary I and Elizabeth I. It was a time in which Sir Thomas Gresham flourished. It was during the reign of Henry VIII, that Sir Thomas Gresham's family first acquired distinction.

The family from which Sir Thomas Gresham was descended, like most other Norfolk families, derived its name for a little village where they had settled for many generations. Tradition points to the ruins of an ancient fortified mansion near Gresham church as their former residence. Tradition also speaks of a John Gresham who was baptized in the year 1340 at Aylmerton, Norfolk and died there in 1410, owning property in Aylmerton and an interest in the manor of Holt. *His* son, also named John Gresham, was born in 1390 and died in 1450. In 1414, this John Gresham was living at Holt.

His son James appears to have been clerk to Sir William Paston, the area judge. James Gresham was lord of the manor of East Beckham, and is said to have settled at Holt, which is only a few miles from the village where his father resided. When James Gresham left the village of Gresham for Holt he certainly exchanged a picturesque surroundings for one that was more bleak and unproductive, for Holt stood in the midst of a wild heathy moor, in the most northern part of Norfolk, being only four miles from the sea. It was here, he erected what would become "the old manor house", which occupied the center of the town. Later the manor would be converted into a free-school.

James Gresham, then had a son, again named John Gresham of Holt who would marry a woman by the name of Alice Blyth, the daughter of Alexander Blyth, of Stratton, Esquire: Alice brought her husband an ample fortune. John and Alice in turn had four sons, William, Thomas, John and Richard. The younger two sons would have the honor of knighthood bestowed upon them by King Henry VIII.

Sir Richard Gresham was Lord Mayor of London in 1537 and it is this Sir Richard Gresham who was the father of subject of this biography, Sir Thomas Gresham, founder of the Royal Exchange and Gresham College, both in the city of London. Both of which still exist today.

Before we enter into the life of Sir Thomas Gresham, it may be proper to give some account of his uncles, who were also quite memorable men in their generation.

Of William and Thomas, little is known other than what is set forth in the family pedigree. The eldest, William was a mercer and merchant-adventurer of London, and the last of the family who resided at Holt, married a lady of the Bodley family. In 1537 he was registered as one of the principal freemen householders of the "Mercers' Company", which we learn more about later in this narrative. In the year 1545, he was ranked among the most considerable merchants connected with the Low-Countries. He died at an early age and was interred in "Our-Lady-Chapel" in the church of St. Pancras, Soper-lane, (now "Bow-Lane,) on the 20th of March, 1548.

The commercial importance which Norfolk acquired at a very early period, and for which it was indebted to its geographical positon, is well known. As far back as the beginning of the twelfth century, many Flemish weavers came over and settled at Worsted in that county, which was then a large and populous town. But at present only remarkable for having bestowed its name on a particular description of woolen manufacture. In the year 1336, a large company of artisans, invited over by Edward III, established themselves permanently at Norwich. Their fleets found anchorage in Kirkley-Road, near Lowestoft, a haven which has been disused ever since the reign of Richard II. Besides their manufactures, the Flemish brought with them the arts of their country of which traces are visible to this day in painted scenes decorating the churches of Norfolk and the style of domestic architecture which they introduced.

About the year 1500, the trade with Flanders had attained its highest degree of prosperity and this may explain why, of the four sons of John and Alice Gresham, three devoted themselves to the commercial career, in which two of them, John and Richard, made such distinguished figures. It serves in particular to explain the origin of their connection with Flanders, which in the end, was productive of such important results to the family.

Thomas Gresham, the second son, entered the church, and was presented to the Rectorship of the adjoining parishes of South Repps and North Repps, in 1515 and 1519 respectively. These villages are only a few miles distance from where the Gresham family derived its name. Thomas became a senior member of the clergy of Winchester and in 1535, advanced to the chancellorship of the cathedral of Lichfield.

John Gresham, the youngest son, was a merchant of considerable importance. he was born in Holt, but apprenticed in London to a mercer by the name of John Middleton, and was admitted a member of the "Mercers' Company in 1517. At that early period, and even earlier, the English traded to Levant. Levant is the name applied widely to the eastern Mediterranean coastal lands of Asia Minor and Phoenicia (modern-day Turkey, Syria, and

Lebanon). John Gresham was one of the principal adventurers and traders. On one occasion, having hired a Portuguese vessel, and loaded it with merchandise for the English market, the Portuguese, to whom the vessel belonged, dishonestly detained it in Portugal. The cargo was valued at 12,000 ducats. Henry VIII deemed this injury done to a British subject not unworthy of his notice and he wrote to the King of Portugal, desiring that the property be restored.

Another illustration of early traffic of the Gresham family with the Levant, is supplied by the will of Lady Isabella Gresham, (Sir John's sister-in-law), where particular mention is made of her "Turkish carpets" – a great luxury for a private individual, in an age when rushes formed part of the decor of the King's Court. (Rushes are a sweet smelling, flowering plant that has been used for a number of domestic purposes including flooring material. When fresh, they added both insulation and a pleasant aroma to cover up the--frequently--muddy earthen floor. When old, some homes/cultures simply strew more rushes over the top to cover them and either rarely if ever cleaned them out.)

John Gresham became sheriff of London in 1537, the year his brother Richard, was mayor, and John was knighted while he was sheriff. One can infer that Sir John Gresham was held in high consideration, and lived as our ancestors would have said, in great worship.

Sir John Gresham was one of the "Esquires of the Body" to King Henry VIII. An Esquire of the Body performed duties as the King's personal attendant. By the time of Henry VIII, the position holders were usually knights, who were entitled to the help of two esquires and a page boy, of which at least two would always be in attendance of the King.

There were six such couriers, with a barber and a page, to attend to the King in his bedchamber when he arose in the morning. They were responsible for dressing the King in his undergarments before he entered the Privy Chamber, or private apartment as such. While the King ate, two esquires would sit at his feet while at least two served the food, and another served the drink in a cup which had been handed to him by the Chief Butler. Other times, the esquires would be on hand to help the King with menial tasks such as carrying his cloak.

During the night the Esquires of the Body had complete control of the King's household and combined in one office the functions which during the day were shared between the Lord Great Chamberlain, Gentle Ushers, and Esquires of the Body. No night-time household business could be conducted and no dispatches could be delivered to the King without the permission of the Esquire on duty.

Eventually the position in the English royal household became more of a formal positon and did not necessarily involve dressing and undressing the monarch. The function clearly needed to change when a female monarch came to the Throne, such as in the case of Queen Mary and Queen Elizabeth. During their reigns they employed "Ladies in Waiting".

While we ordinary "commoners" today, may not think of the position of Esquire of the Body as a particular glamorous job, it was and still is considered to be an honor to serve in that capacity. As Esquire of the Body, Sir John Gresham was privy to the King's most intimate and private conversations and certainly had the King's ear on everything that went on around the King.

As one of the rewards given to Sir John Gresham for his service, Henry VIII granted Gresham the manor of Sanderstead in Surrey, following the dissolution of the monasteries.

Sir John Gresham was one of the jurors who tried Thomas Culpepper and Francis Dereham for treason or "intimacy" with Queen Catherine Howard, one of Henry VIII's wives. Both were beheaded, and their heads put on display on London Bridge. Queen Catherine was subsequently executed as well.

Sir John Gresham, like his brother Sir Richard, became Lord Mayor of London. Before his death he founded Gresham's School in the town of his birth, Holt. Gresham endowed the school with land and money and placed these endowments in the care of the Worshipful Company of Fishmongers, which has continued to carry out his trust to the present day.

Sir John Gresham died of "profuse fever" on October 23, 1556, and his funeral was described as "very grand". His tomb is in the city of London at the St. Michael Bassishaw church.

The brother of Sir John Gresham, Richard was born about 1485 at Holt. He, like his brother John was a mercer or trader of goods. As a matter of fact he and John were partners in exporting textiles and importing grain from the continent. He supplied King Henry VIII with arras, velvets and satins. Most of his trade was with the Low Countries, which were the most significant area for English overseas trade for most of the sixteenth century, and he amassed a great fortune.

Richard Gresham married Audrey Lynne, who was the daughter of William Lynne of Southwick, Northamptonshire. Richard and Audrey had two sons, John, and Thomas, and two daughters, Christian who married Sir John Thynne, and Elizabeth.

Richard served as Sheriff of London, in 1531 and was knighted the same year. He was present at the execution of Anne Boleyn in the Tower of London. The following year he was elected Lord Mayor of London. He was also a member of Parliament.

Sir Richard Gresham and Cardinal Wolsey were the best of friends. Gresham supplied tapestries to Cardinal Wolsey for his new house of Hampton

Court. In October of 1520, he measured eighteen rooms and went to Flanders to order the hangings at a value of 1000 marks or more. In part payment, Gresham asked Wolsey to obtain a license for him to profit by international trade, including the right to send a ship to Turkey. When Cardinal Wolsey died in 1530, Sir Richard paid for his funeral.

After Audrey Gresham died in 1522, Richard married a second time to Isabella Worpfall who was the widow of a knight named Taverson. She survived Richard, with his death in 1549. Isabella Gresham died in April of 1565.

These earlier members of the Gresham family earned their fame and fortunes and laid the foundation of their descendant, Sir Thomas Gresham's celebrity. From them, we now turn to the character and actions of Sir Thomas Gresham, who seems to have inherited all the better qualities of his ancestors, while in his personal merit he certainly far surpassed them all.

CHAPTER I

He was the second son of Sir Richard Gresham, and his first wife Audrey, who was daughter of William Lynne, Esquire and it appears he may have been named after his uncle, the Rector of South Repps.

Thomas Gresham was born in London in the year 1519 it is believed. Of his youth we know nothing, except that his mother died when he was around three years old. He went to Cambridge and was admitted as a student of Gonville Hall. When one considers that period and his father's station in society, it is not unreasonable to presume that, as a young man, Thomas Gresham discovered abilities or inclinations above the common order, or that he should have enjoyed so high a privilege as an education at Cambridge.

At the age of twenty-five, by an arrangement made of Thomas's father, Thomas became an apprentice to his uncle John Gresham learning the merchant business. Thomas was being groomed for the same commercial success that had made his father and uncle wealthy men.

Some ten years later, in a letter to his friend John Dudley, the Duke of Northumberland concerning commercial matters, Thomas wrote:

"To the wise sense, I myself was bound as apprentice for eight years, to come by the experience and knowledge that I have. Nevertheless, I need not to have been apprenticed, for I was like my father, Sir Richard Gresham, being a wise man, I knew that I was like him and so it was of no purpose that I was bound apprentice to do the same thing as my father. Whereby to come by the experience and knowledge of all kinds of merchandise."

In other words, Thomas felt that, although he learned much from his uncle as his apprentice, it most likely was in his blood anyway to follow in his father's footsteps.

The earliest mercer notice of Thomas Gresham occurred when he was mentioned in one of the dispatches of Seymour and Wotton to King Henry VIII, written from Brussels in the month of June, 1543, and he appears already in the character of a merchant of some importance, although but twenty-four years of age. The dispatch read:

"The Regent hath granted a license for the gunpowder and saltpeter bought for your Highness, which we have delivered to young Thomas Gresham, solicitor of the same."

Allusion is made here to Henry's preparations for war with France, which led to the taking of Boulogne in the ensuing year. Thomas is again mentioned in March of 1545, by Secretary Paget, who wrote to Petre from Brussels concerning an arrest of merchandise which had taken place by order of Charles V. This unjustifiable action occurred when Henry VIII having seized certain Flemish ships which were carrying assistance to the French. Secretary Paget was speculating on the consequences likely to result to the merchant-adventurers when he wrote:

"Some indeed shall win by it, as William Lok, Sir Richard Gresham and his son Thomas, and William Gresham, with such other for the most part that occupy silks, who owe more than they have here. But Mr. Warren, Mr. Hill, and others in great number are likely to have a great swoop by it, having much here, and owing nothing or little."

*Author's Note: The spelling, language and style of these letters of antiquity make translation to modern language difficult. As such, interpreting the exact meaning is often left to the imagination as to substance intended.

Between the writing of these two letters, Thomas Gresham's marriage occurred. His wife, Anne, was the daughter of William Ferneley, of West-Creting, in Suffolk. She was the widow of William Read, a mercer of London. It appears William Read was well acquainted with the Gresham family for he appointed Sir Richard executor of his will. Read died in the beginning of 1544, and Thomas married his widow later that same year.

Thomas and Anne appears to have had only one son, named Richard, after Thomas's father, Sir Richard Gresham. Thomas *did* have an illegitimate daughter by the name of Ann, who married Nathanial Bacon, the half-brother of famed Sir Francis Bacon.

These brief excerpts comprise all that is known with certainty of the early life of Sir Thomas Gresham.

It was mentioned earlier of the friendship between Thomas Gresham and John Dudley, the Duke of Northumberland. Dudley was an English general, admiral, and politician, who led the government of the young King Edward VI from 1550 until 1553, and unsuccessfully tried to install Lady Jane Grey on the English throne after the King's death. The son of Edmund Dudley, a minister of Henry VII executed by Henry VIII, John Dudley became the ward of Sir Edward Guildford at the age of seven. He grew up in Guildford's household together with his future wife, Guildford's daughter Jane, with whom he was to have 13 children. Dudley served as Vice-Admiral and Lord Admiral from 1537 until 1547, during which time he set novel standards of navy organization and was an innovative commander at sea. He also developed a strong interest in overseas exploration. Dudley took part in the 1544 campaigns in Scotland and France and was one of Henry VIII's intimates in the last years of the reign.

Beginning in 1548, England was subject to social unrest. A series of armed revolts broke out, fueled by various religious and land ownership grievances.

The two most serious rebellions, which required major military intervention to put down, were in Devon and Cornwall and in Norfolk.

In 1549, Dudley having then the title of Earl of Warwick, was sent to Norfolk to quell the insurrection which broke out there during that year. On the night of August 23rd, he lodged at Intwood-Hall, a house about three miles from the town of Norwich, and which had been built by Thomas Gresham's father. Intwood-Hall was left to John Gresham, the older brother of Thomas, but it is believed that Thomas may very well have resided there and in subsequent years it was frequently his residence and became his property.

Another important character of this period was "Somerset" otherwise known as Edward Seymour, the 1st Duke of Somerset. He was the eldest brother of Queen Jane Seymour, the third wife of Henry VIII and therefore King Edward VI's uncle.

Justification for outbreaks of unrest was voiced throughout the country. The origin of the popular view of Somerset as being sympathetic to the rebel cause lies partly in his series of sometimes liberal, often contradictory proclamations and partly in the uncoordinated activities of the commissions he sent out in 1548 and 1549 to investigate grievances about loss of land, encroachment of large sheep flocks on common land and similar issues.

Local groups often assumed that the findings of these commissions entitled them to act against offending landlords themselves. Whatever the popular view of Somerset, the disastrous events of 1549 were taken as evidence of a colossal failure of government, and the Council lay the responsibility at Somerset's door. In July 1549, Paget of the King's council wrote to Somerset *"Every man of the council have mis-liked your proceedings ... would to God, that, at the first stir you had followed the matter hotly, and caused justice to be ministered in solemn fashion to the terror of others ..."*.

The sequence of events that led to Somerset's removal from power has often been called a *coup d'état*. By 1 October 1549, Somerset had been alerted that his rule faced a serious threat. He issued a proclamation calling for assistance, took possession of the king's person, and withdrew for safety to the fortified Windsor Castle, where Edward wrote, "Me thinks I am in prison".

Meanwhile, a united Council published details of Somerset's government mismanagement. They made clear that his power came from them, not from Henry VIII's will. On the 11th of October, the Council had Somerset arrested. Edward summarized the charges against Somerset in his *Chronicle*: "ambition, vainglory, entering into rash wars in mine youth, negligent looking on Newhaven, enriching himself of my treasure, following his own opinion, and doing all by his own authority, etc."

In February 1550, John Dudley, Earl of Warwick, emerged as the leader of the Council and, in effect, as Somerset's successor. Although Somerset was released from the Tower and restored to the Council, he was executed for in January 1552 after scheming to overthrow Dudley's regime. Edward noted his uncle's death in his *Chronicle*: "the duke of Somerset had his head cut off upon Tower Hill between eight and nine o'clock in the morning".

In contrast, Somerset's successor, John Dudley, made Duke of Northumberland in 1551, was once regarded by historians merely as a grasping schemer who cynically elevated and enriched himself at the expense of the crown. He was later recognized, and he has been credited with restoring the authority of the royal Council and returning the government to an even keel after the disasters of Somerset.

Northumberland's rival for leadership of the new regime was Thomas Wriothesley, 1st Earl of Southampton, whose conservative supporters had allied with Dudley's followers to create a unanimous Council, which they, and observers such as the Holy Roman Emperor, Charles V's ambassador, expected to reverse Somerset's policy of religious reform. Warwick, on the other hand, pinned his hopes on the king's strong Protestantism and, claiming that Edward was old enough to rule in person, moved himself and his people closer to the king, taking control of the Privy Chamber Paget, accepting a barony, joined Dudley when he realized that a conservative policy would not bring the emperor onto the English side over Boulogne. Southampton prepared a case for executing Somerset, aiming to discredit Dudley through Somerset's statements that he had done all with Dudley's co-operation. As a counter-move, Dudley convinced parliament to free Somerset, which it did on 14 January 1550. Dudley then had Southampton and his followers purged from the Council after winning the support of Council members in return for titles, and was made Lord President of the Council and great master of the king's household. Thomas Gresham's friend was now clearly the head of the government.

As for Gresham, it appears that, although for the first few years after his marriage he made London his home, his business frequently carried him to Antwerp – the great focus of commerce during this period. But he was not destined to continue long in a private station. He was already distinguished as a merchant possessing uncommon tact and ability. With a remarkable juncture in the financial affairs of the kingdom having occurred, he was soon called upon to take an important part in its management, and he was only thirty-two years of age.

CHAPTER II

The office of Royal Agent, or as it was sometimes called, King's Merchant, was of early origin. It was created out of the urgent need of an imperfect system of finance which, when the country was threatened with war, or some other source of heavy expenditure, there was but two methods of replenishing the funds of an impoverished treasury. One was to levy support or subsidies by an unjustifiable stretch of arbitrary power as the kingdom saw fit. The other was to induce wealthy merchants to advance the sums required. As the commercial wealth of Europe increased, the practice of obtaining loans from the opulent merchants settled in Germany and the Low Countries became more and more prevalent until it was finally found expedient on the part of the government to employ an agent for the express purpose of negotiating these deals. This person was always someone of high ability, influence and integrity, whose duty it was, in addition to the immediate duties of his office, to supply the state with whatever was required of foreign production.

It was also expected of this servant of the crown, that he should keep the privy-counsel informed of whatever was going on abroad and he was often called upon to act in the capacity of ambassador.

The King's Merchant was one of the highest importance and trust, in as much as it combined the duty of raising money for the Royal Crown by private loans, with that of protecting the sources from which they derived.

Thomas Gresham seems to have been frequently consulted by the Court's Counsel on financial affairs, even before his appointment as Royal Agent or King's Merchant. When in 1551 the mismanagement by Sir William Dansell, King's Merchant to the Low Countries, had caused the English Government much financial embarrassment, the authorities called Gresham for advice thereafter following his proposals.

Besides the care of providing money in Flanders to meet the necessities of the state, Thomas Gresham's correspondence indicated many other duties implored upon him. It was expected of him to keep the counsel constantly informed of all that was passing in his neighborhood or even rumored beyond the seas, a task, which was not easy in the imperfect system of communication in those days, but one in which Gresham performed in the most satisfactorily manner. It was moreover his assignment to supply the country with whatever articles of foreign manufacture were required such as arms, plate or jewelry.

None of Thomas Gresham's family had ever held the office of Royal Agent before him, although his father, uncle, brother and he himself had been repeatedly employed previous to this event, in the service of the Crown as domestic financial agents. Thomas Gresham, mercer of London, is frequently mentioned this capacity in the "Council-book" of Edward VI, long before the Dansell affair, with duties in Flanders. He must therefore, during this period, have been brought under the eye of council and in addition to the favorable testimony afforded by the confidence which had been already bestowed upon him. One may reasonably assume, from his having been sent for on the present occasion, that he enjoyed the reputation of being one of the most enlightened merchants of his day. The experience he must have acquired during the seven years of his life he had already passed mostly at Antwerp, must obviously have made him one of the best choices that could have been chosen to confer with the Lordships on the difficulties which they were now experiencing.

Perhaps never before was the judicious counsel Gresham offered more needed, for the King's financial affairs were beginning to wear an alarming appearance, having been conducted up to that period with very little proficiency, or none at all.

The expensive wars carried out against France had caused Henry VIII to incur debts, which were not always able to be discharged. As a result he was forced often when his bonds became due, to renew them on the most disadvantageous terms.

The annual interest on his bonds amounted to £40,000 (pounds) which, while the exchange was reduced to sixteen shillings Flemish to the pound sterling, he was compelled to pay in English money, and he was required, at every renewal, to purchase jewels or wares, and sometimes both, to a large amount as consideration for deferring the liquidation of the debt. This, combined with the exorbitant rate of interest, resulted much to his disadvantage. Therefore during Henry VIII's reign, debt rose tremendously.

By the time Henry's son, King Edward succeeded to the throne at the age of nine years old, this unfair imposition on the part of the money-lenders was of old standing and sanctioned by the usage of the preceding reigns. It had at last grown into a custom.

But the ministers and advisors of King Edward, who had to conduct the finance of a country impoverished by his father's extravagance, and who were ever at a loss for supplies to meet the annual expenditure, resolved to resist every attempt to repeat it, a resolution, of which Thomas Gresham, in accepting the office of Royal Agent, was unaware of, at first brought him into considerable difficulties.

In December of 1551, or the following January, Thomas Gresham was called upon to serve the King. In order to better attend to the important duties which were now pressed upon him, he moved with his wife and family to Antwerp where he established himself in the house of Jasper Schetz, a merchant with whom he had long been connected by friendship, and under whose roof he had previously had occasion to reside. The Schetz family was one of the most distinguished in the city and Jasper was the most distinguished member of his family. He was in case, principal Factor to the Emperor Charles V.

Antwerp had become the center of international economy and the most commercial capital in Europe. It was no uncommon sight to see two or three hundred vessels loaded with merchandise from every quarter of the globe, on the River Scheldt, which linked to the North Sea.

During the first two years Gresham served King Edward, he wrote to the Court from Antwerp, upon receiving assignments, no less than forty times. Not all of his commercial dealings can be recounted, but of several, we have distinct intelligence. The first we hear of, occurred in January of 1551-2, at which time he was sent a commission to negotiate concerning the payment of certain moneys owed to the Fuggers. The Fugger family was a German family that was a historically prominent group of international mercantile bankers, and venture capitalists. Alongside another German family named Welser, they controlled much of the European economy in the sixteenth century accumulating enormous wealth.

Thomas Gresham discovered much to his displeasure that money that had been taken up for the purpose of paying the King's debt was not being paid by the time agreed upon. This meant that it fell to him to try to prolong payment to creditors and he did not like doing business that way at all. The creditors would then insist on upon the King's purchasing jewels and other commodities to a considerable value as a consideration of prolonging the debt payment not to mention the interest accumulating.

Gresham wrote to his old friend the Duke of Northumberland, the leading member of council and to King Edward explaining his proposal. In the letter he asked if there wasn't some other way to be taken for his Majesty's debts, but to force men from time to time to prolong it. Gresham felt that by doing this, in the end, he would neither be honorable nor profitable to his Highness. In consideration whereof, if there was no other ways going forward, he asked the King that he be discharged of the office of Royal Agent. For otherwise he saw in the end that he would receive shame and discredit which would be his undoing forever. But what would be worse than that would be the King's honor and credit would be spotted, especially in foreign countries.

But, Thomas Gresham had a plan if the council and His Majesty would consent to it, and if they did, he believed he could dissolve the King's debt within two years.

He asked that the King and council to assign to him £1,200 or £1,300 pounds per week, kept strictly secret that he would use at Antwerp. Every day he would be seen to take up in his own name, the sum of £200 pounds sterling at the Exchange. By doing this it would not be brought to the attention of others, nor would it appear to cause the rate of exchange to fall. By the advantageous turn, Gresham said, it would likely *rise* than fall and that he had no doubt that it would continue to do so. As the exchange rises, all the commodities in England would fall. And as the exchange falls, so all the commodities in England would rise. Also, if the exchange rises, it would be the right occasion that all our gold and silver shall remain within our realm. It would also mean other realms shall bring in gold and silver, as they have heretofore done.

How correct Gresham was in the results he had anticipated from these measures. He found the means in a short space to raise the exchange from sixteen shillings Flemish for the pound sterling, to twenty-two shillings at which rate he discharged all the King's debts, and by this means money was rendered plentiful and trade prosperous while the credit of the Crown became established on a firmer basis abroad than it had ever before. All this he foresaw, but the merchants, at the time, complained loudly of his proceedings and it required no slight dexterity to appease them.

Gresham said that "even my uncle, Sir John Gresham had said in a letter to the Duke that he was a little "stormed" with me for the setting of the price of the exchange, and said that it lies in me now to do the merchants of this realm pleasure to increase my poor name among the merchants forever." Gresham added, "I have thought about it and it is no wonder that my uncle Sir John Gresham was stormed about the matter, for he had bought four or five thousand pounds in wools." And to answer the question posed to Thomas Gresham about the matter between him and his uncle – he said "Yes, we had words about it and it seemed likely we were to have a falling out, but before we departed, we drank to each other."

It was so successful that in a few years nearly all King Edward's debts were discharged. The advice of Gresham was likewise sought by the government in all their money difficulties and he was frequently employed in various diplomatic missions. He had no stated salary, but as reward for his service, he received from Edward various grants of lands.

Thomas Gresham continued receiving from the council expressions of the gratitude of his management of the affairs of the Crown. The young King himself was so aware of the services Gresham had done for him that only three weeks before his death, King Edward bestowed upon him lands worth £100 pounds per year and the young king who was fifteen at the time, accompanied the land gift with the encouraging words, "You shall know that you have served a King." It is certain that the preceding was by no means the only instance of bounty Gresham received at his royal master's hands. Westacre-Priory in

Norfolk, which was of much greater value, was also bestowed upon him in the last year of Edward VI's reign.

CHAPTER III

Young King Edward VI became ill during January 1553 with a fever and cough that gradually worsened. The imperial resident at the Court of King Edward VI, Jean Scheyfve, ambassador of the Holy Roman Empire, reported that "He suffers a good deal when the fever is upon him, especially from a difficulty in drawing his breath, which is due to the compression of the organs on the right side". Edward felt well enough in early April to take the air in the park at Westminster and to move to Greenwich, but by the end of the month he had weakened again. By the 7th of May he was "much amended," and the royal doctors had no doubt of his recovery. A few days later the King was watching the ships on the Thames, sitting at his window. However, he relapsed, and on the 11th of June, Scheyfve, who had an informant in the King's household, reported that "the matter he ejects from his mouth is sometimes colored a greenish yellow and black, sometimes pink, like the color of blood". Now his doctors believed he was suffering from "a suppurating tumor" of the lung and admitted that Edward's life was beyond recovery. Soon, his legs became so swollen that he had to lie on his back, and he lost the strength to resist the disease. To his tutor John Cheke he whispered, "I am glad to die".

Edward made his final appearance in public on July 1st, when he showed himself at his window in Greenwich Palace, horrifying those who saw him in his "thin and wasted" condition. During the next two days, large crowds arrived hoping to see the King again, but on the 3rd, they were told that the weather was too chilly for him to appear. Edward died at the age of 15 at Greenwich Palace at 8:00 p.m. on July 6th 1553. It is said his last words were: "I am faint; Lord have mercy upon me, and take my spirit". He was buried in the Henry VII Lady Chapel at Westminster Abbey on the 8th of August 1553, with reformed rites performed by Thomas Cranmer. The procession was led by a great company of children and watched by Londoners weeping and lamenting. The funeral chariot, draped in gold cloth, was topped by an effigy of Edward, complete with crown and scepter.

The cause of Edward VI's death is not certain. As with many royal deaths in the 16th century, rumors of poisoning abounded, but no evidence has been found to support these. The Duke of Northumberland, whose unpopularity was underlined by the events that followed Edward's death, was widely believed to have ordered the imagined poisoning. Another theory held that Edward had been poisoned by Catholics seeking to bring his half-sister, Mary to the throne. The surgeon who opened Edward's chest after his death found that "the disease whereof his majesty died was the disease of the lungs".

When Edward became ill and his illness discovered to be terminal, he and his counsel drew up what was called a "Devise for the Succession". This was to prevent Mary from succeeding to the Throne and having the country return to Catholicism. Edward himself opposed Mary's succession, not only on religious grounds but also on those of legitimacy and male inheritance, which also applied to his other half-sister Elizabeth. He composed a draft document, headed "My devise for the succession", in which he undertook to change the succession. He passed over the claims of his half-sisters and at last settled the Crown on his first cousin once removed, the 16-year old Lady Jane Grey, who on the 25th of May, 1553 had married Lord Guilford Dudley, a younger son of the Duke of Northumberland.

In his document Edward provided for, in case of "lack of issue of my body" (no children), the succession of *male heirs only*, that meant Jane Grey's *mother's* - male heirs, not Jane's or her sister's male heirs. As his death approached, possibly persuaded by Northumberland, he altered the wording so that Jane and her sisters themselves should be able to succeed. Yet Edward conceded Jane's right only as an exception to the male rule. In the final document both Mary and Elizabeth were excluded because they were regarded as bastards, since both had been declared illegitimate under Henry VIII and never made legitimate again.

Lady Mary was last seen by Edward in February, and was kept informed about the state of her brother's health by Northumberland and through her contacts with the imperial ambassadors. Aware of Edward's imminent death, she left Hunsdon House, near London, and sped to her estates around Kenninghall in Norfolk, where she could count on the support of her tenants. Northumberland sent ships to the Norfolk coast to prevent her escape or the arrival of reinforcements from the continent. He delayed the announcement of the king's death while he gathered his forces, and Jane Grey was taken to the Tower on the 10th of July. On the same day, she was proclaimed Queen in the streets of London, to murmurings of discontent. The Privy Council received a message from Mary asserting her "right and title" to the throne and commanding that the Council proclaim her Queen, as she had already proclaimed herself. The Council replied that Jane was Queen by Edward's authority and that Mary, by contrast, was illegitimate and supported only by "a few lewd, base people".

Northumberland soon realized that he had miscalculated drastically, not least, in failing to secure Mary's person before Edward's death. Although many of those who rallied to Mary were conservatives hoping for the defeat of Protestantism, her supporters also included many for whom her lawful claim to the throne overrode religious considerations. Northumberland was obliged to relinquish control of a nervous Council in London and launch an unplanned pursuit of Mary into East Anglia, from where news was arriving of her growing support, which included a number of nobles and gentlemen and "innumerable companies of the common people". On the 14th of July, Northumberland marched out of London with three thousand men, reaching Cambridge the next day. Meanwhile, Mary rallied her forces at Framlingham Castle in Suffolk, gathering an army of nearly twenty thousand by July 19th.

It now dawned on the Privy Council that it had made a terrible mistake. Led by the Earl of Arundel and the Earl of Pembroke, on July 19th the Council publicly proclaimed Mary as Queen and Jane's nine-day reign came to an end. The proclamation triggered wild rejoicing throughout London. Stranded in Cambridge, Northumberland himself, proclaimed Mary - Queen, as he had been commanded to do by a letter from the Council. William Paget and the Earl of Arundel rode to Framlingham to beg Mary's forgiveness, and Arundel arrested Northumberland on the 24th of July.

Northumberland was beheaded on the 22nd of August, shortly after renouncing Protestantism. His recantation dismayed his daughter-in-law, Jane, who followed him to the scaffold on the 12th of February 1554, after her father's involvement in Wyatt's rebellion.

Upon the accession of Mary, Thomas Gresham found himself suddenly ousted from his office as Royal Agent, a circumstance easily accounted for, when it is remembered that his close friend was the Northumberland, who was the very person most hostile to the Queen's succession. Gresham was, besides, personally obnoxious on the score of his religious opinions and found a bitter enemy in Stephen Gardiner, the Roman Catholic Bishop of Winchester, whom the Queen restored to the position, her predecessor had deprived of him.

Gresham wrote to the Queen saying; *"When the King, your brother died, for reward of my service the Bishop of Winchester sought to undo me and whatsoever I said in matters of finance, that I should not be credited. First,* before I was called to save the King's Majesty, (reputation), One Sir William Dansell, knight, was his agent. At that time his Majesty was indebted in the sum of two hundred three score, thousand pounds Flemish. For the discharge whereof, and for other causes to me unknown, Dansell was written to come home, which he refused to do. Thereupon I was sent for unto the counsel and brought by them afore the King to hear my opinion, as they had many other merchants, as to what the best way to lessen his debt. After my advice was declared, the King and counsel required me to take over as Royal Agent.

Secondly: before I was called to serve, there was no other way devised to bring the King out of debt, but to transport treasure out of the realm or else by way of exchange, to the great abasing of the exchange. A pound of our currency was brought down in value. And for lack of payment there at the days appointed, to preserve his Majesties credit withal, it was customary to prolong time also upon interest. The interest, besides the loss of the Exchange, amounted to £40,000 pounds per year.

In every such prolonging, his Majesty was forced to take great sums of jewels or wares, to his extreme loss for interest, yearly. I have, by my travels, clearly discharged the King every penny. Without which prevention, the Queen's Majesty would be indebted at this, her entry into the imperial crown, in the sum of four-hundred-thousand pounds. Besides the saving of the treasury within the realm, without having to take jewels or wares to the King's loss or disprofit.

Thirdly: Whereas at the time of my entry into the office, I found the Exchange at sixteen shillings to the pound, I found the means nevertheless without any charge to the King, or hindrance of any other, to discharge the King's whole debts as they grew due, at twenty-shillings to the pound, whereby the King and now the Queen has saved one-hundred thousand marks clear.

Fourthly: By reason that I raised the exchange to where it yet remains, all foreign commodities have fallen, and sold after the same value, to the enriching of the subjects of the realm in their commodities in a small amount of time.

Fifthly: By reason of raising of the Exchange like in the times passed, the gold and silver was abundantly transported out of the realm by the abasing, even so, contrary wise, now it is most plentifully brought in again by the raising. For there has come already of late, above £100,000 pounds into the realm and more and more will daily.

Sixthly: It is assuredly known, that when I took this service in hand, the King's credit on the other side was small. Yet, before his death, he was in such credit both with stranger and his own merchants that he might have had the amount of money he desired. Whereby his enemies began to fear him, for the commodities of his realm and where his power was not known before. Which credit the Queens Highness has obtained if she were in necessity for money at this present day.

Seventhly: To the intent to work this matter secretly, for the raising of the exchange I did use my own credit with my substance and friends to the extent to prevent the merchants, both stranger and English, who always lay in wait to prevent my devices. Also when the exchange fell, to raise it again, I bore for some time my own losses of my own money as the King and his counsel well know. This was several times done. Besides the credit of fifty-thousand pounds which I took by exchange in my own name without using the King's name, as in my account and letters remaining, which I sent to his Majesty.

Eighthly: For the accomplishment of the premises, I not only left the realm with my wife and family, my occupying and whole trade of living for the space of two years, but also posted in that time forty times, upon the King's sending, at the least, from Antwerp to the Court. Besides practicing to bring these matters to effect—the infinite occasion of writing also to the King and his counsel—with the keeping of reckonings and accomplishments until I had clearly discharged all the foresaid debt and delivered all the bonds clear to the great benefit of the realm and profit of the Queen. For in case this debt had been left alone and differed upon interest four or five years, her Majesty would have found it amounted to fifteen-hundred-thousand pounds at least. Which God be praised, is ended and therefore careless at this day.

For consideration of my great losses and charges and travels taken by me in the causes aforesaid, it pleased the King's Majesty to give unto me one-hundred pounds to me and my heirs forever three weeks before his death and promised me then with his own mouth that he would see me rewarded better, saying "I should know that I served a King". And so I did find him, for whose soul to God I daily pray.

Finally: If upon the consideration of the former articles of my service made, which is all true, you shall think them all met and it shall be her Grace's pleasure to accept them—also as I may have access to her Highness thereby, I doubt not, to do her Grace as good profitable service both for her and her realm, as the former service of her brother. Nevertheless, hitherto I do perceive that those which served before me, which brought the King in debt and took wares and jewels to the King's great loss, are esteemed and preferred for their evil service, and contrary wise myself discontinuance, and out of favor. Which grieves me, for my diligence and good service taken to bring the King and Queen out of debt. The understanding of my service that her Majesty may take in good part is a much as I required.

As I was writing this letter, I received a letter from Flanders whereby I understand that my household stuff, and apparel of myself and my wife which I had sent and prepared to Antwerp is all lost. And now, God help poor Gresham!

Also the Lord of Northumberland owes me £400 pounds for jewels and wares that my factor sold him in my absence. Trusting that the Queen Majesty will be good unto me therein.

That Thomas Gresham had been treated unfairly cannot be doubted, but dismayed perhaps by the ruin of his late patron, and the evil plight of his friends at the court, he apprehended greater misfortune than actually fell to his share.

On the 27th of August, the privy council received Gresham's letter dated eleven days earlier and addressed to the Queen. His enemies had perhaps already begun to realize that their scheming against him might not succeed and may even backfire upon themselves. Whatever the cause of Thomas Gresham's ousting by the new monarch, whether it was actual injury or simple the object of neglect, it wouldn't be long before he was restored to favor of Queen Mary.

Gresham would later confide to his friend William Cecil, the English statesman, and who would become the chief advisor of Queen Elizabeth I for most of her reign, twice Secretary of State (1550–1553 and 1558–1572) and Lord High Treasurer from 1572, that had it not been for a certain "mysterious" man named Sir John Leye, who spoke in his behalf thereby procuring his safety, he, (Gresham) may have been sacrificed after the accession of Queen Mary. "For verily, sir, he was the man that preserved me when Queen Mary came to the crown, for which I do account myself bound to him during my life."

That he should have been the man who preserved Gresham when Queen Mary came to the crown, at a time when the life of many distinguished Protestants were in jeopardy and the whole country was shaken to its very core, is enough to prove that whoever he may have been, Sir John Leye was a Roman Catholic gentleman who possessed the ear of the Queen and to a remarkable degree had her confidence.

It is possible that in the course of his travels, he had occasion to visit Antwerp and while there became acquainted with Thomas Gresham or at least aware of who he was and what he had accomplished there for King Edward.

The death of King Edward doubtless brought Leye in common with many other exiles of the same religious persuasion, into England, and there he became privy to all that passed in the council chamber of the new Queen. Touched with sympathy for a man whose fortunes were suddenly blighted and perhaps whose very existence he perceived to be in jeopardy.

In the month following Mary's accession, she issued a proclamation that she would not compel any of her subjects to follow her religion, but by the end of September leading Protestant churchmen including John Bradford, John Rogers, John Hooper, Hugh Latimer, and Thomas Cranmer, were imprisoned. Mary's first Parliament, which assembled in early October, declared the marriage of her parents valid and abolished Edward's religious laws. Church doctrine was restored to the form it had taken in the 1539 Six Articles, which among other things, re-affirmed clerical celibacy.

By the end of 1554, the Heresy Acts were revived. Under the Heresy Acts, numerous Protestants were executed. Around 800 rich Protestants, including Thomas Gresham, chose exile instead. The first executions occurred over a period of five days in early February 1555: John Rogers on the 4th of February, Laurence Saunders on the 8th of February, and Rowland Taylor and John Hooper on the 9th of February. Thomas Cranmer, the imprisoned archbishop of Canterbury, was forced to watch Bishops Ridley and Latimer being burned at the stake. Cranmer recanted, repudiated Protestant theology, and rejoined the Catholic faith. Under the normal process of the law, he should have been absolved as a repentant. Mary, however, refused to reprieve him. On the day of his burning, he dramatically withdrew his recantation. In total, 283 were executed, most by burning. The victims of the persecutions became lauded as martyrs. Mary earned the nickname "Bloody Mary".

She had always rejected the break with Rome instituted by her father, Henry VIII, and the establishment of Protestantism by her brother's regents. Henry's religious laws were repealed thus returning the English church to Roman jurisdiction.

Reaching an agreement took many months and Mary and Pope Julius III had to make a major concession: the monastery lands confiscated under Henry were not returned to the church but remained in the hands of their influential new owners, which included Sir Richard Gresham. He had obtained several land grants and monasteries as a result of his service to both Henry VIII and to Edward VI.

Evidence shows that during the first few weeks of Queen Mary's reign, financial matters were also among the foremost which occupied her council's attention. It seems that, rather than avail themselves of the services of the late King's financial agent, (Gresham), who was notorious for his strong Protestant bias, they took upon themselves to procure supplies by writing directly to the Fuggers at Antwerp, and commissioning certain persons, men who Gresham had superseded in the former reign, to negotiate the required loans. This turned out to be disastrous however and it wasn't long before they were contacting Gresham for help.

Thomas Gresham found himself in the unique position to be able to set forth terms on which he was willing to resume his office. Terms which would establish Gresham as a financial genius and make him one the wealthiest men in all of England throughout not only Mary's reign but Queen Elizabeth I as well.

CHAPTER IV

No sooner was Gresham reinstated in office, than his services were put in requisition. He was dispatched to Antwerp, to assure the merchants of that town of the validity of all outstanding obligations. In addition, he was to buy ammunition and take up some additional sums for the repayment of which the city cheerfully gave their bonds. His commission assigned to him, as usual, an allowance of 20*s* (shillings) per day, and for the time he has been in the realm, since his last coming over, 12*s* , 4*d* by the day. (perhaps a note should be made here on the monetary values of the time) It should be said that in addition to his salary, Gresham received grants of church lands to the yearly value of £200.

There was no paper money. Coins were minted in gold and silver. The English pound originated from a measure of weight which was used to represent a sum of money. 240 pennies equaled a pound or 20 shillings equaled one pound. The penny was the basic monetary unit of the period. The names of the English units of currency and how they were abbreviated in written form date back to the Roman period.

A pence was expressed as the letter *d* - an abbreviation of denarius, a silver Roman coin.

A shilling was expressed as the letter *s* – an abbreviation for sestertius, a silver Roman coin.

A pound was (and still is) a letter 'L' crossed with a bar, expressed as £ which derives its name from an abbreviation for Libra, the Latin word for pounds.

Just as today, the amount of wages was purely dependent on the job or occupation. The Elizabethan lower class would have only traded in pennies. A pound would have been out of their reach in terms of spendable money and currency. Some examples of the wages during this period are:

A nobleman - £1500 to £3000 per annum.

A merchant - £100 per annum.

A parson - £20 per annum.

A carpenter - £13 per annum.

But enough about such matters. I hope that will help you to understand the monetary values for the period Gresham lived.

So now we find Thomas Gresham back at his old occupation, advising the highest person in the land on the subject which immediately affected the well-being of the government, and which, even by the best informed, was at that time but imperfectly understood. There is something almost patriarchal in the tone and manner of which Gresham addressed the new Queen in his letters where he exposes the origin and progress of an evil, which he had made several vigorous efforts to remedy. But he had to contend with private animosity as well as with the vacillations of Court favor.

A new page however, was now turned in Gresham's history. The Royal lady who had just ascended the throne of her ancestors, had assured him with her own lips of her good opinion and favorable disposition toward him. Once more, therefore, did he briefly expose his views and sketch what he conceived to be her best line of financial policy, closing his address to her with these words:

"And it please you Majesty to restore this your realm into such estate as heretofore it hath been, first your highness hath none other ways, but, when time and opportunity serves to bring your base money into fine standing, and the same with gold after the rate."

"Secondly, not to restore the Steelyard to their usurped privilege." (The Steelyard was the foreign trading post in London)

"Thirdly, to grant as few licenses as you can."

"Fourthly, to come in as small a debt as you can overseas."

"Fifthly, to keep your credit and especially with your own merchants, for it is they who must stand by you, at all events in your necessity"

Queen Mary's instructions to Gresham on being sent to Antwerp to mend the ill actions of Dauntsey were written on the 13th of November 1553.

Where we have been informed that Lazarus Tucker and certain other merchants of Antwerp have of their own good wills offered to lend us diverse great sums of money. We, remembering the great debts left unpaid at the death of our late brother, and considering that as well in respect thereof as for many other great causes, it should be very expedient for the commonwealth of our realm to have a good mass of money in readiness to serve in all events. I have thought to accept the said offers (Gresham's requirements). And for the better understanding of the said merchant's meanings and full concluding with them, have appointed our said servant (Gresham) to proceed in such form as follows.

First: the said Thomas Gresham, repairing to Flanders, shall meet and bargain in our name and for our use with such merchants as he may seem most met, for the sum of fifty-thousand pounds, or so much under that sum as he may get or attain unto, to be lent unto us for one year, to be repaid in Antwerp at the year's end with interest.

And for the arrangement of the repayment, we are pleased that the said Thomas Gresham shall commit to deliver such and like bonds covenants and assurance to be by us signed and sealed with our great seal and with the seal also of our city of London, as he did in the time of my late brother and has in similar cases.

And it shall be also lawful to our servant to take up from time to time during this commission, money by exchange upon his own credit in Flanders, to be delivered in London for our use.

All such sums of money as Thomas Gresham shall take up upon interest or by exchange, shall by him in most secret manner sent to London, in such coins of gold and silver as the said Gresham shall think most met, to be laden in Antwerp to London or Ipswich in every ship that shall depart to either of the said places, not exceeding one thousand pounds sterling in one cargo load. And further it shall be also for our said servant from time to time to send to London over land from Antwerp to Calais (France) and so to London, by every such trusty person or persons as he shall put in trust, the sum of £3000 pounds sterling. The adventure of all such sums of money shall be sent over both by sea and land to be born from time to time at our charge and jeopardy.

And to the intent the said Gresham may better execute the charge committed by us partly unto him or pleasure is that of the money to be by him received by force of this commission he shall retain in his own hands and to his own use, not only the debts for every day, the same to begin the day of the date of these points inclusive and to continue during his abode about our service in this behalf. Also all such money as he shall pay for sending of any messengers, letters or treasure unto us. For the allowance whereof these instructions shall be sufficient warrant to such as shall hereafter have authority to hire his accompaniment for the premises.

On the 23rd of November, Gresham received communication from the council, ordering him to take up his commitment. All of which he accomplished, returning to England before the close of the year.

Of Thomas Gresham, we have, up to now spoken chiefly in his capacity of Royal Agent - procuring military stores for the protection of the country and negotiating occasional loans to meet the necessities of the government. But his employment, as it did not engage all his time, so did it not engage all his attention.

We know he had been bred a mercer, and he exercised that craft up to the period when he was first employed in the service of the government. For the first year or two, after his appointment, he found duties assigned to him, so pressing in nature, that he did not hesitate, as he expressed it, *"to forsake his own trade of living, for better serving of his majesty."* But the necessity for doing so was not permanent.

Throughout a considerable portion of Mary's reign, Gresham pursued his original avocations in Flanders, and after a few years, under Elizabeth I, we shall find him resuming his practice at home. He was able to accomplish this by allowing future management of his affairs in the Low Countries to be managed by Richard Clough, a Welshman, whom he left behind at Antwerp, and in whose zeal and ability he expressed entire confidence.

This interesting individual belonged to a family which had been settled from an early period in North Wales, but which first acquired eminence in his person. His father, Richard Clough, was of sufficient consideration in Denbigh, where he followed the trade of a glover, (someone who makes gloves) to become allied by marriage to two families of worship, the surname of which his first wife was "Holland" and his second wife was a "Whittingham". He lived to a great old age and left by these two ladies, eight children. Gresham's partner—Richard—is believed to be the fifth of these siblings.

In his early youth, he was a chorister in the cathedral of Chester, Wales, where some were so affected by his singing, that they were "loath he should lose himself in empty air", for church music was beginning then to be discontinued. He was persuaded to move to London, where he became an apprentice to,

Thomas Gresham. There is no doubt that Richard Clough earned much confidence and friendship of Sir Thomas Gresham and while he was in his service, due to his abilities, he was able to amass a large fortune. He must have been considered a man of great consideration, for we will see later on, he married into a family of high distinction.

Sir Thomas Gresham continued his role as the Queen's Merchant throughout Queen Mary I's reign, traveling an immense amount of time. One has to wonder how so much travelling affected his marriage. Perhaps his scarcity of being home contributed to his and Anne having only one child between them.

CHAPTER V

Speaking of marriage, at the age of 37, Queen Mary turned her attention to finding a husband and producing an heir, thus preventing her Protestant half-sister Elizabeth who was next in line to the throne, from succeeding her. Edward Courtenay and Reginald Pole were both mentioned as prospective suitors, but her cousin Charles V suggested she marry his only son, Prince Philip of Spain.

Lord Chancellor Gardiner and the House of Commons tried to convince her to consider marrying an Englishman, fearing that England would be relegated to a dependency of the Habsburgs. The House of Habsburg was one of the most influential royal houses in Europe. From the sixteenth century, following the reign of Charles V, the dynasty was split between Austrian and Spanish branches. Although they ruled distinct territories, they nevertheless maintained close relations and frequently intermarried.

In the end, Mary consented to marry Prince Philip, a marriage which was unpopular with the English. Gardiner and his allies opposed it on the basis of patriotism, while Protestants were motivated by a fear of Catholicism.

When Mary insisted on marrying Philip, insurrections broke out. Thomas Wyatt led a force from Kent to depose Mary in favor of her sister Elizabeth, as part of a wider conspiracy now known as Wyatt's rebellion, which also involved Henry Grey, the 1st Duke of Suffolk, the father of Lady Jane Grey.

On the 26th of January, Wyatt occupied Rochester, and issued a proclamation to the county. Many country people and local gentry collected. At first the Queen's supporters, led by Lord Abergavenny and Sir Robert Southwell, the sheriff, appeared to be able to suppress the rising with ease, routing a rebel force of 500 at Hartley Wood on the 28th.

However, Abergavenny and Southwell, were deserted by their men, who either disbanded or went over to Wyatt's side. He now had 3000 men at his command. A detachment from London was sent against him under the command of the elderly Duke of Norfolk. But they also joined the rebels, raising their numbers to 4000, while the Duke fled to London.

Meanwhile Elizabeth had been summoned to the Court and was held without her being in contact with what was going on and in mortal fear. The rising seemed so formidable that the Queen and Council sent a messenger to Wyatt to ask for his terms. He demanded that the Tower of London should be surrendered to him, and the Queen put under his charge. The insolence of these demands turned what was initially a sympathetic London against Wyatt. Mary was able to rally the capital to her cause on the 1st of February by delivering a rousing speech.

When Wyatt's army reached Southwark on the 3rd, Mary's supporters occupied London Bridge in force and the rebels were unable to penetrate into the city. Refusing to give up, the rebels marched to Kingston. The bridge there had been destroyed, but the rebels repaired it and crossed over. They met little resistance as they marched through the outskirts of London, but were stopped by the inhabitants of Ludgate. The rebel army then broke up.

Upon reaching London, Wyatt was defeated and surrendered. He was tried and executed along with approximately 90 rebels, many of whom were hanged, drawn and quartered. Wyatt himself, after being severely tortured in the hope of extracting a confession implicating Elizabeth, was beheaded at Tower Hill and his body quartered. The Duke of Suffolk, his daughter Lady Jane, and her husband Guildford Dudley were executed. Courtenay, who was implicated in the plot was imprisoned, and then exiled. Elizabeth, though protesting her innocence in the Wyatt affair, was imprisoned in the Tower of London for two months, then was put under house arrest for nearly a year at Woodstock Palace.

Under English common law doctrine, the property and titles belonging to a woman became her husband's upon marriage, and it was feared that any man the Queen married would thereby become King of England in fact and in name.

Under the terms of Queen Mary's Marriage Act, Philip was to be styled "King of England", all official documents, including Acts of Parliament were to be signed with both their names, and Parliament was to be called under the joint authority of the couple, for Mary's lifetime only. England would not be obliged to provide military support to Philip's father in any war, and Philip could not act without his wife's consent or appoint foreigners to office in England. Philip was not happy at the conditions imposed, but he was ready to agree for the sake of securing the marriage. He had no amorous feelings toward Mary and sought the marriage for its political and strategic gains only.

The marriage took place at Winchester Cathedral on July 25th 1554, just two days after their first meeting. Philip could not speak English, so they spoke in a mixture of Spanish, French, and Latin.

In September of 1554, Mary stopped menstruating. She gained weight and felt nauseated in the mornings. For these reasons, almost the entirety of her court, including her doctors, believed her to be pregnant. Parliament passed an act making Philip regent in the event of Mary's death in childbirth. In the last week of April 1555, Elizabeth was released from house arrest, and called to court as a witness to the birth which was expected at any time. If Mary and her child died, Elizabeth would become Queen. If, on the other hand, Mary gave birth to a healthy child, Elizabeth's chances of becoming Queen would recede sharply.

Thanksgiving services in the diocese of London were held at the end of April after false rumors that Mary had given birth to a son spread across Europe. Through May and June, the apparent delay in delivery fed gossip that Mary was not pregnant.

Mary continued to exhibit signs of pregnancy until July, when her abdomen receded. There was no baby. It was most likely a false pregnancy perhaps induced by Mary's overwhelming desire to have a child. In August, soon after the disgrace of the false pregnancy, which Mary considered to be "God's punishment for her having tolerated heretics in her realm." Philip left England to command his armies against France in Flanders. Mary was heartbroken and fell into a deep depression.

Elizabeth remained at court until October, apparently restored to favor. In the absence of any children, Philip was concerned that after Mary and Elizabeth, one of the next claimants to the English throne was the Queen of Scots, who was betrothed to Francis II, the Dauphin of France. Philip persuaded Mary that Elizabeth should marry his cousin Emmanuel Philibert, Duke of Savoy, to secure the Catholic succession and preserve the Habsburg interest in England, but Elizabeth refused to comply. Besides Parliament wasn't likely to consent either.

In January of 1556, Mary's father-in-law abdicated and Philip became King of Spain, with Mary as his consort. They were still apart when Philip was declared King of Brussels, but Mary stayed in England. Philip negotiated an unsteady truce with the French in February and the following month, the French ambassador in England, Antoine de Noailles was implicated in a plot against Mary when Sir Henry Dudley, a second cousin of the executed Duke of Northumberland, attempted to assemble an invasion force in France. The plot, known as the Dudley conspiracy, was discovered and the conspirators in

England were rounded up. Dudley remained in exile in France, and Noailles quickly fled England.

Philip returned to England from March to July in 1557 to persuade Mary to support Spain in a renewed war against France. Mary was in favor of declaring war, but her councilors including her financial advisor Sir Thomas Gresham opposed it because French trade would be jeopardized.

The years of Mary's reign were consistently wet. The persistent rain and subsequent flooding led to famine. A series of poor harvests meant England lacked supplies and finances, much to Gresham's despair.

War was declared in June 1557 after Reginald Pole's nephew, Thomas Stafford, invaded England and seized Scarborough Castle with French help in a failed attempt to depose Mary. As a result of the war, relations between England and the Papacy became strained, since Pope Paul IV was allied with Henry II of France.

In January 1558, French forces took Calais, England's sole remaining possession on the European mainland. Although the territory was financially burdensome, it was an ideological loss that damaged Mary's prestige.

Another problem was the decline of the Antwerp cloth trade. Despite Mary's marriage to Philip, England did not benefit from Spain's enormously lucrative trade with the New World. The Spanish guarded their trade routes jealously, and Mary could not condone illicit trade or piracy against her husband. In an attempt to increase trade and rescue the English economy, Mary's counsellors continued Northumberland's policy of seeking out new commercial opportunities. She granted a royal charter to the Muscovy Company, whose first governor was Sebastian Cabot, and commissioned a world atlas from Diogo Homem. Adventurers such as John Lok and William Towerson sailed south in an attempt to develop links with the coast of Africa.

Financially, Mary's regime tried to reconcile a modern form of government—with correspondingly higher spending—with a medieval system of collecting taxation and dues. Mary retained the Edwardian appointee William Paulet, 1st Marquis of Winchester, as Lord High Treasurer and assigned him to oversee the revenue collection system. A failure to apply new tariffs to new forms of imports meant that a key source of revenue was neglected. To solve this problem, Mary's government published a revised "Book of Rates" in 1558, which listed the tariffs and duties for every import.

After Philip's visit in 1557, Mary thought herself pregnant again with a baby due in March 1558. She decreed in her will that her husband be the regent during the minority of her child. However, no child was born, and Mary was forced to accept that Elizabeth was her lawful successor.

Mary was weak and ill from May 1558. In pain, possibly from ovarian cysts or uterine cancer, she died on the 17th of November 1558 aged 42 at St. James's Palace, during an influenza epidemic that also claimed the life of Reginald Pole later the same day. She was succeeded by her half-sister. Philip, who was in Brussels, wrote to his sister Joan: "I felt a reasonable regret for her death."

Although her will stated that she wished to be buried next to her mother, Mary was interred in Westminster Abbey on the 14th of December in a tomb she would eventually share with Elizabeth. The Latin inscription on their tomb, *Regno consortes et urna, hic obdormimus Elizabetha et Maria sorores, in spe resurrectionis* (affixed there by James I when he succeeded Elizabeth) translates to "Consorts in realm and tomb, here we sleep, Elizabeth and Mary, sisters, in hope of resurrection"

At her funeral service, John White, bishop of Winchester, praised Mary: "She was a king's daughter; she was a king's sister; she was a king's wife. She was a Queen, and by the same title a king also." She was the first woman to succeed in claiming the throne of England, despite competing claims and determined opposition, and enjoyed popular support and sympathy during the earliest parts of her reign, especially from the Roman Catholics of England. Catholic historians, such as John Lingard, thought Mary's policies failed not because they were wrong but because she had too short a reign to establish them and because of natural disasters beyond her control. However, her marriage to Philip was unpopular among her subjects and her religious policies resulted in deep-seated resentment. The military losses in France, poor weather, and failed harvests increased public discontent. Philip spent most of his time abroad, while his wife remained in England, leaving her depressed at his absence and undermined by their inability to have children. After Mary's death, he sought to marry Elizabeth but she refused him. Thirty years later, he sent the Spanish Armada to overthrow her, without success.

CHAPTER VI

During this period in history, Thomas Gresham resided in Lombard Street, which was then the handsomest street in London. Like all the other bankers and merchants living in that street, he kept a shop. It stood on the site now occupied by the banking house of Messrs. Stone, Martin, & Co. and over his door by way of a sign, was his crest, a grasshopper. This was not an uncommon practice even at a later period, for we are told that the sign of the house in Bread Street where the father of John Milton, the epic poet, resided and where Milton was born, was "The Spread Eagle", a heraldic symbol which appears in the family arms. The original sign of Gresham's shop continued in existence, we are told, as late as the year 1795, when upon the erection of the present building, it disappeared from the station which it had so long occupied over the door.

At the mention of bankers in the previous section, perhaps now would be a good time to say a word or two about "bankers" during the time of Sir Thomas Gresham.

A banker in early times pursued a very different trade from that which occupies the attention of the opulent and influential class so called at the present day. It is well known that the present day bankers derive their profits from the use of fluctuating sums of money, deposited in their hands for convenience and safety by the public, and for the security of which, the respectability of the banker is a sufficient guarantee. But this is a refinement of comparatively recent introduction, with which our forefathers were wholly unacquainted.

Bankers gave and took a bond on receiving and lending money and made their profit by obtaining a higher rate of interest, or usury as it was called. Ten or twelve per cent was the customary rate of interest during the reign of Queen

Elizabeth. No disrespect is meant when we say that he united in his person, the trades of the usurer, the pawnbroker, the money-scrivener, the goldsmith, and the dealer in bullion. On Lombard Street all sorts of gold and silver vessels exposed to sale, as well as ancient and modern coins, in such quantities as might surprise the visitor the first time he sees it. It is perhaps a curious circumstance that Lombard Street should have retained its character as well as its name for at least five and a half centuries.

The earliest money-dealers in England were the Jews. They in turn were succeeded by the Lombards—which is a generalized name for the early Italian merchants of Genoa, Lucca, Florence and Venice. They obtained a footing in England about the middle of the thirteenth century and established themselves in Lombard Street as it became known. They made it their business to remit money to their own country by bills of exchange. In spite of the prejudices which at first obstructed their reception, they by degrees acquired a firm footing, and in time, became the richest merchants and the greatest money-lenders in the kingdom.

As mentioned, these goldsmiths or bankers as they are sometimes called, differed from those bankers at the present day. The transition period was at about the reign of Charles the First, until which time the whole business of London goldsmiths was to buy and sell plate and foreign coins of gold and silver, to melt and cull them and to coin some at the mint, and with the rest to supply the refiners, plate workers and merchants as they found the price to vary.

In the time of the subsequent troubles, merchants and tradesmen, who before had entrusted their cash to their servants and apprentices, found that practice no longer safe. Neither did they any longer dare, on account of the distresses of majesty itself, to use the Mint in the Tower as a place of deposit. They now began to lodge their necessary cash in the goldsmith's hands, for the sake of greater security.

The Queen's Merchant — Jim d. Jordan

In Lombard Street, at the sign of the Grasshopper, dwelt Sir Thomas Gresham, and hopefully you, the reader, will not lose any respect you may have conceived of him, on being told that he was a banker such as I have described, as well as a mercer and merchant-adventurer, *and* he kept a shop. All the trading community at the time did the same. A banking-house is technically called a *shop* to this day.

But after Gresham was honored with knighthood, he must have begun to look for some other place of residence, and to think of leaving his house in Lombard Street to the care of his apprentices, for we are told that such an abode was considered unfitting the dignity of a knight. We don't know for certain, but judging from the letters of business that subsequently passed between him and his apprentices—dated respectively Gresham House, and London—that his connection with Lombard Street did not cease with his knighthood. He did however, begin to think of moving to some more aristocratic locality and fixed his sights on Bishopsgate Street, where after a year or two, a huge mansion was built to which he gave the name "Gresham House".

Sir Thomas Gresham had been appointed English ambassador at the court of the regent of the Low Countries. He conducted himself in the discharge of the duties of an office which, though not altogether strange to him, was more exalted in its character than any which he had previously filled with his accustomed ability and success. He prepared himself well for all he would have to encounter in his new vocation. This accession of dignity however, brought with it no accession of leisure, but the contrary. His duties as ambassador were now added to those of the Queen's merchant. For example, on the present occasion, he was commissioned to take up for the space of a year and transport to England, the sum of £200,000 pounds to send over the remainder of the armor and stores in his custody, making a present of about 500 crowns to the officers of the customs, in case any serious difficulty should arise in that quarter, and interfere with the transportation of those important commodities. He also ordered the purchase of 500 shirts of mail.

After a month passed in Antwerp, Gresham returned home in the beginning of February, 1559-60, but it was only for a few days. The following mention of his letters is to show Sir Thomas's steady movements over the next several days, a very busy time for him. On the 25th we find him taking his leave from London and writing as follows to Queen Elizabeth.

"It may please your most excellent Majesty to understand, that for the better proof to your Highness for the conveyance of such bullion and gold as I shall provide for you, I have sent you this letter enclosed in the stone-work, being no small comfort unto me that I have obtained to the knowledge thereof, for the better conveyance of your treasure. Which thing must be kept as secretly as your Majesty can devise for if it should be known or perceived in Flanders, it were as much as my life and goods were worth."

We may presume from his words that he had discovered some extraordinary mode of conveying to England with secrecy, the treasure he was commissioned to procure in Flanders. He added at the finish of the letter, *"I shall most humbly beseech you Highness to be a comfort unto my poor wife in this my absence in the service of your Majesty."*

This letter was dated February 25th, 1559-60. On the same day he addressed Cecil from Gravesend as follows:

"Right honorable Sir,

"It may like you to understand that this morning I met upon the Thames, Candiller whereby you may perceive the great scarcity of money upon the bourse, and what ado there is. As likewise, what advertisement the Regent hath out of England of such ammunition and armor as hath been sent home. I shall

most humbly desire you to give great charge to Mr. Bloomflield for the secret receiving of the fine corn powder that daily shall come from thence and of all such other matters as I shall likewise send. (corn powder is a strong kind of gunpowder manufactured from corn, being less finely granulated than serpentine powder.) *There may be no more of my things entered in the Custom-House, whereby any searchers or such knaves might come to the intelligence...Sir, you shall do well that the Queen's Majesty dose use the staples for 15 or £20,000 as you have used the Merchants Adventurers: Which they do stand in much doubt that their needs must serve. For that you honor shall understand that, two days past, both the mayor of Stapell and my cousin Marsh, spoke to me to be good unto them, to be a means unto the Queen's Majesty that they should not serve at this instant—You shall do well to give the attempt, and to demand £30,000. Although you do take by half...I pray you to send me the cypher* (numbers) *by your next correspondence.*

Gresham's next letter is from Dover, dated the 26th. It was addressed to the secretary and contains a memorandum of all that Sir Thomas foresaw he should require in Flanders, as bonds, etc. etc. On the 28th he writes from Dunkirk, Belgium, where he had arrived at eight o'clock that morning after a 'fair passage', observing: *"At this instant I received a letter from Sir N. Throckmorton directed to Sir T. Challoner and me, which I send you here enclosed:"*

His first letter on arriving back at Antwerp mentions the personal danger which his commission obliged him to incur. *"The great brute that runs upon me that I will rob them* [the Antwerp Merchants] *of all their fine gold and silver: by the reason whereof, I will insure you I am half afraid to go abroad, but only at the debtors of the bourse's time. I am credibly informed that the Spanish and Italian merchants pretend to put a supplication up to the Regent against me."*

*The letter which contains this passage is long and curious, but I won't bother you with the details here.

Again we follow Gresham back to London. Having the customary evidence of his presence in the great city—a letter to Sir William Cecil, written on the eve of his departure once more to Flanders. He requests the secretary to give his servant, the license for the twelve tons of beer that he had obtained for him and also to let him have the license for my Lady Dormer and Mr. William Harvey, the Clarencieux for their abode there, (Clarencieux is the title of the officer of arms at the College of Arms in London). This was the last letter Gresham wrote from London for a long period.

From the beginning of April, 1560, until the month of March 1561, he resided almost exclusively in Flanders, as we see from the numerous letters he addressed to Sir William Cecil, Sir Thomas Parry, and Queen Elizabeth during that interval.

We'll take a look at the state of public feeling in Antwerp, when Gresham returned to that city in the spring of 1560. This was a subject of which he always took such a view, and a concern of his, which he always made such remarks as the nature of the duties with which he was entrusted, this might lead us to expect commentary from his pen.

After assuring Cecil how unpopular King Philip was in the Low Countries, he invariably adds some financial intelligence such as the reduced state of his resources, pecuniary and military and the bad odor in which he grew with the people of Flanders. Certain commissioners, he said on one occasion, came from the court of Brussels, for the purpose of obtaining a subsidy of the inhabitants of Antwerp. But the common council of the town having secretly assembled for the purpose of deliberation, the members resolutely determined not to grant any supplies.

The wealth of the new world however, more than once came most effectually and opportunely to the relief of the Spanish nation. Gresham wrote:

"*Here are letters that come from Sevill advertising that there has arrived at Cadiz, Spain, eight ships from the Indies, laden with fine gold and silver. As likewise, they are looking for four more ships, wishing for my part, it were all in the Queen Majesty's coffers, or in the Exchequer.*"

What must have added in no slight degree to promote the bad understanding which it is obvious existed between the Spanish monarch and his Flemish subjects, was his restless spirit which kept them in a state of perpetual anxiety and ferment.

"*On the 17th of this instant,*" Gresham said, writing to Sir William Cecil from Antwerp, "*I received you letter of the 13th, whereby I perceive that King Philip's preparations is now apparent to the Queen Majesty, for the aid of the French King to subdue the Scots, whereof our merchants and others had knowledge of, as soon as I had. So that here is such ado amongst our nation and others, to preserve one another, as it is wonderful and the most part of all the merchants of this town be ready to borrow, to content and pay themselves with our commodities.*"

The unsettled state of affairs in Flanders coupled with a degree of uncertainty as to what hostile circumstances might induce King Philip to take, was no doubt in part the cause of why Thomas Gresham was commissioned, about this period, to purchase military stores in so large amount, and forward them to London. The progress he was making in the fulfillment of this object forms, in fact, the theme of all his letters during a considerable time, for his operations, which were conducted upon an immense scale, not only gave full occupation to himself, but also to the numerous agents who were constantly employed in his service in different parts of Flanders and Germany.

While Gresham was acting temporarily as ambassador, his letters to Cecil dealt almost entirely with foreign complications. He perceived the impending storm between the Spanish government and their Flemish subjects. He bribed Spanish officials to obtain information, and with the knowledge of the council took into his pay his friend Gaspar Schetz, Philip's factor at Antwerp. He kept a watchful eye upon the Spanish king's movements, and reported his suspicions that a force of 4,400 Spaniards, stationed at Zealand, would be dispatched to the assistance of the French garrison at Leith, then besieged by the English and Scotch. He assured Cecil of the popularity of Elizabeth and her people with the Netherlander, although the Queen's credit had suffered by delaying the payment of her debts.

It was not so much any direct aggression on the part of the King of Spain which the English apprehended, as the danger which might result from his aiding France with his powerful support. The cause of Mary of Guise, with the accession of such an ally, would have become formidable, and this was the real reason why Gresham watched so narrowly the movements of the Spanish soldiers in Zealand, lest by one of those strokes of policy of which King Philip was so capable, a fair wind should have been availed of to transport his veterans to Leith—a stronghold at the time in the occupation of the French army, from which it was the object of the united forces of England and Scotland to dislodge them.

King James V had died in 1542 when the heir to the throne Mary (Queen of Scots) was only six days old. His Queen Consort, Mary of Guise ruled as Regent until such time as Mary was able to take up the throne. Mary was French with strong family connections so the bond between Scotland and France, the 'auld alliance' was stronger than ever.

This did not please the English and the Protestant movement in Scotland which had been gathering momentum for some time. As the situation worsened Mary called for support from her home nation. France responded and 3000 troops arrived in Leith and set up a garrison there.

English troops, assisted by the Protestant Scottish factions had been camped around the entrance to the River Forth and the French (crack troops fresh from European wars) set about routing them. The French were commanded by Monsieur D'Essé, he quickly realized the strategic importance of Leith and set about building massive fortifications around the town. The French mounted a successful assault on the island of Inchkeith, killing the garrison commander, and returning in triumph. The Scots had mounted batteries around the Leith fortifications and once again the skilled French broke out to attack them. They easily captured cannons mounted on Calton Hill. Fighting raged across Leith links and up onto the higher ground by Hawkhill and Prospect Hill. The protestant Scots began to feel that their God had deserted them. A more convenient excuse rather than the reality that their relatively inexperienced and ill-disciplined army were no match for the French.

Gradually though the English and Scottish alliance began to gain the upper hand. English warships blockaded the port and stopped supplies from reaching the French garrison. Fortified batteries and siege trenches grew nearer to the French positions. Three massive batteries were set up surrounding them; Mount Falcon (near Leith hospital) Mount Pelham and Mount Somerset (situated on high ground to the south of the current Leith links). The constant bombardment wore down the French and the terrified Leithers still living in the town. Despite several successful French raids they were beginning to starve, reduced to eating horsemeat the end was in sight. (an excavation in recent times at the bottom of Easter road discovered an old well full of horses heads).

Nevertheless the French had been given orders to defend the town to the last man and no amount of force was going to remove them. The English, tired of the conflict and of the constant jibes from the French ramparts looked for a different route to victory and looked towards their diplomats to settle the issue.

Mary of Guise had fallen ill by this time and Queen Elizabeth's secretary, Sir William Cecil was sent to negotiate a truce. Gresham says on the 18th of April, 1560, *"I am glad to hear that the Queen Dowager (Mary of Guise) is entered into communication, and the Queen Majesty's army is at Leith."* As might be expected, the reports which subsequently prevailed at Antwerp of the progress of the siege, obtain frequent notice in the course of this correspondence. Such passages as the following cannot fail to be interesting to English ears. *"Here is a secret talk that the town of Leith had yielding by our men and the Scots' assault. Whereas was lost 1000 men, as they say here. Sir I most humbly beseech you, if there is any good news, I may hear it from you first, for here there is no other talk but of England and Scotland, and all men wish Scotland were once English...and all men wish Leith to be taken, and the French men to be put out of Scotland. They do lament the fact that Queen Elizabeth has suffered this matter for so long."*

Cecil along with some of the leaders of the Lords of the Congregation arrived at Edinburgh Castle on the 12th of May 1560, and had dinner with Mary and the keeper of the castle, Lord Erskine.

They discussed a plan that had been made before the troubles, in which Mary would travel to meet with Elizabeth in England, and her brother would have been made Viceroy in Scotland. The Lords again complained about Frenchmen being appointed to Scottish government posts. Negotiations to end the siege of Leith and demolish new fortifications at Dunbar Castle continued.

But the next day, the talks ended when permission was refused for the French commanders in Leith to come to the castle to discuss the proposals with Mary.

While continuing to fortify Edinburgh Castle, Mary became seriously ill, and over the course of the next eight days her mind began to wander; some days she could not even speak.

On the 8th of June she made her will.

Mary of Guise died of dropsy on June 11th 1560. Her body was wrapped in lead and kept in Edinburgh castle for several months.

However the story was not over yet. Mary, Queen of Scots who had become Regent on the death of her mother refused to accept the treaty; this was down to one condition, that she ceased using the coat of arms of England. This may seem a minor point but with her later marriage to Lord Darnley in 1565, who was grandson to Margaret Tudor, daughter of Henry VII. Mary's claim to the English throne had become stronger – coupled with the Catholic belief that Elizabeth was illegitimate this would make Mary the true heir to the English throne. Elizabeth never forgave her cousin for this and it would later become one of the reasons for her execution.

CHAPTER VII

The English merchants at Antwerp were in constant fear of the seizure of their goods, and Sir Thomas Gresham had increasing difficulty in procuring the military stores, which Elizabeth's government ordered on an immense scale. He urged the council to set up powder-mills in England, and advised Cecil to keep all English ships and mariners within the realm, adding that he had spread the report that the Queen had two hundred ships in readiness well-armed.

After he had procured large quantities of ammunition and weapons, which he disguised in his dispatches under the name of 'velvets,' he still found much difficulty in exporting them to England. More than once he complains of the want of secrecy at the Tower in unloading his consignments, whereby the authorities at Antwerp were informed of his acts, and both Gresham himself and the Flemish custom-house officers, whom he had bribed, put in considerable danger.

On one occasion he abstracted some two thousand armor corselets from the king of Spain's armory at Malines. Gresham was strictly cautioned by Cecil to communicate only with him, or in his absence with Sir Thomas Parry, and the secrecy with which his correspondence was conducted certainly raised some suspicion at court.

His old enemy the Marquis of Winchester charged him before the Queen in council with using his position to enrich himself at the expense of the state, and with holding £40,000 of the Queen's money. Gresham replied by letter that he had not £300 remaining in his hands, and Parry led the Queen to disregard the accusation. But Gresham's financial dealings were not always above suspicion, even to the Queen.

The raising of loans was still Gresham's main occupation. Count Mansfeld, a German nobleman, who owned silver and copper mines in Saxony, offered to lend the English government £75,000. The council referred the offer to Gresham, who sent his factor, Clough, into Saxony to arrange the terms. Clough was magnificently entertained, and concluded the bargain at ten per cent., returning to Antwerp on the 2nd of July 1560. But according to Gresham's letter to Parry on the 26th of August, it appears that the count did not keep his word. The government had, therefore, to fall back upon Gresham's old device of procuring a compulsory loan from the merchant adventurers and staplers by detaining their fleet.

Though altogether devoted in general to the discussion of affairs entrusted to his management, Thomas Gresham's correspondence is occasionally enlivened by details of a somewhat more relaxed character. One example of this is when a courtier of the Queen's court had requested Gresham to procure for him some "elegant articles of foreign manufacture', or other objects which was more easily obtainable on the Continent than in England, and sometimes he was called forth by other circumstances.

In another letter to William Cecil in 1560, Gresham wrote, *"It may please you to do my most humble commendation to my Lord Robert Dudley, and to declare unto him that the Queen Majesty's Turkish horse is beginning to mend in his foot and body. Which doubtless is one of the readiest horses that is in all Christendom, and runs the best."*

About a month later, Gresham wrote to Sir Thomas Parry, *"It may please you to tell my Lord Robert, that the Queen Majesty's Turkish horse waxes a very fair beast."* (in other words, it is a fine, beautiful horse) *"With the Queen Majesty's permission, I intend to bring it home to the Queen myself."*

In a letter addressed shortly after, again to Sir Cecil, he says, *"I thank you for the gentle entertainment you gave to my poor wife, who I do rightly know molests you daily for my coming home, --such is the fondness of women! And whereas your honor would have a great iron chest bought for the Queen's Majesty, with a little key. I have sent you the key of the fairest chest that is to be had in all this town, if it is not too big. If the Queen's Majesty would prefer less, (smaller) let me know the size, and I will have one made."*

In the following August, addressing the same person, Gresham says, *"I sent you on the 17th overland, to Dunkirk, the young cortall, (a little horse) I gave you, with the Queen Majesty's Turkish horse. As likewise, I have sent you four dozen of the black buttons you spoke to me of, which cost you 48s the dozen."*

"The man that maketh the clock is out of town this Easter holiday" observes Gresham, addressing Sir William Cecil. *"I trust to send you one within ten days."* In still another letter, he says, *"I have written to Spain for the silk hose for both you and my Lady your wife."* Silk stockings were, in fact, at this time, a great rarity and value. In another part of the letter Gresham says, *"I trust you received your seven pieces of tapestry I had made in Germany, the 100 shirts, corselets, blue and white that your honor spoke to me for, and subsequently the six velvet chairs and six Spanish leather are being made for you now."*

Sir Thomas Gresham appears to have written letters nearly every day to someone and many addressed to Sir William Cecil.

During his extended periods of absence from England, Gresham often expressed his concern for the welfare of his wife, such as in this passage in one of his letters to Queen Elizabeth. *"I shall most humbly beseech your Highness to be a comfort unto my poor wife in this—my absence in the service of your*

Majesty." Similar passages frequently occur in his correspondence with Secretary Cecil and the Treasurer of the Queen's household, Sir Thomas Parry. On one occasion to Cecil he writes, *"With my most humble commendations to my Lord Keeper and to my Lord Robert, so that my wife be not forgotten,--whom I will assure you, was very sorrowful to see me depart, therefore I shall humbly beseech your honor, according to your promise, to be a stay and some comfort unto her, in this my time of absence."*

One can see from these passages from the letters of Sir Thomas Gresham that occasionally things like Turkish horses, clocks, custom made chests and even silk hosiery, occupied some of his time while away on business of the throne, but we know most of Gresham's effort was occupied with procuring military stores for England and providing for their safe transportation, a matter as it would appear, of great difficulty and danger.

He writes the following relative to his proceedings from which it is sufficiently obvious what great hazards he ran into providing England with those implements of warfare, which be put to good use a few years later. It should be observed that in serving the state which he represented, he was acting in direct violation of the laws of the Low Countries, and could bring about their severest penalties, should he get caught. In order to deceive the reader, should any of his letters have been intercepted, in his correspondence with Sir William Cecil he customarily made use of the word *velvets* to indicate in secrecy, *gunpowder*. He would also use terms such as *silks, damasks,* and *satins,* in the same manner.

"I have secret knowledge from one of the searchers," Gresham writes, *"how the court here has given orders that all such ships loaded for England should be searched. Which is only to take me in a trip, as I am credibly informed. I can no more write to you of this matter now, but well fares the penny given, that saves one hundred!* (In other words, the small amount he pays

informants for information is well worth the cost.) *I had thought to have shipped in this float of ships, which number ten or twelve, all the Queen Majesties' corselets, morions, and cuirass that are remaining in this town.* (corselet is piece of armor, a morion is a steel cap, and cuirass, is a piece of armor consisting of a breastplate and backplate fastened together.) *"But now I will stay until this worst part has passed. In the last ships that sailed from here I sent you ten pieces of velvets—five pieces of dobbill, and five pieces of pill and a half." "You wrote back saying you didn't understand and you were hoping that Candiller could inform you thereof, wherein I stand in doubt you shall understand that every piece of velvet is one thousand lbs. weight of corn powder, and one piece of velvet of pill and a half is one lbs. weight of serpentine powder." ...... "Sir, you must devise some way whereby things that are sent from here may be secretly conveyed to the Tower or else such matters I shall not be able to stand her Highness in small amounts from now on. I have heard reported that there is a parish church in the Tower, whereunto does resort all the Dutch men of St. Katherine's, and in my opinion, where such a number of strangers does resort, it cannot be chosen, but there are some false brethren among them. Therefore sir, if it stood with the Queen Majesties' pleasure to remove that access from thence to some other church in St. Katherine's, I believe things would be more secretly used."*

In June, Gresham writes, *"According as I have written your Honor, I have corrupted the chief searcher, whom is all my doer and who has right honestly desired a worthy reward. So by him and through his advice, I am doing daily, as by my proceedings to you may appear. If it is discovered, there is nothing short of death of the searcher and with him whoever enters customs. So that there shall be no ship depart, but I shall give the adventure of 3 or 4 pieces of velvets in a ship: likewise, I trust the three ships from Hambro, with £9000 worth of provisions."*

Notwithstanding Gresham's precautions, and he repeated injunctions that the greatest possible secrecy should be observed at the Tower, the periodical arrivals of large quantities of ammunition did not fail to attract notice. and the intelligence soon found its way to Antwerp. To use his own words, he was now "wholly at his wits end."

In the middle of June, 1560, Gresham was notified by his informant that there was an Englishman snooping around and implying that Thomas Gresham may be smuggling arms and ammunition aboard ships leaving the harbor. Fortunately this Englishman, whoever he was, told this to the very man in Gresham's pocket as his spy. Gresham's man told Sir Thomas that he would try to find out the man's name.

Gresham had his suspicions. He wrote to Cecil saying, *"Sir, I am right assured that there comes nothing into the Tower, but that Sir John York and others doesn't know of. And they have their agents and factors here in Flanders. I do mis-trust Mr. York's factor here whose name is Gardiner."* Sir John York had held in succession several high appointments in the Mint, which at the time was situated within the Tower. He was once "Master of the Mint".

It had been alluded to that there was some amount of jealousy on behalf of York of Gresham in Antwerp by certain merchants of that city, but this sentiment towards him was by no means confined to Flanders, and with no one does it seem to have prevailed in a greater degree than with William Paulet, 1st Marquis of Winchester, the former Lord-Treasurer.

The old marquis being the chief financial officer in the kingdom and having, in the discharge of his functions, amassed an immense fortune, regarded with no slight dissatisfaction the conspicuous part a private merchant, Gresham, was taking in directing the financial operations of the state. Paulet had successively served Henry VIII, Edward VI, Mary and Elizabeth. The esteem in which he was held at court, rendered him a dangerous enemy, so that Gresham trembled, not without reason, when he discovered about this time that his lordship was exerting his influence with the Queen and her ministers, in endeavoring to effect his ruin—an attempt which he had twice unsuccessfully made before. What seems to have principally vexed Paulet was the secrecy with which (in accordance with Queen Elizabeth's express commands) Gresham conducted all his operations, making no one privy to them but Sir William Cecil, or in his absence, Sir Thomas Parry.

The treasurer took care, of course, to assign a less unworthy motive than jealousy for his harmful proceedings against the Queen's Merchant. He threw out suggestions that Gresham was availing himself unfairly of his advantageous position, and had defrauded the state. Also, that he had remaining in his coffers, £40,000 of the Queen's money. Whereas Gresham declared that he had no £300 remaining by him and said that if Sir William Cecil, to whom he had transmitted his accounts, had not been in Scotland, he could have proved the fact immediately. But being forbidden even to leave Antwerp—a circumstance which he says much disquieted him—he wrote to Sir Parry the following:

"Sir, I do perceive by my servant that my Lord Treasurer is offended with me because he is not privy to all my doings, which I cannot do withal, for that I was commanded by the Queen's Majesty to make no man privy to them but you and Sir Cecil. This is the third time that my Lord Treasurer has served me this. – Once in King Edward's time, and once in Queen Mary's time and when his Lordship came to see the state of my account and found the Prince rather in my debt than otherwise. I assure you honor of my faith and pure honesty. .... "I *trust in God, her Majesty according to her promise will keep one ear shut to hear me, till it please her Highness to listen when I come home."*

Parry was a good friend to Gresham. He not only counteracted the evil intentions of the lord treasurer, by speaking to Queen Elizabeth in favor of Gresham, but he conciliated the Lord Hunsdon, who, instigated probably by Paulet, had not hesitated to express his dissatisfaction openly.

Henry Carey 1st Lord Hunsdon, was an English nobleman and courtier. He was the son of Mary Boleyn, Anne Boleyn's sister. Carey served twice as Member of Parliament, representing Buckingham during 1547–1550—entering when he was 21—and 1554–1555. He was knighted in November 1558 and created Baron by his first cousin Elizabeth I of England on the 13th January 1559. His sister, Catherine, was one of Elizabeth's favorite ladies-in-waiting and the Queen was very generous to her Boleyn relatives.

His Baronial estate consisted of the manors of Hunsdon and Eastwick, Hertfordshire and possessions in Kent. Hunsdon had previously belonged to Elizabeth's predecessor Mary I. He was also granted an annual pension of £400. Hunsdon was prominent in all the court tournaments and jousts of 1559 and 1560.

On 31 October 1560, he was appointed Master of the Queen's Hawks, making him "the Queen's master falconer." Elizabeth would later appoint Carey Captain of the Gentlemen Pensioners in 1564, a position making him effectively her personal bodyguard for four years.

Gresham wrote to Parry: *"My factor, Richard Candiller, writes me that my Lord Hunsdon said to him that he did much marvel that I had much disappointed her Highness and that he thought I had sold her imports to the merchants in London, for liquor and gain! Sir, I cannot but marvel that his Lordship would make any such report of me. For as the Queen's Majesty and* you do right well know, I have already sent home form this town of Antwerp 7,000 corselets and then passport being banished, I was forced to transport all my armor, and other munitions out of Germany, whereas there has been for the space of three months, five or six thousand pounds of other provisions, for the sum of £20,000. And daily there is transported there from all places, as they can get carriage. And yet for the further expenditure fearing that things should be called for as they are now."

"I have adventured upon my own head, one thousand pounds more in a ship, which I have caused to be assured upon the Bourse of Antwerp. So that I trust in God it shall most plainly appear to the Queen's Majesty I have done my duty and diligence according to the trust her Highness has reposed in me. Being right assured, the like was never done by no subject, and here, writing unto your honor, there is as much done as may be done, by wit of man... Therefore, I shall most humbly desire your Honor, as to give my Lorde Hunsdon to understand how all things stands, and all others that has the charge of the receipt of those provisions I have made, for my life lay on it, I can do no more."

"Assuring you Sir it is no small grief unto me to hear of any complaint to be made of me. Considering the great care and travel and sorrow I have had, to bring all these things to so good purpose, wherein I must confess I have done nothing but my duty to her Majesty, and ten times more."

The subject of dissatisfaction with Lord Hunsdon is quite in character, and was just such as might have been expected to have had most weight with that high-spirited, warlike peer. But he soon reconciled with Sir Thomas Gresham.

Gresham wrote again to Parry on the 2nd of July saying, *"The Queen's Majesty and you are fully satisfied in that behalf as also, you have satisfied my Lord Hunsdon, and he has always been my good Lord, and will so continue, for* which I thank him. To whom it may please you to do my most humble commendations."

The letters from where these passages are extracted, also conveyed intelligence of Gresham's progress in the shipment of military stores. *"The ships wherein was laden with thirty pieces of velvets, black damask, (a quilting fabric), satin, to be departed from here without search, amounting to the sum of £25,000. Trusting in God that they have all arrived safely. Most humbly beseeching your honor that there may be all the secrecy used that may be, for the receiving thereof into the Tower. Wishing there were no man privy to this but only Mr. Bloomfeld whom is a very honest, secret gentleman in all his doings. Doubtless this matter cannot be to secret kept considering the great care and adventure it is in the transporting of it from here."*

Shortly after, he announces a further shipment of "velvets" and ads, *"Tomorrow I intend to send fifteen pieces of velvets more, and one thousand bolts of black damask, so I trust you shall lack no more of that kind of silks."* By this means of codes, it will be remembered that a certain quantity of ammunition was signified.

CHAPTER VIII

The Treaty of Edinburgh also known as the Treaty of Leith was a treaty drawn up on the 5th of July, 1560 between the Commissioners of Queen Elizabeth with the assent of the Scottish Lords of the Congregation and the French representatives of King Francis II (husband of Mary Queen of Scots) to formally conclude the Siege of Leith and replace the Auld Alliance with France with the new Anglo-Scottish accord, while maintaining peace between England and France.

The representatives were Jean de Monluc the Bishop of Valence, Charles de la Rochefoucault, and Sieur de Randan, for France, with William Cecil, and Nicholas Wotton, the Dean of Canterbury and York, for England. The French deputies were authorized to discuss the withdrawal of their troops with the Archbishop of St. Andrews, John Bellenden of Auchnoul, and William Maitland as representatives of the Congregation. The French delegation was also permitted to meet and console the bereaved ladies-in-waiting of Mary of Guise's court.

The cessation of hostilities during the negotiation was marked by two cannon shots from Edinburgh Castle at 7:00 o'clock in the evening on Monday June 17th.

It was agreed between France and England that all their land and naval forces would withdraw from Scotland. Mary and Francis should not use the arms and signs of England and Ireland in their heraldry, and they would fulfill the representations made by the nobility and people of Scotland on the 6th of July, 1560.

On the 16h July 1560, the French troops marched out of Leith after sacking it and so twelve years of French involvement in Scotland came to an end.

The treaty was not ratified by Mary, the reigning monarch at the time, despite considerable pressure upon her to do so. Even so, it had the intended effect of the withdrawal of the French Troops from Scotland at the time and the eventual fall of the Roman Catholic Church in Scotland.

Mary may not have wanted the treaty to be ratified as she was heavily attached to France, having been its Queen Consort, and viewed the Lords of the Congregation as rebels against her mother Mary of Guise. She also did not ratify the treaty because it officially declared Elizabeth the monarch of England, a position Mary herself desired.

Prior to the treaty being drawn up, Sir Thomas Gresham had written to Parry on the 22nd of June, which included the following passage: *"On this day at 7:00 o'clock in the morning, Mr. Beaumont, (Mr. Secretary Cecil's friend), came to me and said that yesterday he had come to town with the French King's ambassador. He informed me that his coming is only to practice with some Scottish man, to send into Scotland, letters from the French King to the Earl of Aran, wherein he offers him the whole government of Scotland—so far forth he will proceed no further with the Queen Majesty and claims that all Frenchmen shall depart out of Scotland."*

During that summer of 1560, negotiations between Sir Thomas Gresham and his agent and Count Mansfeld by his agent, took place for the purpose of levying a loan of 300,000 gold florins and £400,000 in Germany for the Queen of England, which Gresham declared took no effect on account of the Count's demand for additional security, and also through his telling Gresham's agents that he expected that the money should be laid out in Germany for the levy of the troops. The money was to go towards the defraying of the Queen's debts,

£35,000 was to be paid and lastly 40 or £50,000 was to be paid by the Merchant Adventurers upon their cloths, and £25,000 by the Staplers upon their wools.

Count Mansfeld was a German nobleman of the highest rank and distinction, to whom, in the distribution of the government of the provisions, the Dukedom of Luxemburg had been assigned, but the estates on which he generally resided, and from one of which he derived his title, were situated in Saxony and were particularly rich in mines of silver and gold.

The Count employed as his negotiator in this business, one Hans Keck after considerable deliberation.

Gresham had written to Queen Elizabeth concerning sending a representative to Count Mansfeld saying: *"My factor Richard Clough, whom it may please you to credit in all things he shall declare, as though I came in person myself. I will insure you he has taken great pains in the Queen's Majesty's service in my absence and has deserved some consideration at her Majesty's hands."* Clough returned from London to Antwerp immediately but Keck lingered in England to Gresham's great annoyance. At last he made his appearance, commending Sir William Cecil to Gresham.

The documents which Hans Keck carried with him, included Count Mansfeld's letter, on which Gresham noted Sir William Cecil's handwriting where Cecil referred the Count wholly to Sir Thomas Gresham as negotiator.

During his meeting with Keck, Gresham explained that just as he had done twice before in King Edward's time, he planned to raise the Exchange from twenty-six shillings to twenty-nine shillings four pence. Whereby, all foreign commodities and ours cheapened, thereby, we robbed all Christendom of their fine gold and silver. And by raising the Exchange and keeping it so, the gold and silver remains forever within our realm. *"Sir"*, Gresham said to Hans Keck, *"If you will enter upon this matter, you may in no way relent, by persuasion of the* merchants. You may keep them in fair and good order, for otherwise, if they get the upper hand, you will never rule them."

"I would ask the Queen's Majesty to give license for our English merchants to ship. For the sooner they do begin, the sooner they will be laden and for license of long cloths, the Queen's Majesty to grant them liberally."

"Sir, this matter is of so great importance, as it must be kept secret. For if the merchants have any inkling of it, they will never ship their goods, but dispatch them otherwise."

"To conclude with this practice—first, you shall raise the Exchange, to the 'enrich' the Queen Majesty, and the realm forever. Secondly, you shall defray the Queen Majesty's debt. Thirdly, you shall ask only King Philip and the French King, whereof her Highness has felt the commodity. I cannot express unto you enough this matter is of so great importance for the Queen Majesty's honor and for the profit of her realm."

In addition to the expedience here recommended, which had been already successfully practiced, Gresham was naturally anxious to discover some channel through which he might be enabled in the future with less publicity to accomplish the objects of his commission. The practical difficulties which he had to encounter as often as it became necessary to negotiate a fresh loan with the Antwerp merchants, were of the most discouraging nature. It was with eagerness, therefore, that he availed himself of an offer which was at last made to advance a considerable sum for the use of the English government.

Gresham accordingly dispatched his servant, Clough, to Count Mansfeld, with a letter to that nobleman in Latin from himself. Clough wrote from Eisenach, that he was at that time, sixteen miles from the town of Mansfeld, where he expected to arrive on the 3rd of June, 1560. A day or two after, passing through the Nassone and lodging in Syggen, Clough wrote again. He had traveled through the south of Germany until he entered Saxony. From there, he proceeded directly to Mansfeld.

Gresham did not hear from Clough for quite some time after that, so much that he became quite anxious concerning his absence. The long absence was later explained by Clough who told Gresham in a letter that the Count had provided "marvelous entertainment" by taking him on a half-day's journey of the Count's copper and silver mines. He said he had been received well by the Count and was given one of the "fairest chamber" in his house to stay in while he was there. Clough went on to explain how the Count had showed him his towns and castles, whereas at diverse places, Earls and Noblemen of his house met him. He was treated with banquets as well. This well accounted for Clough's unable to write for a few days as to his whereabouts and dealings. Clough finally returned to Antwerp on the 2nd of July, full of further details of his visit to the Count.

Clough brought with him a letter of instructions to Sir Thomas Gresham from the Count, written in the German tongue of which Gresham sent a French translation to Parry. Clough said there were many things not contained in those instructions which the Count was unwilling to commit to in writing, these had been confided to Clough. What is known of the result of his mission has already be stated: namely that the Count had pledged to furnish Queen Elizabeth with 300,000 in gold florins, which he promised to deliver at Antwerp by the 15fth of August. The loan was for the space of a year, on interest at the rate of ten per cent, per annum, on the security of the Queen's bond and that of the city of London, as usual. He offered £400,000 more, provided the Queen would give him the bond of the merchants of the Steelyard as an additional security, but Gresham objected to this, foreseeing that if the proposal were accepted without protest, a similar concession would be required by the merchants of Antwerp also, in all future bargains.

Notwithstanding the fair promises and flattering proposals of Mansfeld, this negotiation proved fruitless. Weeks went by and no money exchanged hands. Finally, the period fixed by the Count himself expired, and the necessities of the State became more urgent than ever.

Gresham's feeling of unease is apparent from his correspondence. He implicitly relied on the good faith of Mansfeld, and how completely he depended on this resource for accomplishing his purpose, will be seen from the following extract from a letter which he addressed to Sir Thomas Parry on the 7th of July 1560, with reference to his intentions: *"...for as the payment is but little considering the great debt, so I will insure your honor it will not be a little spoken of throughout the world, that Her Majesty, in her wars, does make payment of her debts, when neither King Philip or the King of Portugal, in peace time, pay nothing. And they owe no small amount of money, which causes money to be here as scant as the like was never seen before."*

"Therefore, now, a payment of £25,000 to be equally divided among the Queen Majesty's creditors, will do more good to Her Highness's credit than the sum of £25,000 is worth. By this means, her debts grow less, and the interest is saved. So, the £25,000 deducted out of Count Mansfeld's money, will leave remaining £50,000, which I will see transported by Exchange or else in fine gold and silver, which shall fall out to the Queen's profit."

The following letter to Parry serves to show how the negotiation with County Mansfeld terminated.

"Right Honorable Sir,"

"After my most humble commendations it may be necessary for you to understand that Count Mansfeld did not accomplish his bargain for £400,000

according to his promise. What shall come thereof, our Lord knows, and I do not. But I do perceive by one word that Hans Keck said, the money is here already, which is let out upon interest to the town of Antwerp I guess. Which will not help the Queen Majesty's credit. Nevertheless, I have so travailed that I have given full contention to all the Queen Majesty's creditors, as by my prolongations sent to Mr. Secretary you many see."

But the "contention" Gresham alluded to here, was only to be procured by having the recourse to a scheme, practiced as we have seen on former occasions, by which a compulsory loan was extracted from the Merchant-Adventurers. On the 2nd of August, we find Gresham addressing Parry in London. *"I will not bother your Honor with all the details, but it may please you to remember the Merchant-Adventurers, and Staplers. To proceed with first, the Merchant-Adventurers who begin now to enter in the Customs-House and to be laden by the 25th of this month, they shall have their ships loaded and sailed. You will remember that in case the Queen Majesty does mean to refine her base monies within this three months that you do demand, of the merchants at least, for every 20s. sterling, 26s. 8d. filmish, and as her Majesty is therein minded to govern the price of the Exchange. Otherwise the Queen Majesty may lose money."*

CHAPTER IX

After the treaty with Scotland was signed, Queen Elizabeth set out on progress through Surrey and Hampshire spending a few days at Basing House, a major Tudor palace built in 1531 as a new palace for William Paulet, 1st Marquis of Winchester, whom we have already met.

While the Queen was a guest of Paulet, he wrote a letter to Cecil telling him of "black counsels" or those who were trying to turn the Queen against Cecil. Even though Cecil had successfully negotiated the treaty in Scotland, upon his return to England he found himself no longer in such high favor with the Queen. Some in the Court resented the influence he was beginning to exert over Elizabeth and were talking against him. In particular, he found himself being supplanted by Lord Robert Dudley who had aspirations to marry Elizabeth.

In his letter to Cecil on the 24th of August, 1560, Paulet wrote that there would never be sound counsel until there was a smaller number of councilors in whose advice the Queen had absolute trust. He believed that they would all work for reward and that Cecil, who gave the most of himself, would receive the least thanks. Indeed the benefit of Cecil's good counsel was hindered by the lack of esteem in which the Queen now held him. Paulet continued by advising Cecil to bear with the situation, while he would "play the part of a good servant and tell the Queen the truth."

Three days after Paulet wrote the letter, Cecil arrived at Basing. When he was at Court and close to the Queen he felt it was more difficult for his enemies to talk against him.

For Paulet, the Queen's visit to Basing was a memorable success and the Queen was most splendidly entertained with all manner of good cheer. Indeed she was so impressed with his house and hosting, that she commented of Paulet that *"If my Lord Treasurer were a young man, I could find in my heart to have him for my husband before any man in England."* To the 26 year-old Queen, Paulet, at the age of 76, must have truly seemed ancient.

Part of the reason for the Queen's visit to Paulet was no doubt to discuss the concern of the purity of the coinage. Much of the "good coins" – that with a higher silver content – was either overseas or hoarded and at the time of Elizabeth's accession, there were at least four different standards of coin in circulation. Re-coinage began in September of 1560 to restore coins to "fine money".

In October the justices in each town were commanded to collect together four or five hundred pounds of base money and send it sorted to Paulet and Thomas Sackville, Lord High Treasurer, with a guard of one or two 'substantial men' and the coins would be replaced by new money. Paulet, Mildmay, Sir Thomas Parry, Cecil, and Sackville were to oversee the minting and the issue of the new coinage. The coins collected, were melted down and refined and then made up in new proportions with a higher percentage of silver to lead.

Sir Thomas Gresham, as might be expected, was in on the plans of re-coinage, long before it became generally known. Indeed it seems no unfair inference that he was the originator of the plan from the beginning. As far back as July 7th, Gresham had written to Parry saying: *"Tomorrow departs from here, Daniel Wolstat, to confer with you if it shall be the Queen Majesty's pleasure to refine all her highness' base money...he is an honest man, to whom I am much beholding......Albeit, the enterprise is of great importance, and the sooner it is put into place, the more honor and profit it will be to the Queen Majesty and the Realm. For this will doubtless raise the exchange at the least."*

At your honor's commandment,
Thomas Gresham.

Gresham was certainly correct when he said the new coinage would raise the exchange, for within a year the re-coinage was almost completed and the new coin to the value of £758,102 was issued for £666,267 of base coin used, so even allowing for expenses, the government made a profit on the exercise. Such successful management reflects the greatest credit on those who accomplished this difficult feat. Daniel Wolstat of Antwerp, was chief refiner, hired by Gresham on the understanding that he would receive five percent on the value of the reissued coinage. The work was executed more rapidly than would otherwise have been possible.

By now, you must have some idea of the nature and extent of the services which were continually required of Sir Thomas Gresham. It has been shown that he discharged the duties of not only Agent, negotiating loans for the State, and of Queen's Merchant, in which capacity the task of furnishing the country with military and other store continually was put upon him. He corresponded constantly with Sir William Cecil, as the ambassador at foreign courts, and provided Cecil with a tremendous amount of intelligence of the concerning the often secretive actions of foreign countries' trading, enterprises, councils and resolutions. Antwerp, Thomas Gresham's home base to conduct business from, was then, in short, what London is now—the center of intelligence. So in addition to Flemish news, Gresham conveyed home to Cecil and the Queen, the freshest intelligence respecting of the Pope, derived from Rome, Naples or

Venice, respecting the Turks, derived from Constantinople or Tripoli, Spanish news from Seville or Toledo, and not least often, tidings of what was passing or rumored in Sweden, Denmark, Germany and France.

Many were the strangers engaged by Sir Thomas Gresham to gather information on friends and foes. But it must be said that Gresham did not altogether depend on strangers however, for his intelligence. There is abundant evidence of the activity of his disposition and the personal exertions he constantly made to accomplish his objects. Today, he might be in Antwerp, and on the slightest summons, in less than four days, in London. Or, as was often the case during his protracted duties beyond the seas, he was found writing from Brussels, and other towns in Flanders where he judged his presence necessary.

On such occasions, the only mode of travel was by horseback, and in October of 1560, on one of his hasty journeys he took a nasty fall from a horse, breaking his leg. This accident would leave him lame for the rest of his life. Even Queen Elizabeth made mention of his leg in one of her letters to him four months later when she wrote: *"We trust after the prolongation of the February date, your leg will be able to carry you shipboard, to return to us, where both your recovery, and for intelligence of your doings, we shall be glad to see you."*

Soon after this period, Thomas Gresham was able to leave Antwerp and go home to England. He had at long last obtained permission to return, after an almost unbroken absence of eleven months, during which nine of those, he had vainly petitioned for that favor.

During this protracted absence from England, namely the year of 1560, Sir Thomas Gresham lost his elder brother, Sir John Gresham.

His brother John, born in 1518, had been knighted by Lord Protector Somerset, on the field after a victory of Musselburgh, in 1547.

Isolated since his break from Rome and Catholic Europe, Henry VIII sought to secure his northern borders though an alliance with Scotland. Henry's proposal involved the marriage of son, Prince Edward to the young Scottish Queen Mary.

When the Scottish Parliament rejected Henry's plan, he sought to change their mind through a show of force.

When Henry died in 1547, his will had named sixteen executors who were to form a regency council, along with twelve other advisors, until nine year-old Edward VII came of age. The plan was that the council would rule collectively with every member having equal power and rights. However, the will also allowed the executors to grant themselves lands and honors. Edward Seymour, uncle to the new King Edward VI, took advantage of this and made himself Duke of Somerset and Lord Protector of his nephew's council, with the agreement of 13 out of the 16 executors. Seymour now called "Somerset", then went on to rule by proclamation, making all of the decisions himself. He was now, effectively ruling England as its Lord Protector.

Like Henry VIII, Somerset liked the idea of an alliance with Scotland, but the Scots rejected his proposal it would have meant them adopting the Reformation and breaking their links to the Papacy.

Somerset gathered the English army at Berwick before marching his force of around 18,000 men north, along the east coast road to Edinburgh, closely supported by a fleet of thirty warships.

It fell to the Earl of Arran to organize the Scottish defenses, who managed to muster an army estimated at 22,000 strong in response to the English invasion. Moving out of Edinburgh, Arran organized his troops on the west bank of the River Esk, blocking Somerset's march on the Scottish capital.

The main action began on the 10th of September 1547 with a charge by the English cavalry which was driven off by the Scottish pike-men. The artillery pieces from both sides were now brought into the action, including the canons from the English ships lying offshore. Battered now from three sides and unable to respond, the Scottish resistance began to crumble.

In the last pitched battle to be fought between the English and the Scottish armies, the English offered precious little mercy to the retreating Scots. Estimates claim Scottish losses at around 6,000, earning this epic defeat the title of "Black Saturday". The English refer to it as the "Battle of Pinkie Cleugh"

It was at this battle, that Somerset knighted Sir John Gresham, while still on the field of battle. This suggests that Thomas's brother had done something heroic, deserving to be knighted without delay.

Perhaps it should be noted here that Somerset's eventual downfall was the result of widespread social unrest in England, such as the "Prayer Book Rebellion" in the South West in 1549, something which the rest of the council blamed him for. After his arrest, Somerset was succeeded as the leader of Edward VI's council by John Dudley, the Earl of Warwick, and although he was later released and restored to a place on the council, he was eventually executed on the 22nd of January 1552, after plotting to overthrow Dudley.

As far Sir John Gresham, like the rest of his family, he was a mercer and merchant-adventurer, having been brought up in the business under his father, like Sir Thomas Gresham had been.

Sir John Gresham was survived by his widow, Lady Frances, daughter and heiress of Sir Henry Thwaytes. It would appear that he did not leave her in affluent circumstances, for Sir Thomas Gresham bestowed upon her an annuity of £133, 6s, 8d, which in those days was a very considerable income. John and

Frances' only daughter and heir, Elizabeth, married Sir Henry Neville of Billingbere, in Berkshire.

On the 5th of July 1561 with Sir Thomas Gresham back in London, he wrote a memorandum to Cecil requesting for an audit of his account and approval for expenses against the Mercer's Feast. This first request was not rapidly complied with however.

Toward the latter end of July Gresham became aware that his five month presence at home would be coming to an end, as he would soon be again required in Flanders. As the accustomed sheet of instructions was being drawn up by Her Majesty the Queen, Gresham was preparing for his departure.

So much has been already said in respect to the financial transactions in which, especially at this period of his life, Gresham was engaged, that there nothing to suggest that what kept him occupied during this visit to London was anything but of a financial nature.

CHAPTER X

The correspondence of Richard Clough, Gresham's man in Antwerp, was maintained throughout
Gresham's absence, with unabated vigor. It is curious to observe to how great a degree, in that age, the wealth which resulted from the Commercial eminence of the Flemish people had engendered a taste for pageantry and extravagant apparel. Beginning on the 3rd of August, soon after Sir Thomas Gresham had returned to London, Antwerp held another of the grand festivals, this one perhaps the grandest of them all.

Formal competitions within individual cites Chambers grew into formal competitions between Chambers. A "Chamber" was a dramatic society much like today's theater groups, writers groups, poetry clubs etc. These competitive festivals, called Landjuweels which literally meant "jewel" or "prize of the land", pitted chambers against one another in a series of contests strictly governed by rules of form.

A Landjuweel could last for several days or sometimes for several weeks. Performances were open to the public, and everyone attended. Contestants competed for prizes in a number of categories including, the best play, the best farcical entertainment, the most beautiful costumes, the best acting, the best poem, the best reader of a poem, the best song, the best singing. At one festival held in 1607, there was a prize for best fireworks display. A typical Landjuweel also included a number of parades and banquets.

The city of Antwerp spent more than a hundred thousand guilders on preparations for the festival which lasted the entire month of August. Nine cities competed, and the streets of Antwerp were decorated as for a King…or Queen.

Richard Clough wrote to Gresham on the day after the opening of the festivities describing everything he saw. He first explained that Antwerp had three "Chambers". One was called "The Painters" another, The Marigolds (who wore marigolds in their armbands), and the third was called The Olive Branch, (and wore on their arms a branch of olives).

On the opening day of the Landjuweel, in Antwerp, the members of the "Painters" host Chambers, rode outside the city on horses to welcome the visitors.

"As the 3rd day of August, being yesterday, all the lords of the town of Antwerp, or the most part were, at one o'clock in readiness, upon their pageantry or standing place where they were to judge the competitions." wrote Clough. "At the same hour, all the towns of Brabant, with their Chambers, must be in a readiness outside the gates, where at one o'clock, the gates were opened. The Chamber that are first upon the market—to say, the trumpeters, and the heralds—do come and declare unto the lords that they are ready at the gates, they shall come first, and pass throughout all the town and so before the lords. So that being done, the "Chamber of Painters" must go to the gates and fetch them in at once and present them to the lords. Then another Chamber is fetched from the gates by "The Marigolds", where sixty horsemen dressed all in crimson satin and velvet, in short cloaks lined with white satin, white satin hose and doublets, red hats with white feathers and white boots. All of their horses were draped accordingly. In addition there were twelve trumpeters and heralds and at least forty footmen, all appareled accordingly."

"After them, the next Chamber of Antwerp, "the Olive Branch", fetched in another company. They were sixty horsemen, dressed in green satin and velvet, lined with white, with white hose and doublets. In all points, every bit as costly as the other, both for footmen and the trimming of the horses."

"Next came in the town of Bourbourg with forty horsemen, all in tawny satin damask and velvet, and with them twelve wagons covered with tawny cloth and in every wagon, two men were setting in tawny silks carrying torches. All of the Bourbourg had red hose and doublets, and red hats with white feathers, very costly."

"After them, came in the town of Mechlin all appareled in coats of carnation color, made after the English fashion, being well tied with yellow parchment. All, had yellow hose and doublets, red hats and yellow feathers, and white boots. They came in with 360 horses, riding two by two together, the first two carried burning torches and the other two held flowers. Among them were a hundred and twelve gentlemen, every one of them with great chains of gold around his neck and his coat guarded with fine gold."

"They had twelve trumpeters, four minstrels, four heralds and others, many of them carrying arms and banners, which was wonderful to see. After them, sixteen wagons covered with yellow carnation cloth made of a very strange fashion, like a canopy and around each wagon hung twelve shields very costly engraved. All the waggoneers dressed accordingly. The matter was so strange, that it is too long to write about. They were in number, at least 450 horses and rather at least 600 persons!"

"After them came in the town of Liere all in green coats, trimmed with white, white hose and doublets, green hats with red feathers. Four pageants with trumpeters, heralds, and footmen accordingly, and with them sixteen wagons covered with green and white, with torches and crests in very good order."

"There came after them from diverse towns, some in green, some in black, some in orange, some in yellow—to the number of fifteen towns and companies. But the principal of all came was Brussels, which methinks was a dream."

"First, they came in with many trumpets, heralds, footmen, standard-bearers and carriers of arms, with diverse other kinds of officers. After them came seven pageants being carried by 150 men and the pageants being so trimmed with young children in cloth of gold, silver and satin of all colors, so embroidered and wrought that I cannot tell what to write of them. About every pageant rode four men on horseback with torches in their hands, appareled in long coats after the manner of Poland, of crimson satin, embroidered with gold and silver. Their hats were red, trimmed as the rest with white feathers, white satin doublets and white boots. They had great girdles of gold taffeta with their swords. After every seven of these pageants came seven wagons all covered with red cloth and trimmed with white. In twenty-one of these wagons were very fair persons, some in armor, some like nuns, some like monks, priests, bishops, cardinals and all kind of religious men with wonderful devises which I could not see well, for it was two o'clock after midnight before they came in, so that I could not very well see everything by torchlight."

The rest of the wagons being at least 200, were covered with red as the others and in every wagon, two men sitting, sometimes three—in crimson satin, holding torches"

"After the wagons, came 380 on horseback, all in crimson satin, embroidered with gold and silver. In fact I judged there to be a p persons and riders all together."

"This was all the strangest matter that ever I saw, or think I shall ever see, for the coming of King Philip to Antwerp with the cost of all the nations together in apparel was not to be compared to this done by the town of Brussels. I wish that our gentlemen of nobility of England had seen this."

"The ceremony ended between two and three o'clock in the morning."

"The following day, the city fathers gave a reception for the officers of the societies. The opening ceremonies continued on August 4th with each Chamber's procession to church, exhibiting their specially designed emblem blazons, pageant wagons, and allegorical devises." (devises that convey hidden meanings through symbolic figures, actions, or imagery).

"Generally performances took place in a large hall or on an open platform in the public square. The platform, which was also used for the performance of songs, poems, and other entertainments, was backed by an elaborate architectural facade. Places were reserved on the facade for a number of shields of honor usually including those of the emperor or king, of the city, and of the Landjuweel's host society. Thus the facade served as a way of proclaiming and celebrating the festival's pedigree rather than providing mere decoration or realistic backgrounds for the performances."

"Atop the facade typically was a throne for the figure in whose honor the contest was held. The throne might be occupied by figures representing the Virgin, the Holy trinity, Honor, Wisdom, or Lady Rhetoric. Apparently, these figures were portrayed by human performers at least for part of the festival for contemporary accounts report that several contest featured Lady Rhetoric or Lady Victory descending to the stage in a cloud machine to award prizes."

On the opening day of play competition, the "Painters Chamber", who did not compete in their own festival, presented a play of welcome. Each Chamber then presented its entry in the theme play category. These presentations lasted through August 23rd when the award for best play was presented in a dramatized ceremony. The Landjuweel at Antwerp, concluded on September 2 with a farewell play presented by the "Painters Chamber".

Whether or not our Sir Thomas Gresham was disappointed to have missed the festivities we can't be sure of, but for sure we can be that he was nevertheless glad to be home in London once again.

Correspondence between Gresham and Clough continued with Clough writing:

"I wrote your mastership by my last, that there was some news from Rome, which I could not learn. So that now I have learned what the matter was,--Of late, certain Cardinals in Rome have conspired against the Pope. Intending to have chosen a new Pope and having called a consistory, where they thought to have sent him off and to have made a different one. The Pope learned of the conspiracy against him and sent for them all and said; "The cause that I have sent for you is this, I have somewhat to say to you, but I do command you, upon the pain of death, that what so ever I do say unto you, that you do make me no answer, nor that you do ask no question, for my pleasure is so. The cause that you have called this council is (I know right well) to put me off, and to make a new Pope. Whereof I have great marvel. I have done, and will do my best to observe such orders as others have done before me. If I do amiss—tell me, and I will amend. Well, for that is past, I do forgive you, for I do know who they are that were the doers hereof. But and if I may hear that the like, look for no pardon!"

"So—they that are in fault, are in much doubt and fear of the Pope. Whereas yet, it is thought will be more news very shortly." Richard Clough wrote to Gresham.

The most dramatic proceedings of the reign of Pope Pius IV revolved around the denouncement and destruction of Cardinal Carlo Carafa and his brother Giovanni Carafa.

Pope Pius IV summoned all the Cardinals then in Rome to a secret consistory, (council house) for Friday morning the 7th of June 1560. They assembled at the Vatican Palace and awaited the Pope. Aurellio Spina, a chamberlain of Cardinal Borromero, informed Cardinal Carlo Carafa that the Pope wished to speak to him in an audience hall on the upper floor. Taking a small, winding staircase, he hurried off, but the Pope was not in the hall.

Carlo was told to wait. Presently his nephew Cardinal Alfonso entered the hall. Instead of their receiving the good news Carlos had obviously expected, the Pope's Swiss guard came up to them and arrested them for leading the conspiracy.

In another letter Clough writes to Gresham, he tells: *"The Prince of Orange is departed for Deutschland to be married to the daughter of Duke Maurice with a small company. For whereas he thought to have had diverse noblemen of this country with him, there is commandment given by the King that no man in all these Low Countries, bearing any office, shall go with him in paying by losing his office, and incurring the King's displeasure besides, with express words, because they shall not be infected with any of the heresies that is used in that country."*

"Which matter it is thought that the Duchess will not take in good part. Which in the end, may fall out ill. For the Prince is now waxing great by this marriage, and presently his officers do sell most of the lands that he had in this country. Which is much spoken of now."

The Prince of Orange is a title originally associated with the sovereign Principality of Orange, in what is now southern France. William the Silent held the title of Prince of Orange in 1561.

A wealthy nobleman, William originally served the Habsburgs as a member of the court of Margaret of Parma, governor of the Spanish Netherlands. Unhappy with the centralization of political power away from the local estates and with the Spanish persecution of Dutch Protestants, William joined the Dutch uprising and turned against his former masters. The most influential and politically capable of the rebels, he led the Dutch to several successes in the fight against the Spanish.

One can see why King Philip, the King of Spain, detested the Prince of Orange. and forbid any officers in the Low Countries from following going with William on his travel to wed the Duchess.

On the 25th of August, 1561, William the Silent *"Prince of Orange"*, married his second wife, (his first had died in 1558). His new wife was Anna of Saxony, who was described by contemporaries as "self-absorbed, weak, assertive, and cruel". It is generally assumed that William married her to gain more influence in Saxony.

King Philp so hated William the Silent, that he would later, in 1580, offer a reward of 25,000 crowns to anyone who killed him. King Philip referred to William as a "pest on the whole of Christianity and the enemy of the human race".

On July 10th, 1584, a man named Balthasar Gérard would assassinate William the Silent by shooting him twice with a pistol. The story of Balthasar Gerard is an interesting tale itself and should be mentioned here.

After the reward offered by Philip was published, Gérard left for Luxembourg, where he learned that another man, Juan de Jáuregui had already been preparing to attempt the assassination, but this attempt did not succeed. In March 1584 he went to Trier, where he put his plan before the regent of the Jesuits but another Jesuit convinced him to change his original scheme and go to the prince of Parma.

In Tournai, after holding counsel with a Franciscan, Father Gery, Gérard wrote a letter, a copy of which was deposited with the guardian of the convent, and the original presented personally to the Prince of Parma. In the letter Gérard wrote, in part, *"The vassal ought always to prefer justice and the will of the king to his own life."*

At first the prince thought him unfit but after consulting Haultepenne and others with the letter he was assigned to Christoffel d'Assonleville, who spoke with Gérard, and asked him to put this in writing, which he did on 11 April 1584. He requested absolution from the prince of Parma *"as he was about to keep company for some time with heretics and atheists, and in some sort to conform himself to their customs"*.

For his first expenses he begged for 50 crowns, which were refused. "I will provide myself out of my own purse", Gérard told Assonleville, "and within six weeks you will hear of me." Assonleville responded: "Go forth, my son ... and if you succeed in your enterprise, the King will fulfill all his promises, and you will gain an immortal name besides."

On Sunday, 8 July 1584, Gérard loitered in the courtyard of the Prince of Orange examining the premises. A guard asked him why he was waiting there. He excused himself by saying that in his present shabby clothing and without new shoes he was unfit to join the congregation in the church opposite. The guard unsuspectingly arranged a gift of 50 crowns for Gérard, from the Prince of Orange himself. Gérard, the following morning purchased a pair of pistols from a soldier, haggling the price for a long time because the soldier couldn't supply the particular chopped bullets or slugs he wanted.

On Tuesday, July 10th, William the Silent climbed the stairs to the second floor, he was spoken to by the Welsh captain, Roger Williams, who knelt before him. William put his hand on the bowed head of the old captain, at which moment Gérard jumped out of a dark corner. He drew his weapon and fired three shots.

William the Silent collapsed. His sister knelt beside him, but it was too late. Asked whether he commended his soul to Christ, he answered in the affirmative. His last words were, *Mon Dieu, ayez pitié de moi et de mon pauvre people* (*My God, have mercy on me and on my poor people*).

Gérard fled through a side door and ran across a narrow lane, pursued by Roger Williams. Gérard had almost reached the ramparts, from which he intended to jump into the moat. On the other side a saddled horse stood ready. A pig's bladder around his waist was intended to help keep him afloat. However, he stumbled over a heap of rubbish. A servant and a guard of the prince who had raced after him caught him. When called a traitor by his captors, he is said to have replied, *"I am no traitor; I am a loyal servant of my lord."* "Which lord?" they asked. *"Of my lord and master, the king of Spain"*. At the same time more pages and guards of the prince appeared and dragged him back to the house under a rain of fists and beatings with the butt of a sword. Hearing his assailants chatter and convinced he heard the prince was still alive, he cried *"Cursed be the hand that missed!"*

At the house he immediately underwent a preliminary examination before the city magistrates. Upon being interrogated by the magistrates, he reportedly showed neither despair nor contrition, but rather a quiet exultation, stating: *"Like David, he had slain Goliath of Gath."*

At his trial, Gérard was sentenced to be brutally – even by the standards of that time – killed. The magistrates decreed that the right hand of Gérard should be burned off with a red-hot iron, that his flesh should be torn from his bones with pincers in six different places, that he should be quartered and disemboweled alive, his heart torn from his chest and flung in his face and that, finally, his head should be taken off.

Gérard's torture was also very brutal. On the first night of his imprisonment Gérard was hung on a pole and lashed with a whip. After that his wounds were smeared with honey and a goat was brought to lick the honey off his skin with his rough tongue. The goat however refused to touch the body of the sentenced. After this and other tortures he was left to pass the night with his hands and feet bound together, like a ball, so sleep would be difficult.

During the following three days, he was repeatedly mocked and hung on a pole with his hands tied behind his back. Then a weight of 300 metric pounds (150 kg) was attached to each of his big toes for half an hour. After this half hour Gérard was fitted with shoes made of well-oiled, uncured dog skin; the shoes were two fingers shorter than his feet. In this state he was put before a fire. When the shoes warmed up, they contracted, crushing the feet inside them to stumps. When the shoes were removed, his half-broiled skin was torn off.

After his feet were damaged, his armpits were branded. After that he was dressed in a shirt soaked in alcohol. Then burning bacon fat was poured over him and sharp nails were stuck between the flesh and the nails of his hands and feet.

Gérard is said to have remained calm during his torture. On 14 July 1584, Gérard was executed.

Upon later hearing of the fate of Gérard, King Philip II gave Gérard's parents, instead of the reward of 25,000 crowns, three country estates in Lievremont, Hostal, and Dampmartin in the Franche-Comté, and the family was raised to the peerage.

Philip II would later offer the estates to Philip William, Orange's son and the next Prince of Orange, provided the prince continue to pay a fixed portion of the rents to the family of his father's murderer; the notion was rejected with scorn. The estates remained with the Gérard family.

The apostolic vicar Sasbout Vosmeer tried to have Gérard canonized, to which end he removed the dead man's head and showed it to church officials in Rome, but the idea was rejected.

The village of Vullafans, renamed the street where Gérard was born, "Rue Gérard" in his memory.

We resume now to the letter of Richard Clough to Sir Thomas Gresham, where we find written at the end of the last excerpt, *"Here enclosed, you shall receive a parcel of letters which I received from Sir Thomas Chamberlain, out of Spain."*

"-The Exchange passes at 22s. 4d. uses; small store of money, and takers. Having nothing else to bother your mastership at this present, sending your mastership and my Lady Gresham, good health and long life to the honor of God, and to your heart's desire."

"Your mastership's servant, Richard Clough"

CHAPTER XI

When last we heard of Sir Thomas Gresham, he was preparing to return to Antwerp on the Queen's orders for duties desired of Her Majesty.

Before leaving he composed two letters, sent to Sir William Cecil as follows.

"Right Honorable Sir,"

"It may like you to understand that I sent you my last [letter] on the first of this present [month] and there enclosed, a letter from Mr. Earl' by the order of Sir Richard Sackville. Wherein I desired your honor to be good unto me for the rate of the Exchange, for such money as was disbursed and paid here in London. So I shall humbly desire you to have consideration. Also it may please you to be aware, that my Lord Treasurer has appointed me to pay the 27th of August in Antwerp, the sum of £44,784. 6s. whereof the Merchant Adventurers pays £30,000 sterling. For, being rated at 22s. to the pound, I shall thereby lose money."

"As likewise, whereas the Queen Majesty has appointed me, by my instructions, fifty-thousand pounds to be prolonged until February next, my Lord Treasurer will have that set over until August 1562, with the rest of the debt due this August and November, which amounts to one-hundred-thousand pounds. And for the rest of the Queen's debts to be prolonged, to pay in June 1562, £14,094. 19s. 4d. and in November, 1562, £14,094, 19s. 4d. and in December 1562, £14,094, 19s. 4d."

The second letter from Gresham was as follows:

"Right honorable Sir,"

"Since the writing thereof, 1 have received two letters from my factor, Richard Clough, which 1 send to you here enclosed for you to consider at your leisure, for that it is much noted that the King of Denmark has altered his purpose, and taken up all the ships he can come by at Hamburg and Bremen."

....

Frederick II, King of Denmark, had inherited from his predecessor, the Livonian War, where he installed his younger brother Magnus of Holstein, whom he considered "troublesome", as Bishop. Lest Danish efforts create more insecurity for Sweden, Denmark made another attempt to mediate a peace in the region. Magnus at once pursued his own interests, purchasing the Bishopric of Courland without Frederick's consent and trying to expand into Harrien–Wierland . This brought him into direct conflict with Eric XIV, King of Sweden.

..."After my most humble commendations, it may like you to understand that 1 wrote you my last upon my arrival at Dunkirk, and as the 17th 1 arrived in this town...The occurrence that the King of Sweden has sent commissioners into the lands of Wurtemberg (in Germany) *to take up a great number of horsemen and footmen, some men 1 think to give war against the King of Denmark."*.

"Both the King of Denmark and the Duke of Holst do arrest and take up all the ships they can come by at Hamburg and Bremen: to what purpose it is not yet here revealed. The Duke of Augustus has sent the County of Swartzenburg and another County in post to the King of Denmark. The Duke Augustus and nobles in Germany do take in very ill part that King Philip would suffer none of his nobles of this country to accompany the Prince of Orange to his marriage of the Duke Maurice's daughter, for fear that any of them should

be corrupted with their heresy. The saying is, that the French King has sent the order of St. Michael to the King of Denmark."

"Of other news I will not bother you with, but that I have shipped your four chairs of leather and two of velvet and the rest of the velvet, will be ready this next week. Most humbly beseeching you, at the Queen Majesty's coming to Enfield, to remember me for the passing of my account. As I trust in in God and you. That it may please you to write for Sir Walter Mildmay to be there. Thus, with my most humble commendations to my Lord Admiral Clinton and to Sir Frances Knollys, and to my Lady your wife, I commit to God, to preserve you with increase in honor."

"From Antwerp, the 19th day of August, 1561."

"At your honor's commandment,"

"Thomas Gresham"

Thus we follow Gresham back to Flanders, where he proceeded in order to receive £30,000 of the merchant-adventurers, to pay a portion of the Queen's debt, and to persuade her creditors to postpone for the space of a year the liquidation of the sums due in November and December. In less than a fortnight, (two weeks), we find him addressing the secretary from Antwerp, as follows:

August 24, 1561, Gresham wrote to Cecil:

"Wrote last on the 19th, instant. The Kings of Sweden, Poland, and Denmark, and the Duke of Saxony, the Landgrave, and other noblemen of Germany have joined together against the Emperor of Muscovy The Council of Trent goes forward, where it is thought nothing will be concluded. The King of Spain requires from the States of this land a subsidy of money towards paying his debts and has been answered that they will grant nothing unless the Inquisition is put down and the land not be molested with the new Bishops in religious matters."

"Wrote last that the merchant-adventurers had received order for the payment of the £30,000 at the day agreed upon. As of yet, they have not paid one penny. On the 22nd instant, the Governor and three others appointed by the company came to me and said they could only pay £20,000. I told them there must be no delay, for it stood with the Queen's honor and credit. I have heard nothing of them since."

Letter to Cecil written August 30th, 1560:

"Wrote last on the 24th instant. It is certain that the King of Sweden will come to England and that he has departed from Stockholm towards is haven of "Newles" which is a distance of 400 English miles, and takes with him one of his sisters and his youngest brother and the youngest Duke of Saxony with other noblemen and gentlemen. He has made the Duke, his brother, who was in England, governor of all his countries."

"The merchant-adventurers and staplers have paid about £25,000. I trust they will accomplish the rest next week, which is a worthy service, considering the scarcity of money that is here, and the bankruptcies that have been since my last time here."

Letter to Cecil, September 2nd, 1561:

"Sent my last on the 30th of August, wherein I mentioned having received of the adventurers and staplers £25,000, since then I have received of the staplers the whole sum, and this week I trust the merchant-adventurers will clear the rest, which I assure you Sir is as worthy a service as ever they did, considering the little credit and great scarcity of money here. The Bourse of Antwerp is quite altered, for there is no credit to be had. There are likely to be more bankruptcies expected because the Kings of Spain, France and Portugal owe us more than they are worth."

"I have much to do with the Queen's creditors to content them with this little portion of money" Gresham wrote, "I nevertheless brought my charge to a good purpose, and prolonged the debts due the 20th of August into two payments. To pay the 20th of February next £37,069, and on the 20th of August 1562, £74,187, as appears by the note sent herewith."

"This instant [month], Mr. Harvey that was in Spain, came to me and said—"For as much as you are here wholly the Queen Majesty's administer, I come to give you to understand that I was commanded by the Queen Majesty's ambassador, Sir Thomas Chamberlain, to make my preparations for home, for her Majesty's pleasure was such. As likewise, I received a letter from Sir William Cecil, by which he promises me that I might safely come. For as much as I have no other assurance from her Majesty than by the Ambassador, I have written to Mr. Secretary [Cecil], my full determination therein."—

"I did persuade him that I could [assist him]," Gresham writes, "that your letter was more than sufficient, and that, if I were in his case, I would upon your letter presently make my preparations for home."

"But as far as I can perceive, he will not come home unless he has some other assurance, even with all my persuasion."

"So herewith you shall receive his letter, and a letter that he gave to me to be delivered to Lord Montague. He remain at Louvain."

Four days later Gresham wrote again. *"The saying is here that the King of Sweden for certain is coming to England with a great navy of at least one-hundred ships and brings with him two million dollars at least. Whereof I do right well know your honor has better intelligence of this by your ambassador than I can give you from here."*

"There is great talk here that the Emperor has become a Protestant, and has consented that priests shall marry throughout his dominions. Some say it is done more for fear of the Protestants for preserving his empire, others say it is a color to bring the Bishop of Rome's pretend purposes to pass."

Gresham received a letter on the 6th of September from Sebastian Spydel letting him know that they will shortly be finishing the refining of the base money in England and in two or three months will have the copper ready to take into Germany to extract all the rest of the silver. Spydel told Gresham that during the three months, they would have to pay all they owe in ready money, and to discharge all their obligations and securities. He asked Gresham to procure for them, the payment from the Queen, and that he would give notice, so that they could take up by the Exchange at Antwerp by the 20th or 25th of October as much as the Queen owes them. He added that in the event of not being able to discharge the whole sum, they would be obliged to ask the Council to take the debt as a set off for the silver and copper which they have to produce.

Letter to Cecil, September 10th, 1561:

"Sent my last on the 6th of September with a duplicate of the Queen's debts that I have managed to prolong in which there is a bond to be made to Conrad Schetz for 58,756 florins, payable on the 20th of February next. I have now

agreed with him to pay half thereof at six months, and the other half at twelve months, for which there must be two bonds made according to the enclosed."

"Since writing hereof, I have received a letter from Sebastian Spydel, who is doing the refining of the money among Daniel Wolstat and the others at the Tower. The Queen owes on the 20th of November £2,146. 13s. 4d. He desires his payment here or to be rebated at London, as by his letter enclosed may appear. I told him that I intend to be home by the 20th of October."...

"There has been talk here of a great earthquake that has occurred in Naples and has destroyed towns and castles. They say many people have died."

The preceding letters were written during a period of two months, made by Gresham at Antwerp in the Autumn of 1561. From October until the end of the ensuing February, he was in London and on New Year's Day, he and Lady Gresham presented Queen Elizabeth for the Christmas season. Elizabeth likewise presented the Greshams with gifts as well.

The active mind of Sir Thomas Gresham seems to have been as much on the watch as ever, for opportunities to benefit the State. One cannot help but wonder at the esteem he must have held, when the number and importance of his services are considered. During his long residence at Antwerp, however successful he had been in evading them, he had witnessed the superiority of the custom-house regulations in that city, or those same establishments in London. He wrote to his factor, Richard Clough, asking him to obtain complete information as to the system pursued in Flanders and to communicate to him the result of his inquiries in writing. This produced the following composition, which will be viewed with interest for the contrast it affords between the commercial usages of that age and the present, as well as on account of the interesting proposal with which it concludes. Nor will the reader fail to give Clough due credit for his intelligence and activity, when it is mentioned that a very few days after the receipt of his master's inquiries, he returned to him the answer from which an extract is here.

31st December, 1561 in Antwerp:

"Right Worshipful Sir,"

"It may please you to know that 1 sent you my last [letter] by our English post, wherein 1 wrote you of all things at large. Since which 1 have received your mastership's letter of the 20th, well understanding the effect thereof."

"First, whereas your pleasure is that 1 shall make inquiry among your friends here, for the order, and how they do use the matter in hiring out of their toll or customs here, with the whole system thereof,--1 have, through the friendship of your gossip, Christopher Pruen, now being Treasurer of the town of Antwerp, gotten the principal particulars thereof."

Clough proceeded to enter details of his discovery which covered sixteen pages of description. But for our purpose here, we shall only take up three or four.

"Sir, 1 am glad to hear that this thing is called for. Hoping that such order shall be taken therein, that it shall be for the Queen Majesty's profit, and the honor of the realm. For as the matter is now used, it is against conscience to hear that talk goes, how the Queen is deceived. Which, must be true considering the order that they do use, which is to no reason. Namely that the Queen's customs must stand upon the report of five or six searchers The searchers are known to be men that will be corrupted for money. For, in the opening of a vat full of silks, sometimes 1 doubt it is brought over to the customs house for such other wares. But and if the Queen Majesty will thus let out her custom, 1 do not

doubt but she shall feel shortly how the matter has passed. Otherwise, and if her Majesty is not disposed to do so, and if I might be credited therein, and if the Queen Majesty would bestow but two or three thousand pounds once, I would not doubt but to save her five thousand pounds every year at least."

"For were as the matter is used at London by so many Quays, crown-searchers, waiters and other polling officers in such order that all the world does cry out upon us, as you right well know. Here is in Antwerp but one or two searchers."

"Yet, I dare say there is more customs stolen in London in one month, than is here in Antwerp in one whole year! That is because they do things here in order and we don't in London."

"I doubt whether Mr. Secretary Cecil or other lords of the counsel, know of some of these usages which I have heard both Englishmen and strangers complain much about. One is when men have their goods at home in their houses, they must run sometimes ten days before they are able to get a searcher to come and see the opening of the goods. And unless he, the merchant, will give four or five groats to the searcher, he will possibly not come for fifteen days. There should be no reason a stranger or Englishmen ought to pay but one custom instead of one to the Queen and to the searcher both."

"This is a daily occurrence. And when the question is asked of the searcher or waiter, why he does that, they say that "they have but £6. 13s. 4d. wages, which they cannot live on."

"In my opinion, better it were that the matter were so used that men might be served as they ought to be! For I dare say that not on Englishmen, but strangers also are more grieved over the trouble, than they are in paying of the custom. One thing is certain, it must need be much against the Queen's profit."

"A merchant, whatsoever he is, having a vat or package of silks in his house for six or seven days, and considering the great customs that they 'do' pay for it, it is not to be thought the contrary, but that he will seek all the means he can to take out those silks and put in other goods in their place."

"Some men will say,--'No, because the searcher has put his seal on it.'-- he that made the searcher's seal, can make the like and it is to be thought that merchants are not the simplest kind of people there is. I know both here, in Spain and Denmark, men seek out the best headed men they can to do business with, especially abroad in foreign countries. In England, many will say these are customs that has been used a long time, yet in my opinion, and if they are never so old, and not for the honor or profit of the realm, they may well be broken."

"I write this much to your mastership to remind you that when the time comes, you may mention some of these matters to Mr. Secretary. For indeed it is a wonder we have so good orders as we have, considering what rulers we have in the city of London, such a company that do study for nothing else but for their own profit. For example, considering what a city London is, and that in so many years they have not found the means to open a Bourse! But must walk in the rain, when it rains, more like peddlers than merchants. In this country and all others, there is no one that have occasion to meet, that doesn't have a place to meet for that purpose."

"Indeed, if your business were needed done, and I had the leisure to go about it and you had the means to have the favor of Mr. Secretary, I would have no doubt but to make so fair a Bourse in London as great as the Bourse is here in Antwerp, without bothering any man more than he should be indisposed. Herein I am somewhat tedious, desiring you to pardon me for being once entered into this matter, I cannot seem to stop myself."

"Occurrences there is none, except that by letters out of Italy, they write of little doubt of war between the Venetians and Milan. For the Venetians have a town which some say has pertained to the Dukedom of Milan, which town they have lately fortified with a great number of men"

"And to the contrary, they write that the Marquis of Pescara doth make all the frontiers of the Dukedom of Milan strong and hath furnished them with men and ammunition, but it is though all will be seized, for the Venetians have too much money in that respect."

"They also write that the Pope makes great labor to have a general counsel, and that there is already at the Counsel of Trent more than 200 Bishops."

"As touching all other of your affairs, I wrote you at large yesterday by the English post; having nothing else to write you at this present time, but praying God to send your worship with my Lady, grace, health and long life, to the honor of God and to your heart's desire."

"Your Mastership's Servant,"

"Ryc. Clough."

The result of this correspondence does not appear to have made an immediate change of the customs system which had prevailed at the custom houses, but after a few years, a great change was wrought in this department, which was attended by an enormous increase in the revenue.

That a vigilant eye had for some time been kept on the merchants, is sufficiently evident, and the wealthy foreigners who had become naturalized in the city, but who were always regarded by their English neighbors in the light of rivals, had been the objects of peculiar scrutiny.

They were, it seems, in the habit of taking out a license to export a certain quantity of merchandise, paying the same duty as English subjects. It being always understood that the said merchandise was to be their own property.

The most interesting, if not the most important point of Richard Clough's letter, is his suggestion relative to the building of an Exchange or Bourse for merchants in London. Granted the idea originated with Sir *Richard* Gresham, Thomas's father, yet Clough's suggestion was no less a general expression of passion. As we now know from history and shall soon see here in this memoir to Sir Thomas Gresham, it is to his shoulders the completion of this idea will rest. It can be said with assurance that it was Cough's letter to his mastership that planted the seed in Gresham's mind.

From the month of October 1561, until the ensuing February, as perhaps already stated, Sir Thomas Gresham was back in London, but on the 4th of March, 1562 we find him on his way to Antwerp, addressing Sir William Cecil at five o'clock in the morning from Dunkirk, where he arrived after a stormy passage. To pay some of the Queen's bonds, and to renew others, was as usual the object of his journey. What seems to have caused him considerable anxiety, were four cases of treasure in sovereigns, which he carried with him in order to satisfy certain creditors. Carrying large sums of money was always dangerous.

The month of March kept him quite busy in Antwerp. On the 27th of March (having already written on the 21, 22nd and the 23rd), he announced his intention of returning home as soon as Clough returned form Deventer. With the Queen's indulgence, he proposed to call himself to account again, it being now twelve months since he had so done. Gresham writes: *"Trusting that now her Majesty will bless me with her Royal give for my service, in such sort as King Edward, her late brother and Queen Mary, her late sister did. As you know, they gave me and my heirs forever, between them, the sum of £300, in land per year. When I* took charge of this business, the Queen Majesty promised me, by the faith of a Queen, that if I did for her the same service I did for her late brother and sister, she would give me as much land as they both did."

In reality, Gresham rendered Queen Elizabeth more important services than both her predecessors. Gresham goes on to write: *"A brief account of Sir Thomas Gresham, knight, the Queen Majesty's agent in Flanders, for three whole years, one hundred-fifty-nine days. Determined the 22nd day of April."* – Gresham listed several rather hefty "charges" and "discharges" along with two items of which we have some knowledge, from an earlier mention in this narrative of Gresham. *"...an iron chest - £20, Charge of a Turkish horse - £10."* and finally,

"Writing and postage charges...£1,627. 9s. 0d.
House-hire [rent].................200/ 0.   0.
Diet [food] and Necessities.........<u>1,819. 3.   5.</u>
                       £ 3,646. 12s. 5d"

With regard to the second of these, it is worth mentioning that Sir Thomas Gresham's house at Antwerp was situated in the "Long New Street", or, as it is laid in the plans of that city, *De Lange nieu strate,*--which exist to this day and preserves it ancient character, and was in Gresham's time, the principal street in Antwerp.

During the intervals between his late journeys to and from London, he may be presumed to have been busy in the building of his mansion in Bishopsgate Street, to which he afterwards gave his name – "Gresham-House".

More will be spoken of "Gresham House" later, or by which it is known today as "Gresham College". This huge mansion was capable of accommodating so many people and yet we have to remember, living there was only Sir Thomas Gresham, his wife Lady Anne, Richard their only son, and Anne, the daughter. At the time the Gresham's lived here, it would have likely been more picturesque than it is today. Whereas today, looking at the college building, it is hard to imagine it once being a home to a family of four, surrounded by spacious gardens.

Directly opposite of the "Gresham-House" stood another mansion called "Crosby-Place, at the time in all its glory, and occupied by one of Sir Thomas Gresham's relatives. His cousin Cicily Gresham, daughter of Sir John Gresham, lived there with her husband Jarman Sewell, reported to be a Spanish merchant. Sewell, who likely came over from Spain in the company of King Philip, was at this time an opulent person of some not, and in Queen Mary's days had been employed in the service of the State. But from the following passage in a letter which Gresham addressed to Cecil from Osterley in 1566, Jarman Sewell appears to have subsequently experience some severe reverses of fortune. *"I am so bold,"* wrote Gresham, *"as to send you a letter that my cousin Cecily Sewell has written unto me, wherein I pray you, for my sake, to help her husband Jarman Sewell, to his money, if it is possible, in his great necessity, whom I will assure you has fallen in decay only by loss of sea and bankrupts."*....

This explains why, in 1566, "Crosby-Place" passed into other hands and why Sir Thomas Gresham left in his will to his cousin Cecily, of whom he was extremely fond, a considerable legacy. She continued to reside in Bishopsgate-Street until her death in January of 1610.

Before we leave "Crosby-Place", we should recall the many historical associations with it and to which Sir Thomas Gresham, having been often entertained within it, will add another. The medieval mansion was built in 1466 by the wool merchant Sir John Crosby. In 1483, the Duke of Gloucester, later known as Richard III, acquired the Bishopsgate property from the original owner's widow. It was the setting for a scene in William Shakespeare's *"Richard III"* Among other owners of note was Sir Thomas More and Antonio Bonvisi.

Sir Thomas More, honored by the Catholics as "Saint Thomas More", was an English lawyer, social philosopher, author, Statesman and noted Renaissance humanist. He was councilor to Henry VIII and was Lord Chancellor of England from October 1529 to May 1532.

More opposed the Protestant Reformation, and Henry VIII's separation from the Catholic Church, refusing to acknowledge Henry as Supreme Head of the Church of England and the annulment of his marriage to Catherine of Aragon. After refusing to take the Oath of Supremacy, he was convicted of treason and beheaded.

Antonio Bonvisi was an Anglo-Italian merchant in London, also a banker and employed by the English government, as well as being an agent for the Italians appointed as Bishop of Worcester. He was also a close friend of Thomas More. He at first leased the property to the priory of St. Helen's, a lease he bought from More. After the dissolution of the priory, he purchased it from the King.

At the beginning of the reign of Edward VI, he settled his affairs and later left for the continent, the lease of Crosby-House was made over to his tenants William Roper and William Rastell. He also conveyed ownership, but almost all involved were Catholics who when into exile before he did. The house was seized by the sheriffs of London, on February 7th, 1550 and came into other hands. Bonvisi soon recovered it during the Reign of Queen Mary. At the time of Bonvisi's death it passed into the hands of his nephew and eventually into the hands of Jarman Sewell and his wife Cecily, (Thomas Gresham's cousin).

Following a fire in 1672, only the Great Hall and parlor wing of the mansion survived. The Great Hall, still impressive, still exists today.

CHAPTER XII

Foreign travel began, about this period, to be fashionable with younger members of nobility and private families of distinction. It may have been observed in some preceding letters which Thomas Gresham addressed to Sir Thomas Parry, that the treasurer's eldest son, being on his travels, spent time in Antwerp apparently under the watchful eye of Gresham, who repeatedly requested Parry to increase the young gentleman's yearly allowance to "one hundred crowns more by the year". About the same time, Thomas Cecil, the Secretary's eldest son was similarly engaged, who having pursued his education under Thomas Windebank, his tutor, for a year or two in Paris, made his appearance in Antwerp a few days after Gresham's return to that city.

This young gentleman, afterwards made Earl of Exeter, was the only son of Secretary Cecil and his first marriage to Mary Cheke. He was at this time about twenty years of age.

So little is generally known respecting this young person, when one considers his illustrious parentage. Young Thomas Cecil's connections with Gresham, to whom he became eventually related, warrant his being mentioned in the life and times of Sir Thomas Gresham. A few extracts are given here from correspondence, which until now went unnoticed for their historical content, however, they are certainly illustrative of his character and history.

Sir William Cecil, his father, was one of those men who preserve everything in the form of a written document which came into his possession. It was a habit to which we are indebted, in a great measure, for our minute information in respect to many occurrences during Queen Elizabeth's reign. A great part of the letters which he addressed to his son, as well as many of those he received in reply, in addition to a considerable portion of his correspondence with his son's tutor, Windebank, have in consequence been preserved. The following is an early specimen written by the Secretary to his son in 1560.

"I wish you blessing from God, and to deserve it through his grace. I marvel that I have so few letters from you. Seeing, in writing either in French or Latin, you should profit yourself. Will desire Windebank to advise me of your expenses, that I may see how your money is spent. If you find in that country any things meant for my garden, send me word of it. And so, God keep you."

Your loving father,
W. Cecil

It is to be wished that 'son Thomas' [as Cecil called his elder son], had never given his father occasion for more serious rebuke that this letter contains. It is needless however, to anticipate reflections which we shall be compelled presently to make on this subject. For the moment, it suffices to say, that the young man having made a short tour, and visited in his progress Dieppe and Rouen, (of which towns Windebank sent the Secretary some account), the travelers returned to Paris on the 24th of June, 1561. The following brief extract is from one of the tutor's letters:

"Sir, I humbly beseech you, in your letters to Mr. Thomas, to remind him that he does not lease the commodity of the morning for his profiting in any kind of thing. I cannot perceive he has any great mind to the lute; but to the cistern, he has.....We received the 9th of this month, a bill of credit for 300 dollars from Mr. Gresham's man at Antwerp, to be received by us at our pleasure. I pray God we may bestow them well."

"As yesterday, being the 9th, my Lord Ambassador, Sir Nicholas Throckmorton, went to the court, to speak with the Queen of Scotland, to whom he presented Mr. Thomas."

In the Secretary's letter to his son, four days later, we read:

"To my son Thomas Cecil
in Paris"

"I have received three overall letters from you, but none make any mention at what charge you live at. Anyway, be serviceable, but not chargeable to Sir Nicolas Throckmorton. Begin by making time to translate into French, serve God daily, take good heed to your health, and visit once a week your Instructions. Fare ye well. Write ever so often to my wife."

Your loving Father,
W. Cecil

It could be said, up to this point there does not appear to have been sufficient motive for the displeasure which Cecil expressed towards his son. Perhaps he considered it the most likely means of making his son approach nearer to the high standard he had proposed for his son's attainment.

Cecil's complaints of him were that he was careless in his money matters, a fault of the greatest magnitude in the eyes of Queen Elizabeth's future Lord-Treasurer. He wrote in one of his letters to Windebank that he thought his son was a "spending sot", not fit to run a tennis court. Cecil also considered his son too idle. A sentiment he expressed in his next letter to Windebank.

"I know not what to judge, but I have had a watch word sent to me out of France that my son's being there shall serve him little purpose, for he spends his time in idleness, not in profiting himself in learning. If this shall be confirmed to me again, I shall think myself much deceived in you. And therefore, as you mean to have credit with me, look into this. If it be true, I would revoke my son. I pray you to write to me plainly."

"William Cecil "Lord Burghley"

Two weeks later Cecil wrote again to Windebank:

"Surely I have up to now had small comfort in him. If he deserves no better by doing well, I will learn to take less care than I have done."

"My trust is you will not, being thus charged, leave me deceived no matter how you feel of my son. But truly and plainly advise me of his faults. I know some of his old faults were to be slothful in keeping his bed, negligent and rash in expenses, and careless of his apparel. He was also loves frequenting seedy places with cards and dice. In study, my son is weary—in game, never."

"If he continues or increases in this, it would be better if he were at home than abroad. It is time to end this manner of writing, for it increases my grief. I have written herein little to him, and I wish he would change his ways, that I might sometime have cause to write comfortably."

"Fare ye well,"

William Cecil "Lord Burghley"

The correspondence of Sir William Cecil and his son's tutor having been briefly examined, we now look at the connection this had with Sir Thomas Gresham. The following letter is from Windebank addressed to Gresham from Paris. This letter must have reached Gresham a few days before he returned to England in April of 1562.

"*Mr. Gresham,*"

"*We have received your letter of the 20th of March by Mr. John Fitzwilliams, (Governor), together with the iii c crowns which you sent to us by him for which Mr. Cecil chiefly has cause to thank you. I have no less cause than he for that being furnished with money, you may think what a lightening it is to me of care that I have in this charge, that my Master has appointed me in a strange country. But seeing that I now speak of myself, surely Sir, I cannot but with great shame confess a great slackness, or rather a whole negligence in me, in that I have not for a long time, written to you as I should have.*"

"*For next to my Master, I acknowledge myself as much beholden unto you, as to any man in England. Not only for your great good and for the benefits you bestow upon me, but also for a singular affection that is within me, which I cannot constrain. But Sir, I desire you not to regard my fault in not writing sooner. If I may be any service unto you I am most ready.*"

"*I send to you herewith, a bill of my hand acknowledging the receipt of your iii c. [$300.] and so I will not trouble you further at this time.*"

"*Windebank*"

It so happened that on the very day Windebank wrote the preceding lines to Sir Thomas Gresham, Cecil wrote a letter of heavy complaint to Windebank regarding his son. The next two letters we look at are Cecil's letter to Windebank and Windebank's reply. As painful as it is to read these letters of Cecil complaining about his son Thomas, it should be noted that Thomas became much improved in character as he aged.

He served in government under Elizabeth I of England, first serving in the House of Commons in 1563 and representing various constituencies for most of the time from then until 1593. He was knighted in 1575 and appointed High Sheriff of Northamptonshire for 1578. He accompanied the Earl of Leicester to the Dutch Republic, where he was distinguished for his bravery. In 1585 he served as governor of Brielle.

His father's death in 1598 brought him a seat in the House of Lords, the 2nd Lord Burghley, as he then was, served from 1599 to 1603 as Lord Lieutenant of Yorkshire and Lord of the Council of the North. It was during this period that Queen Elizabeth made him a Knight of the Garter in 1601. He was created Earl of Exeter on the 4th of May 1605, the same day his half-brother Robert Cecil, 1st Viscount Cranborne President, was created 1st Earl of Salisbury.

Thomas Cecil married, firstly, Dorothy Neville, the daughter of John Neville, 4th Baron Latimer, by his wife, Lucy Somerset, daughter of Henry Somerset, 2nd Earl of Worcester; and, secondly, Frances Brydges, the daughter of William Brydges, 4th Baron Chandos, of Sudeley Castle, Gloucestershire, and widow of the Master of Requests, Thomas Smith, of Abingdon, Berkshire (now Oxfordshire), and Parson's Green, Middlesex. By his first wife, Thomas Cecil had eleven children:

William Cecil, 2nd Earl of Exeter.

Catherine Cecil.

Lucy Cecil, who married William Paulet, 4th Marquis of Winchester.

Mildred Cecil.

Sir Richard Cecil of Wakerley.

Edward Cecil, 1st Viscount Wimbledon.

Mary Cecil, who married Edward Denny, 1st Earl of Norwich.

Dorothy Cecil, who married Sir Giles Alington.

Elizabeth Cecil, who married firstly Sir William Newport *alias* Hatton, and secondly, Sir Edward Coke.

Thomas Cecil, esquire.

Frances Cecil, who married Nicholas Tufton, 1st Earl of Thanet.

But to return to Cecil's letter which is as follows:

"Windebank,"

"I am here used to pain and trouble, but none creep so near my heart as does this of my lewd son. I am perplexed what to think. The shame that I shall receive to have such an unruly son, greaves me more than if I lost him by honest death."

"Good Windebank, consult with my dear friend Sir Nicholas Throckmorton, to whom I have referred the whole matter. I could be best content if he would commit him secretly to some sharp prison. If that shall not seem good, yet I would rather have him sent away to Strasburgh, if that could be possible, or to Lovain, for my grief will grow double to see him, until some kind of amends may be."

"If none of these will serve, then bring him home, and I shall receive that which pleases God to lay on my shoulders. That is, in the midst of my business, for instead of comfort, a daily torment. If you shall come home with him to cover the shame, I rather desire to have this summer spent though it were but to be absent from my sight. I am so troubled, as will what to write, I know not."

"Yours assured,"
"W. Cecil"

Shortly after receiving the letter above, Windebank replied to Cecil the following:

"Sir,"

"After so many uncomfortable letters, for so I take them to be unto you, I wish to God I could with just cause, write to you that which might take away, if not all, at least some part, of your grief. But sir, I may not."

"Mr. Thomas' behavior doth continue as such. Notwithstanding all your severe letters—all counseling and threatening of My Lord Ambassador—all the shame in the world and all danger in inconvenience that both come and yet to come, that the same being known to you, it cannot diminish your grief, but increase it."

"And because it is most necessary, a remedy to be most speedily provided which lies not in me nor, in my Lord Ambassador. If he continues in this country, I cannot but let you understand that he is come to this extremity, that if good watch had not been kept, he would have fled away from us all and you."

"The means for money was, that he would have sold all his apparel and mine. And by the means of a merchant, using rather good will than otherwise, he was upon the point to have a couple of horses, upon credit of the merchant."

"And when a man is in an evil state of mind, he casts the worst that may come to him, as Thomas does. He says that he is sure of his position and that you cannot disinherit him. I leave it to be thought what hope there is of such a person!"

"His behavior is such to me, that I can be sure of nothing in my own custody, which makes me very perplexed. I am sorry that you will not have him home."

Young Thomas Cecil and his tutor are brought into closer connection with Thomas Gresham by a visit they paid him on the 7th of August and stayed with him until the 16th. They had come from Paris to see the principal towns of the Low Countries and Germany.

Gresham commented in a letter to William Cecil on how much Thomas had grown since last he saw him. He also mentioned that how well Thomas spoke French and that he seemed to be full of civility and virtue. Certainly a different view of Thomas Cecil from what we have seen in his recent past. It would seem from letters that Thomas and his tutor, Windebank and Gresham got along very well.

"The Queen's Merchant"

Sir Thomas Gresham

Served as financial advisor to King Henry VIII, King Edward VI, Queen Mary, and Queen Elizabeth I.

Founder of "The Royal Exchange."

Lady Gresham - Wife of Sir Thomas Gresham

Anne Ferneley

Above: King Henry VIII
Ruler of England from
1509 - 1547
Married six times.

Right: Edward VI
Son of Henry VIII and Jane Seymour - Ruler of England from
1547—1553

Above: Mary Tudor daughter of Henry VIII and his 1st wife Catherine of Aragon.
Ruler of England from 1553 - 1558

Above: Elizabeth I daughter of Henry VIII and his 2nd wife Anne Boleyn.
Ruler of England from 1558 - 1603

Sir William Cecil 1st Baron Lord Burghley, Chief advisor to Queen
Elizabeth I, Secretary of State (1550–53 and 1558–72)
Lord High Treasurer from 1572.

Sir Richard Clough

Close friend and Merchant (Factor or Manager) for Sir Thomas Gresham. Stationed in Antwerp he ran the affairs of Queen Merchant in Gresham's absence. Credited for planting the seed for the construction of a Bourse in London in the mind of Thomas Gresham.

Mary, Queen of Scots, also known as Mary Stuart or Mary I of Scotland, reigned over Scotland from 14 December 1542 to 24 July 1567.

Robert Darnely

He was a first cousin and the second husband of Mary, Queen of Scots, and was the father of her son James VI of Scotland, who succeeded Elizabeth I of England as James I.

As husband of Mary Queen of Scots, he was king consort of Scotland from 1565 until his murder at Kirk o' Field in 1567

Robert Dudley, 1st Earl of Leicester KG (24 June 1532 or 1533[note 1] – 4 September 1588) was an English nobleman and the favorite and close friend of Elizabeth I's, from her first year on the throne until his death. He was a suitor for the queen's hand for many years.

Philip II became king of Spain in January 1556. He governedSpain in her so-called "Golden Age". However, his reign saw the economic decline of Spain, her bankruptcy and a disastrous decade from 1588 to 1598 which included the disaster of the Spanish Armada.

The Low-Countries (Antwerp)

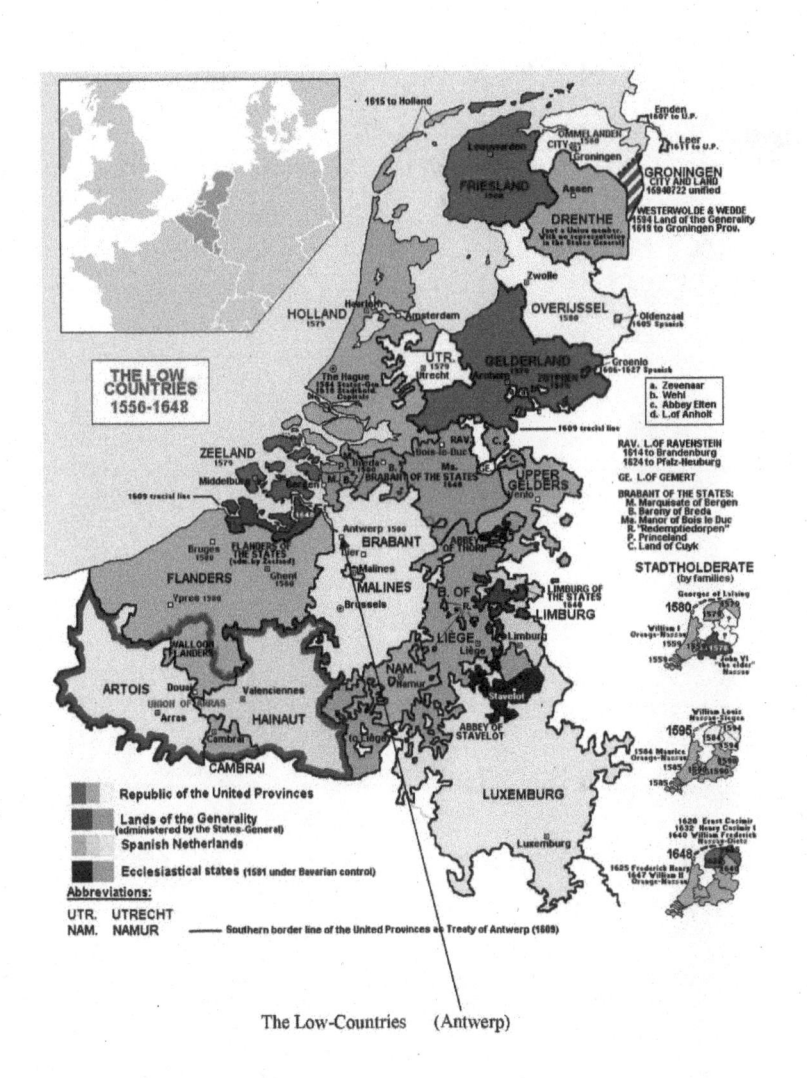

Above: The Royal Exchange as it most likely appeared in Sir Thomas Gresham's day.
Below: Inside the mezzanine of the Royal Exchange as it appears today.

CHAPTER XIII

When last we heard of Sir Thomas Gresham he was taking his leave of young Robert Cecil and his tutor, who left Antwerp in order to proceed to Germany on the 16th of August 1562.

Gresham was witnessing trouble brewing in Antwerp at this time. Having now reached the period when the seeds of discontent had already been noticed in Flanders and had now ripened into dissension among the people and the faction among their rulers.

Cardinal Granville, Bishop of Arras and King Philip's favorite minister, had proved himself particularly obnoxious to the Flemish—commoners as well as individuals of rank. The latter, in fact, had so labored to effect his ruin, that they would eventually succeed at last in procuring his removal from Antwerp, but not for a couple of years yet. Nor would it be without earning for themselves a deep resentment of the King of Spain.

The mischief, in the meantime had been done. The cardinal had fostered, measures of the most unpopular and repugnant to the spirit of the age, and these, with their long train of consequent evils, slowly worked their way, long after his departure from Antwerp.

First in order, was the establishment of twelve new bishops in the Provinces. That this scheme—for which the papal bull was obtained with considerable difficulty and delay—had been for years a favorite project with Philip, is certain. And that he and no one else, was to blame for this infringement on the rights and revenues of the established clergy of Flanders, seems equally clear. But the population, in their hatred of the obnoxious cardinal, attributed the measure entirely to him. When they witnessed his elevation to the archiepiscopal in 1561, they required no further confirmation of their suspicions.

Next and this was by far the most formidable of the evils with which Flanders was threatened, came the projected introduction of the Spanish Inquisition into that country. The Inquisition was an organization within the Roman Catholic Church that existed from 1542, created to punish people whose religious beliefs were considered wrong. This odious project exasperated all classes, and aroused, as might be expected, the indignation of the population to the last degree. They made up their minds that their enemy, the cardinal, was at the root of this grievance also, and that he had proposed the measure to King Philip. It was a scheme for making himself Inquisitor-General, while the twelve bishops were to become Inquisitors, each over his respective diocese. The motive for the introduction of this system, was the same which had been assigned for the formation of the new bishops, namely, the security of the established Roman Catholic religion. But whereas the latter measure, however unpopular at first, proved in a short span of time, so far palatable, that at the Council of Trent it encountered very little opposition, the affair of the Inquisition was soon found to be altogether intolerable. It admitted no compromise, and became eventually the grand pretext for rebellion. So loud and so general throughout the Low Countries was the outcry raised against the proposed introduction of this.

It is impossible to discuss the state of Flanders in the year 1562, without mentioning the religious conflict which was raging at the time in France, between the Papists, headed by the Duke of Guise, on one hand, and the Huguenots, under the Prince of Condé, on the other. What deserves our notice is the share which England took in the quarrel. Alarmed for its national safety if the Roman Catholics should prevail, the English government at first sought to bring about a pacification between the contending parties, but when the attempt proved unavailing, it became a measure of self-defense to grant to the endangered Huguenots the aid they solicited.

Queen Elizabeth entered into a convention with the Prince of Condé, in the month of September, announcing her intention to possess herself of all those harbors in Normandy, whence a descent on the English coast by the papal faction might by apprehended, but promising at the same time not to retain them beyond the period of danger, and pledging herself to recall her forces when peace should be re-established in France and the town of Calais restored, according to the covenanted stipulation. A naval armament was sent to Newhaven, on which the Huguenot chiefs delivered the town, as they had agreed, peaceably, into the possession of the English.

The aid thus granted by Queen Elizabeth to the Protestant party was of the highest importance. Philip regarded the cause of the Duke of Guise as his own and urged forward by his religious zeal, was for the extermination of the Huguenots. Now that one can see how the occurrences of this period gained the attention of all of Europe and especially of the northern portion, where the scene of our story chiefly lies. How fatal they were to the commerce of Antwerp, may easily be understood.

On Gresham's arrival at that city in July of 1562, he found the inhabitants all in a ferment. The letter which he addressed on that occasion to Sir William Cecil follows:

"Right Honorable Sir,"

"After my most humble commendations, it may like you to understand that, as of this day, I arrived here at 11:00 o'clock in the morning and at that instant, I received this packet of letters from Doctor Monte to be sent on to you with all the speed that may be."

"Letting you know that, as yet, I have not spoken with one of the Queen Majesty's creditors, neither for the prolonging, nor taking up, which matter will take some time, therefore you must have patience."

"The occurrences here that by the practice of Monsieur de Guise, the five forts in Piedmont which were kept to the French King's use, were delivered to the Duke of Savoy. The said Duke has sent the soldiers that were in the five fortresses, under the conduit of the Prince of Mantua, to the assistance of the Duke of Guise, which news of this comes today from Paris by letters of the 21st this present."

"The said Prince of Mantua has in two places, overthrown twelve thousand men of the Prince of Condé, which news I take it, to be of the devise of some papist. I know that you have better intelligence from my Lord Ambassador, than I can likely give from here. Of further news, nothing is certain."

"Likewise, here is no news other than the Queen Majesty will have wars with Monsieur de Guise, and take part with the Prince of Condé and that the Queen Majesty has above twenty-thousand men in the readiness."

"Finally, if a man should write of all things that passes here, it would be too much to bother you with. For, at this instant, I can write you of nothing certain, but that every man speaks according to his religion. And thus, desiring you to do my most humble commendation to my Lord Robert Dudley, I commit you to God."

"From Antwerp the 27th of July, 1562"
"At your honor's commandment,"
"Thomas Gresham"

P.S.

"They write out of Germany that the 7th of September next, the Emperor's son Maximillian shall be crowned King of Bohemia in the city of Sprague. As also, the 27th of October, the Emperor with the Princes will meet at Frankfort, for the electing of a new Emperor."

In Gresham's next letter, which is dated the 1st of August, he mentions that Count Mansfeld was actively engaged in raising troops of horsemen for the King of Spain. You remember Mansfeld don't you? The man who welched on a deal to loan money to Queen Elizabeth. With the same piece of intelligence he commences his next letter, written eight days later, with the following passage which deserves mention here.

"I am right glad I have passed over that the store of ammunition is done. For here comes news out of France daily, that every man cannot tell what to say or do. Here is now told about, that the King hath sent to Monsieur de Guise 4,000 Spaniards out of Spain, and that the King of Spain was provided 3,000 horsemen by the Count of Mansfeld. There has arrived to the Duke of Guise 6,000 Germans, brought by Ringrave. So that now, they think the Prince of Condé too much under foot to withstand this business, except the Queen Majesty doth assist him."

"Answering you, the gravest and wisest men here hesitate not to say, that if the Queen Majesty doesn't help, having this opportunity, if Monsieur de Guise and the papists should have the upper hand—let her Majesty make her reckoning, they will visit her for religion's sake! Which has made such an alteration of credit as this pen cannot write you. Beseeching the Lord to put into her Majesty's head and you, and the rest of my Lords of her most honorable council, to do the thing that may be for the best. For now is the time, (they say here) to recover those pieces that we have lost of late in France, or else better pieces. Being right assured her Majesty has provisions of men, munitions and

armor to do it withal. Which is not hidden, but well known to all princes of Christendom."

"I will not enlarge any further in this matter, by pointing out what a treasure and strength it is to her Majesty and her realm, because I have been the doer thereof. But if I were of such credit with her Majesty as to be able to persuade her Highness, I would wish there were provided three hundred or four hundred-thousand pounds weight of salt-peter more, for all events. I know her Majesty has brimstone enough to make two hundred-thousand weight of salt-peter. It will be the only thing she shall lack, if wares should change, which should be foreseen in time. Her ships are nothing without powder. For as your honor knows, here will none be suffered to pass out of the King of Spain's dominions."

It should be remembered that Gresham's main concern was financial business and how circumstances happening between Spain, France, and England affected that business. In another of his letters, he spoke of how the 'money men' in Antwerp were afraid to deal any further with the Queen Majesty, by reason they cast so many doubts of the troublesome world.

Gresham said that there in Antwerp there was no other communication but that, if Monsieur de Guise gets the upper hand of the Protestants, then the French King, the King of Spain, the Pope, the Duke of Savoy and those of that religion, meaning Catholicism, will set upon the Queen Majesty only for religion's sake, whether she takes part or not.

Gresham was concerned that there was such a great amount of doubt cast upon England that the credit of Elizabeth and of the whole nation was at a standstill. Word had reached Antwerp that de Guise had taken the town of Poiters in west-central France, and that two-thousand persons had been killed or injured. They also heard that de Guise was increasing his power daily.

In one communication Gresham said, *"Here is now great communication that the Queen Majesty has twelve great ships abroad and that her Highness sends to the aid of the Prince of Condé ten-thousand men which is marvelous and well liked of all this country of Flanders. For now, every man says the time and opportunity her Majesty is never likely to have, whereby to come by Calais, or some other such place. Which I pray to God to send us."*

P.S.

"Monsieur de Guise and his part begins to grow in great necessity of money, for all the great assistance he has received from the Bishop of Rome, the King of Spain and others. Trusting in God, he will cut his own throat for lack of money!"

"August 16, 1562"

"Thomas Gresham"

For whatever the reason, the tide did seem to turn in favor of Prince Condé about this time, for in a letter dated August 20th from Gresham stated the following.

"Here is news come that Ringrave and de Guise have fallen at great dissention by the reason his men will not fight against the Prince of Condé, for the profess the same religion! And likewise, there is intelligence come out of Italy that the Duke of Florins and the Duke of Farrara have fallen out and that the Bishop of Rome will take the side of the Duke of Florins in that quarrel. The state of Venice will take part with the Duke of Farrara. The certainty of the quarrel at this present, I cannot tell, but by my next letter I trust I shall know if it is true. To conclude, here there is such joy at this incredible news."

"The men that was provided in Germany for the Prince of Condé remains in one estate. I understand they will not leave until they have been paid for their service."

"Here, every man's head is so full of this matter of France, that they cannot tell what to do. Fearing this matter will not be so ended, but that it will set all Christian princes together by the ears. For now, the saying is that the Prince's protestants of Germany be resolved and agreed with Monsieur Dondelot, and that the forty-thousand horsemen and thirty-thousand footmen should march the 25th of this month. Also, there is news come out of France, that the Queen of Navare and the wife of the Prince of Condé should be encamped with ten thousand men and that they have laid siege to Toulouse, and have won the town again by assault."

"As also, the saying is here, that New Haven and Diep should be delivered up to the Queen Majesty and that her Highness's ships should be there, which I pray to God to be true."

"August 22, 1562"
"Thomas Gresham"

Such was the state of affairs in Flanders about the close of the year 1562, at which time Sir Thomas Gresham once more returned to England. He seems to have left Antwerp on the last day of August or during the first few days of September, for the Council-Book (MS.Vol. 58) states that he made his appearance at Greenwich on the 6th.

CHAPTER XIV

After the numerous extracts from Gresham's correspondence which have been already given, it becomes superfluous to observe that the events, or the rumors of the day form the general topic of his letters. Added to the occasional notices of the progress he was making in the queen's affairs, which now became so difficult to manage as to be almost impracticable. He remained in England until the following spring.

As if the war with the Duke of Guise and the King of Spain wasn't enough to keep Elizabeth and her privy council, and even Sir Thomas Gresham, occupied with concern, another matter was about to occur which would be the cause of much distress.

On October 10th 1562, twenty-nine year-old Queen Elizabeth was taken ill at Hampton Court Palace, with what was thought to be a bad cold. However, she developed a violent fever and a doctor was sent for. He diagnosed her with smallpox, to which she swiftly dismissed him, denying that she had the dreaded decease that was sweeping through the kingdom, killing and disfiguring tens of thousands.

By the 16th, she was worse and was having trouble speaking. She lapsed in and out of consciousness. Fearing the worse, other medical experts were summoned and the diagnosis was confirmed. The Privy Council sent for Sir William Cecil to discuss the possibility of the Queen's death and whom would succeed her. Over the next few days the councilors were panic stricken.

Even Elizabeth herself felt she was dying and during one of her conscious moments as the Privy Councilors gathered around her bedside, she commanded them to appoint Robert Dudley, Lord Protector of England in the event of her death. The councilors were greatly opposed to this, but promised to follow her instructions so as not to distress her with their arguments. The truth of the matter however, was there was no way her request would ever been applied.

Robert Dudley had been a thorn in the side of the Privy Council because of his close romantic relationship to Queen Elizabeth. In the spring of 1559 it became evident that Elizabeth was in love with her childhood friend. Sir William Cecil in particular did not like Dudley due to his influence over Elizabeth. By the autumn of 1559 several foreign suitors were vying for Elizabeth's hand; their impatient envoys engaged in ever more scandalous talk and reported that a marriage with her favorite was not welcome in England. The public could not forget nor forgive that Robert Dudley was the son and brother of traitors to the throne of England, and that his father, John Dudley (Northumberland) and his brother Guildford had been executed as traitors under Queen Mary's reign.

Another problem with Robert Dudley was the fact that on June 4th, 1550, he had married Amy Robsart, the daughter and heiress of Sir John Robsart. It was claimed that his wife Amy suffered from a "malady in one of her breast" and that the Queen would likely marry Dudley if his wife should die.

Amy Dudley in fact, did die. On Sunday 8 September 1560, Amy was found dead at the bottom of a flight of stairs with her neck broken. This turned into one of the most intriguing unsolved mysteries of the Elizabethan period which struck right at the heart of the royal court and the queen herself.

Amy was staying at Cumnor Place, a medieval manor house in Berkshire which was owned by George Owen, one of the royal physicians who had treated Henry VIII, but had been rented by Sir Anthony Forster, a friend and a member of Robert Dudley's household.

Amy awoke early that morning and her servants noticed that she was agitated and determined to be alone. In the nearby town of Abingdon four miles away, the Fair of Our Lady was taking place, and Amy instructed her entire household to attend. One of her gentlewomen, an elderly widow named Mrs. Odingsells, refused to go. She told Amy that 'it was no day for gentlewomen to go in' – Sundays were usually reserved for the common people at the fair. It would be best if they attended the following day: 'the morrow was much better,' she remarked.

Hearing this, Amy grew 'very angry', replying that she 'might choose and go at her pleasure.' She insisted that the rest of her household should leave for the day and that Mrs. Owen, the sister of George Owen, would join her for dinner.

Once all the household had left for the fair Mrs. Odingsells and Mrs. Owen sat down to play cards when they heard a crash.

Amy's body was discovered at the foot of a staircase which was just eight steps high. She was dead of what appeared to be a broken neck but the oddest thing was, her headdress remained intact upon her head and no other mark was found upon her body.

A man named Bowes, a retainer of Dudley's, was present at Cumnor Place when Amy's body was discovered. He set off immediately for Windsor to inform his lordship of his wife's death. On the road Bowes ran into Thomas Blount, Dudley's household officer who was already riding out on the road from Windsor. He revealed all he knew to Blount who then decided not to travel directly to Cumnor that evening. Instead, he stopped off at an inn nearby in Abingdon for an evening meal and also to listen to any rumors that were circulating about Amy's sudden death. 'I was desirous to hear what news went abroad in the country,' he later wrote to Dudley. At supper, Blount took the opportunity to strike up a conversation with the landlord, concealing his identity by pretending that he was not local to the area, and was merely passing through. He asked the landlord what news there was.

"There is fallen a great misfortune within three or four miles of the town,' the landlord replied, 'my Lord Robert Dudley's wife is dead."

"How?" Blount enquired.

"By a misfortune,' the landlord had heard. 'By a fall from a pair of stairs."

"By what chance?"

The landlord did not know. "What was his judgement?" Blount asked, "and what did the people think had happened?"

"Some are disposed to say well, and some evil."

"What is your judgement?" pressed Blount.

"By my troth, I judge it a misfortune because it chanced at that gentleman's house," the landlord replied, referring to Anthony Forster.

"His great honesty doth much curb the evil thoughts of the people."

"Methinks that some of her people that waited upon her should somewhat say to this," Blount ventured.

"No, sir, but little, for it is said that they were all here at the fair, and none left with her."

"How might that chance?" Blount asked.

"It is said how she rose that day very early, and commanded all her sort to go to the fair, and would suffer none to tarry at home; and thereof much is judged."

This was very intriguing to Blount and he suspected that there was more to Amy's death than he had expected. He wrote to Dudley, who was waiting anxiously at Windsor for further news: *"The present advertisement I can give to your Lordship at this time is, too true it is that my Lady is dead, and, as it seemed, with a fall; but how or which way I cannot learn."*

When Blount reached Cumnor Place he spoke with Amy's maid, Picto, whom he noted 'doth dearly love her', he asked 'what she might think of this matter'. Picto replied that she believed Amy's death was entirely accidental. 'By faith she doth judge very chance and neither done by man nor by herself.' Amy was, she said, 'a good virtuous gentlewoman', who had been seen to pray on her knees daily; sometimes she had even been overheard asking God 'to deliver her from desperation.'

Those last words were too important to go unnoticed. "That she might have an evil toy in her mind?" Blount asked.

"No, good Mr. Blount," Picto replied. "Do not judge so of my words. If you should so gather, I am sorry I said so much."

The jury was chosen and they viewed Amy's body and the evidence but would they have been qualified to judge whether Amy had met her death by accident, suicide or by more sinister means. Eventually their findings ruled that Amy's death had been an accident.

According to the report, the inquest into Amy's death had opened at Cumnor on 9 September, the day after her death, but was postponed until 1 August 1561. The verdict was finally given at the local Assizes in August 1561.

The aforesaid Lady Amy on 8 September in the aforesaid second year of the reign of the said lady queen [Elizabeth], being alone in a certain chamber within the home of a certain Anthony Forster, Esq., in the aforesaid Cumnor, and intending to descend the aforesaid chamber by way of certain steps of the aforesaid chamber there and then accidentally fell precipitously down the aforesaid steps to the very bottom of the same steps, through which the same Lady Amy there and then sustained not only two injuries to her head (in English called 'dyntes') – one of which was a quarter of an inch deep and the other two inches deep – but truly also, by reason of the accidental injury or of that fall and of Lady Amy's own body weight falling down the aforesaid stairs, the same Lady Amy and then broke her own neck, on account of which certain fracture of the neck the same Lady Amy there and then died instantly; and the aforesaid Lady Amy was found there and then died instantly; and the aforesaid Lady Amy was found there and then without any other mark or wound on her body; and thus the jurors say on their oath that the aforesaid Lady Amy in the manner and form aforesaid by misfortune came to her death and not otherwise, in so far as it is possible at present for them to agree; in testimony of which fact for this inquest both the aforesaid coroner and also the aforesaid jurors have in turn affixed their seals on the day.

This report reveals that Amy had two deep cuts on her head, one was a quarter of an inch deep (approximately 5mm), the other an extremely deep gash of two inches in depth (5cm). How did Amy get these cuts? Did she sustain them by falling down the stairs, even though her headdress was still in place? Or was she hit from behind by a sharp instrument, then either thrown down the stairs to make it look like she had fallen and the headdress placed on her head to hide the gashes or, was she just simply placed at the bottom of the stairs by her attacker? No other marks, apart from the cuts to her head, were found on her body. You would expect that had she fallen down stone steps, she would have some bruising to her arms or wrists and face, but there were none.

Despite the coroner's inquest finding that it was an accident, many people suspected Dudley to have arranged her death so that he could marry the Queen.

Elizabeth seriously considered marrying Dudley for some time, However, William Cecil, Nicholas Throckmorton and some conservative peers made their disapproval unmistakably clear.

Now that the Queen was feared, close to death, the thought of making Robert Dudley the Lord Protector of England and therefore in charge over the Privy Council was out of the question.

Soon afterwards, the doctor entered her bedchamber to examine her and it was noticed the first of small pustules had appeared on her hands. The doctor assured the councilors that was a good sign, that the worst was over and the pustules would dry up and scab over. From that point on, she did seem to recover rapidly to the relief of the council and Parliament.

Throughout her illness, Elizabeth insisted only a minimal of her Ladies in Waiting attend her, as she feared spreading the disease. One of the most dedicated of those ladies was her friend, Lady Mary Sidney, wife of Sir Henry and sister to Dudley. To great despair, as Elizabeth's pock marks faded, Mary contracted the dreaded smallpox. In Mary's case, she became terribly disfigured by it, and never appeared publically in the Royal Court again. Elizabeth felt terrible about it, and remained Mary's friend, visiting her often.

Mary's husband, Sir Henry was abroad throughout Mary's illness and when he returned home he was horrified at her appearance. He later wrote: *"When I went to Newhaven, I left her a full, fair lady, at least in my eyes the fairest, and when I returned I found her as foul a lady as the smallpox could make her, which she did take by continual attendance to Her Majesty's most precious person. Now she lives in solitary."*

As for Dudley, who very nearly became ruler of England, Elizabeth made him a Privy Councilor and in order to preserve the peace, she did the same for his rival Norfolk. Although their rivalry remained intense, they displayed in public a cordial appearance.

Elizabeth resumed her full duties on the 25th of October, fully aware of the battle she faced over a suitor for marriage and, or who should be next in line of succession to the throne.

During this time, Mary, Queen of Scots, consistently wrote letters of support to her "dear sister, so tender a cousin, and friend", having resisted all attempts by the Guise faction to draw her over to their side. After Queen Elizabeth had recovered from her smallpox. Mary wrote to Elizabeth on November 2nd to express her relief that her cousin had recovered from her illness and that "your beautiful face will lose none of its perfections".

Mary was still enthusiastic about meeting with Elizabeth, and even more anxious to persuade her cousin to declare her successor to the throne of England.

Elizabeth wrote affectionate letters to Mary and after Parliament had been prolonged in April, she ordered the imprisonment of John Hales, a lawyer who wrote and circulated a pamphlet deriding Mary's claim to the throne and supporting Lady Katherine Grey. Elizabeth also temporarily banished his patron, Sir Nicholas Bacon, from court. (The wife of Sir Nicholas Bacon, Jane Ferneley, and the wife of Sir Thomas Gresham, Anne Ferneley were sisters it should be noted.)

Elizabeth's stubbornness at not wanting to marry and satisfy the question of who would succeed the throne was complicated even more in regards to Mary Queen of Scots. The succession was not a thing she could bestow as a gift, it was a right under the law, and there was much dispute over whose claim was the strongest, Mary Queen of Scots or Katherine Grey, both relatives of Elizabeth.

Elizabeth complained to Cecil that she was "in such a labyrinth" with regard to the problem of Mary and the succession that she had no idea what course to follow, yet Cecil could offer little comfort. He did not trust Mary because of her Catholicism, but he had also told Elizabeth that if she excluded her cousin from the succession, the result would likely be war. Cecil again, suggested to Elizabeth that it would be best if she would marry. Which is not what Elizabeth wanted to hear from her lead councilor.

For Parliament to accept Mary as Elizabeth's heir, Mary would have to prove that she had England's interest at heart, and her marriage plans so far had done little to reinforce this. Unaware of his sadistic tendencies, Mary was still pursuing negotiations for a marriage to Don Carlos, the son of King Philip of Spain, which was seen in England as being directly opposed to English interests. Elizabeth's wanted to see Mary married to a loyal Englishman, and it was around this time that she first conceived the idea of proposing Robert Dudley as a husband to the Scots Queen. This was probably her way of getting back at him for inciting Parliament into pressing her on the marriage issue. Gradually she grew to like the idea and began pursuing it seriously.

It was not such a preposterous idea. Robert Dudley was the one man who could be trusted to promote England's welfare north of the Border. He was indebted to Elizabeth for his rise to power as a member of the Privy Council. He was not likely to forget the woman for whom he felt such great affection, if not true love. Dudley was hungry for a crown and had a penchant for attractive red-heads. By marrying him, the Queen of Scots would remove herself from the European marriage market and the threat of foreign interference in Scotland would go away. England and Scotland would grow closer together in friendship. As a Protestant, Dudley would be able to hold the Scots Catholics in check.

The drawback of course was Elizabeth would have to give him up, but it seems she had already decided that she was married to England. Few people shared her view of the situation. Only Cecil, who perceived what good could result from the match and who, for reasons of his own, wanted Dudley out of the way, supported the plan. When, in the spring of 1563, Elizabeth first broached the subject to William Maitland, the renowned Secretary of State to Mary, Queen of Scots and ambassador at Elizabeth's Court, he thought it was some sort of a royal joke. When he realized she was serious, he stuttered and stammered that "this was a great proof of the love she bore of his Queen, that she was willing to give her something that she so dearly prized for herself, but he felt certain that Mary would not wish to deprive her cousin of all the joy and solace she received from his company."

Elizabeth said it was too bad that the Earl of Warwick, Ambrose Dudley, was not as handsome as his younger brother, for had he been so, Queen Mary could have married Ambrose while she herself became the wife of Robert. Maitland, maintained that Elizabeth should indeed marry Robert Dudley herself. Maitland's private opinion was that it was an insult that Elizabeth would try to pawn her discarded lover off on the Queen of Scotland, a man who was a commoner, with a reputation as a former traitor and suspected in his wife's death.

When Maitland returned to Scotland, he said nothing of this outrageous plan to Mary, but he did tell Bishop de Quadra who informed King Philip.

Dudley was still enjoying his bit of success, when in June, Elizabeth bestowed upon him Kenilworth Castle in Warwickshire. Kenilworth was a huge medieval fortress that had been converted by John of Gaunt in the fourteenth century into a luxurious palace. Northumberland had owned it briefly and Robert Dudley had had his eye on it for some years. Now, he would have his own county seat, just five miles from Warwick Castle, the residence of his older brother Ambrose. Dudley wasted no time in drawing up plans to renovate his castle, He wanted to make it a place fit to entertain the Queen. It would be ten years before Kenilworth was ready to receive her, and it would be the most magnificent of all Elizabethan mansions.

Elizabeth sent word back to Scotland to persuade Mary to allow her to choose her a husband. If Mary would consent that Elizabeth would be as a mother to her and would proceed to the inquisition of her right and title to be the next heir to the throne of England. The only clue as to who the chosen husband would be, was that he would be someone of noble birth within the realm.

Mary didn't understand what was being implied and begged for clarification. "Who, among the English aristocracy, would her good cousin regard as suitable?" But Elizabeth was playing for time, not divulging any more than she had to. As long as it kept Mary from pursuing other marriage plans, Elizabeth could keep Mary guessing for months.

In the coming weeks, Don Carlos fell seriously ill and this appeared to signal the end of Mary Stuart's hopes for a Spanish marriage. Carlos's illness was more than a convenience for Elizabeth, who had done everything she could behind the scenes to delay Mary from marrying until a safe husband could be found for her.

CHAPTER XV

Gresham was indebted to Richard Clough, as usual, during the interval, for Flemish intelligence. One short extract shall be given from a letter which Clough wrote on the 7th of March, 1563, because it communicates an event which arrested the progress of the religious troubles in France—namely, the death of the Duke of Guise, which occurred two weeks previous to the date of the letter. That eminent commander was engaged in the siege of Orleans, which he would probably have brought to a successful termination, when he was assassinated as he was riding from the camp to his lodging.

"For occurrence," says Clough, "*It follows that the Duke of Guise is departed, (whose soul may God pardon!) and that the Duke of Namor is appointed in his place. Yet some do affirm that Monsieur de Tumpase should be made general. But yet, to this day, they are not satisfied here, how he was slain.*"

The letter from which the foregoing short extract was made, met Gresham at Dover, on his way back briefly to Flanders on the 10th of March, 1563.

Illustrating the relative position of England and the Low Countries at this period, the troubles rendered insecure the property of the English commerce at Antwerp and elsewhere.

The pirates which infested the seas made the trade between the two countries both difficult and dangerous. This, added to the constant rumors of an approaching breach with England proved nearly fatal to commerce, that, for a time, it could scarcely be conducted at all, making Thomas Gresham's job that much more difficult.

This positon of affairs in Flanders must have operated to render a residence in that country particularly unpleasant, and Gresham was doubtless glad to find himself again residing in England in June of 1563. However, just two months later, residing in London would prove even more treacherous when the Plague broke out on August 2nd.

It had apparently been brought in by English soldiers from Newhaven, where it raged so hotly, that Cecil, in writing about it called it a "den of poison" and congratulated himself on the recent evacuation by the English.

In order to escape the infection, Gresham hastened with his family to his house in Intwood, near Norwich.

Plagues devastated Elizabethan England. They were a constant threat to the people and the land. The most devastating to England was the bubonic plague, which had originated in Central Asia, where killed 25 million people before it made its way into Constantinople in 1347. From there it spread to the Mediterranean ports such as Naples and Venice. Trade ships from these Mediterranean ports spread plague to the inhabitants of southern France and Italy. By 1350, all of Europe had been hit by plague.

In 1563, London experienced another outbreak, considered one of the worst outbreaks the city had ever seen. The bubonic plague took almost 80,000 lives, between one quarter and one third of London's population at that time. Statistics show that 1000 people died weekly in mid-August, 1600 per week in September and 1800 per week in October. One of those who died from the plague was Bishop de Quadra, who succumbed in August. His reports to King Philip had done much to weaken the relationship between England and Spain.

Fleeing from the cities and towns was common, especially by wealthy families such as the Greshams, who had country homes. Queen Elizabeth was no exception. She took great precautions to protect herself and the court from the plague by moving her court to Windsor Castle. She erected gallows and ordered anyone coming from London was to be hanged. She also prohibited the import of goods as a measure to prevent the spread of the plague to her court.

Gresham addressed a letter to Cecil on the 15th of August as follows:

"After my most humble commendations, it may like you to understand that I have received your letter of the 9th of this present. Being very sorry for your great heaviness, which I shall most humbly desire you to put no nearer your heart than you are able to shake off, seeing it will not help. For that it is well known to all men how careful you were to bring all things to quietness to the great honor of the Queen Majesty and the realm. Whereas you wish me there, I would have presently waited for you, but I have no house to put my head in, but in London, for me and mine, which I would loath to come to as yet, considering the great sickness that is there."

"Therefore I have sent to you by courier, my servant John Conniers, the note of prolongations for the making of the new bonds, seeing as there is no other remedy. I intend, (if we rest in peace with those countries, and hat I may in safety pass, to resort from hence toward Flanders, for the better preserving of the Queen Majesty's honor and credit, and the satisfaction of the creditors. Doubtless, my being there shall somewhat satisfy them."

"Most humbly beseeching her Majesty, if it stands so with her Highness's pleasure that I shall go, that I may have two or three good ships of wares to carry me over with her bonds from Yarmoth to Zeeland. I understand there are French ships of war abroad."

"Having appointed Conniers to resort there with the said bonds, and my Instructions, which I have drawn by a note of my formal instructions, for my better dispatch."

"Good sir, the more haste there is made in the writing of the bonds, the sooner they will be there. And by reason, the payments be in hand. Because of this plague, there is no money nor credit to be had in the streets of London. I understand from my servant Candellier that everyone is afraid to even speak with one another. Therefore it may please you to move the Queen Majesty to see it presently paid and hereafter, when the plague has passed and everyone falls to his trade again, money will be easier to be had."

"The poor citizens of London were this year plagued by a threefold plague—pestilence, scarcity of money, and war. No doubt the poor will remember it, the rich, by flight into the countries, made shift for themselves."

"I thank you for my warrants and for your bill obligations, which I received by Candelier. Praying for you. If there is any other service or pleasure I can do for you let me know."

"Give my most humble commendations to my very singular good Lord, my Lord Robert Dudley. From my house in Intwood, the 15th of August, 1563."

"At your honor's commandment,"

"Thomas Gresham"

One has to be amused by the fact that quite often, Gresham asks Cecil to give his regards to Robert Dudley, considering how Cecil feels about Dudley. You'll recall that Robert's father, John, or "Northumberland" as he was also known, was a close friend of Gresham. Therefore Sir Thomas must have also been friends with Robert Dudley as well.

It appears Gresham remained at Intwood a little over a month before resuming his duties to the Queen for we find his next correspondence dated the 28th of September, where he states he is in the suburbs of Antwerp. As indicated at the beginning of the letter to Cecil, we find that on the 25th, at five o'clock in the evening, he had taken some shipping goods from Harwich, aboard her Majesty's ship the "Swallow". He says Captain Handshew had arrived at Armu in Zeeland on the following day, at eleven o'clock at noon, Gresham had taken his passage the day after, to Bourburg and finally arrived at his destination at four o'clock in the afternoon. But once there, Gresham discovered he was not allowed to enter the city of Antwerp due to the plague that was still raging strong in London.

It would be two months before Gresham was allowed to enter Antwerp. His next letter is dated the 3rd of October where he says, since he wrote last, *"it had pleased the Lords of the town to license him to come into town to his house, with all his servants,"* and that he had succeeded in contenting all the Queen's creditors except Rantzowe and Brocketrope. *"I could by no means bring the factor of the said men to conclude with me, by this reason his commission extended only to be paid, or else to arrest me, and to proceed in justice."* He related how he had persuaded this agent to repair to his masters, and see if he could not persuade them to agree to the prolongation of the debt, by promising to defray the expenses of his journey, and to give him on his return a chain of gold, and he insists on the indispensable necessity of the Queen's getting ready by the 20th of November, £20,000 in gold, to be sent over to Antwerp for the purpose of being coined there, he said, than paying by exchange.

But a private concern of his own, which occupied all the rest of the letter, remains to be noticed. Queen Elizabeth (probably with the connivance of 'Master Secretary Cecil') in pursuance with that spirit of retrenchment, amounting to meanness, which characterized so many of her proceedings, had thought it proper to reduce her merchant's salary of twenty shillings a day. This Gresham terms as *"abridging me of my diet,"* for which he adds, *"methinks the Queen Majesty deals very hard and extremely with me….Your honor hath been* only privy to all my devices and doings, and considering how much I have always been beholding unto you in the declaring thereof to her Highness, so sir, I am the bolder to molest (bother) you with my grief and to open my poor meaning unto you, that it may please you to be a main (spokesman) now unto the Queen Majesty for me. And to put her in remembrance of my service done this five years, that she may have some remorse upon me. According to her Majesty's promise that she made me, before you, at her Highness's house at Hatfield on the 20th of November, 1558, when I took this great charge upon me."

"That was if I did her the like service as I did either to the King, her late brother or to the Queen, her late sister. She promised me by the faith of a Queen, she would give me as much land as both the King her brother and the Queen her sister did. Thereupon her Majesty gave me her hand to kiss, and I accepted this great charge again."

"Now finding that I have done her Majesty more service of greater importance and of greater charge and mass all manner of ways than I have done either to the King her late brother or the Queen her late sister, put both their doings together—for that their charge put them both together, did amount to the sum of £760,000. And her Majesty's doth amount alone, by accounts already passed, as your honor right well knows, to the sum of £830,000—which I will, with your honor's permission, partly touch for your better remembrance."

"First, at her Majesty's coming to the crown, I had taken up by me in Antwerp, the sum of £25,000 for which I caused her Highness to make a bargain with her merchants to receive in England, and to pay here: wherein I saved her a good piece of money, and served in turn for her coronation."

"Secondly, I took diverse other sums for the saving of her turn, diverse and sundry ways, and then made it a practice with the merchants to make payment here, of their cloths, as otherwise, which did not a little redound to her Majesty's profit."

"Thirdly, for furnishing her Majesty with all kinds of armor and munitions for the defense of her Majesty and the realm, whereby all Christian princes hath her Majesty and the realm in estimation."

"Fourthly, since she ceased to use the merchants for payment of her debts, how I have charged with my own credit by Exchange, for some time, £1,000, £11,000, £30,000, £25,000, and £20,000 at diverse times."

"Fifthly, I took up in one day in Lombard Street, upon my own bills and credit, £25,000 for her use, to her Majesty's great profit."

"Sixthly, whereas the King's Majesty, her father, and King Edward her late brother and Queen Mary, her late sister, did always pay fourteen upon the hundred and were feign to take jewels for one part or else they could come by no ready money, for the serving of their thrones. Since she came to the crown, I have brought down her interest to twelve upon the hundred, whereby I saved her in ready money in her coffers at times that should have issued out at times as good as twenty-thousand marks as the accounts will show."

"Seventhly, I have by her commandment otherwise lent my credit to all her ambassadors for no small sums of money, as to, Sir Nicholas Throckmorton, Sir Thomas Smith, and Sir Thomas Chamberlain, whom owe me £1,000, lent to them in Spain, whom would not been able to come home if I had not been there. Which I am yet repaid and cannot get my money."

"Eighthly, This is the 24th journey I have taken over the seas for her Majesty, of no small charge, diverse times in great danger of my life with drowning. I have always accomplished her Majesty's commandment and instructions in all points, to her Majesty's great honor and credit through all Christendom. And besides this, my leg was broken in her Majesty's service, whereby I have become lame, and now am getting older. Seeing that my service extends a great benefit to her Majesty and her realm than her Majesty did require of me at first, I trust her Highness will be as good to me as the King her late brother and the Queen her late sister was, for so her Highness promised me."

"Wherein good Sir, I shall most humbly beseech your honor that you will be my spokesman to her Majesty, as I may have my old accustomed allowance, and that I may have such reward for my service. And that it may not be put in oblivion as methinks now it is, seeing her Majesty begins thus to abridge me my diets in England."

"I have written a letter to her Majesty, wherein I have touched my grief as fair as I dare. Whereas I am allowed 20s a day, I have not, nor do not escape with the £40. a day—all my charges both here and in England accounted. I have sent you a copy of the Queen's letter, for your honor to consider whether you think it convenient to be delivered or not. Praying you now that you will stick with me, for this is the thing that I have in my head to trouble you with. I mean for the recompense of my serving, to be obtained at the princes' hands, having oftentimes, through your goodness, conferred with you in that behalf."

"I can say nor write no more, but the will of God and her Majesty be fulfilled! For my part, howsoever I shall be considered, I shall remain her faithful true servant to do her Highness the best service that lies in my power to do, as long as God shall send me life."

"Praying to you good Sir, to bear with me that I am so long and tedious unto you in this matter, for I will assure you, it has and does yet disquiet me."

"Thomas Gresham"

It was stated here at the beginning of this letter that it was probably with the connivance of Sir William Cecil that Queen Elizabeth reduced Gresham's income, but this is by no means certain. For as strange as it may appear, at about this same time, Cecil was lamenting in a confidential letter to Windebank, his son's tutor, the narrowness of his own circumstances. His words are these: *"I am driven in service here into such lack as I never looked for. I am forced to sell men office in the common place,* [Court of Common Pleas], *which was the stay of my living. I cannot carve for myself but if I might avoid the Court, and service, I should recover my losses."*

Cecil cannot be supposed to have been a party to his own ruin, and it therefore only remains to suppose that his royal mistress, acting with her accustomed independence, and inherited sense of high prerogative, was "abridging the diets" or curtailing the income of her servants, both at home and abroad.

Without much more discussing of this subject, one has to note that years later, Sir William Cecil declared of himself, that during the twenty-six years of Queen Elizabeth's reign, he had not been "benefited" so much as he had during the short space of four years under King Edward.

It is remarkable to know that as such disclosers as mentioned here of Throckmorton, Smith and Chamberlain, indeed all of the statesmen employed on foreign missions about this period, were in the constant habit of sending home, their letters of discontent. Their salaries did not by any means enable them to meet their necessary expenses, and they were all compelled to incur debts.

It is therefore, by any means to be regarded as indelicate or unreasonable, much less as singular of Gresham for remonstrating so openly with Cecil on the Queen's treatment of him and for so pointedly requesting the fulfillment of the Queen's promise to him that she would see him well rewarded for his services.

Gresham was well experienced in writing expressively to Queen Elizabeth on the subject of his grievances.

One may wonder if Queen Elizabeth rescinded her decision to cut Sir Thomas Gresham's pay. While it may not be clear in this instance, we do know that Gresham *was* and remained a very wealthy man and would do great things with his great amount of wealth.

With the object of Gresham's journey to Antwerp this time being accomplished rather quickly, he lost no time in returning home to Intwood again. The trip on the sea must have been stormy voyage, for when he arrived home nine days later, he reported how sea sick he was, but was glad to be home to his wife.

CHAPTER XVI

It appears by the following letter, that Gresham didn't leave the shores of England again until the 1st of January, 1564.

"Right honorable Sir,"

"After my humble commendations, it may like you to know that as of the 1st of this month present, at ten o'clock at night, Sir Thomas Cotton and I, with four of the Queen Majesty's ships, took to the seas at the land's end and arrived in Zeeland on the 2nd day at three o'clock in the afternoon."

"On the 3rd day, I arrived with my charge at Harrowgate and carried it overland by wagon to Antwerp, arriving there on the 4th. I have spoken with the agent of Brocketrope and Rantzavi, who will reserve no bullion nor gold, but coin. It shall be put into the mint with as much speed as may be."

"On this day, I will take my journey to Brussels and sense my coming, I have learned which of the noblemen hold together against the Cardinal, and who holds with him. I have directed the Queen's letter to the Prince and to them all accordingly. The copy thereof, you shall receive herein enclosed."

"Here is a proclamation come forth that no English ships shall be laid here, as long as there is any Dutch ships. Also diverse goods prohibited that none shall come into England. As by the proclamation that Clough sent you by his last letter, your honor shall further perceive. Which causes the common people to think there will fall out some breech between us and this country, than which I think they mean nothing less. For here is no provision of ships, nor other things for wares. Whereunto I shall endeavor to learn from time to time of their proceedings and tell you about them."

This brings us to the period at which the Low Country's troubles began more directly to affect England, by interfering on the part of the Duchess of Parma, regent for King Philip, her Highness having prohibited by a public proclamation, dated the 28th of November, 1563, the importation into Flanders of English cloths and wools. The alleged reason of it being issued was a dread of the plague, which for some time previous had been so prevalent in London.

But perhaps the real reason for the proclamation was an act of Parliament passed some time before, which prohibited the importation of pins, knives, hats, girdles, ribbons, and other small items already manufactured in England. This was encouraged by some of the eminent merchants, among whom was Sir Thomas Gresham, having lately set up those manufactures at home.

This may have been, and probably was, the immediate cause of the proclamation but the motive of it is to be sought deeper in the long-stifled, but never completely extinguished animosity between King Philip and Queen Elizabeth. In proof of this, it is to be observed that frequently, before issuing this proclamation, there had been misunderstandings more or less significant between the two powers. Not infrequently, encounters at sea occurred and whether Englishmen or Spaniard, the weaker was plundered regardless of the circumstances.

Gresham pointed out that so numerous and so loud were the complaints which awaited him upon his next arrival at Antwerp by the inhabitants of the city. He said, they were sorry for the stay against their cloths and other merchandise, from which they would suffer more than even themselves expected.

Gresham sent a letter to Cecil saying the Lords of the town of Antwerp had sent him (Gresham), a present of expensive wine, in hopes that he would be their spokesman to Queen Elizabeth asking her to be good to their town, as her ancestors had been. And to tell her they would do her Majesty any service they could. They were at her Majesty's commandment to the utmost of their power.

The Regent's next step was to prohibit the exportation to England of the merchandise which had been shipped before the uttering of her memorable proclamation, and on which the customs had already been paid.

Gresham had supposed that such goods for England having been shipped before the proclamation should pass, which proved untrue, for she would let nothing pass.

On the 26th of January, Richard Clough wrote to Gresham the following:

"The ambassador at Brussels was very honorably received. His lodging was appointed by the Regent herself. He received an audience with the Regent the next day after he came. Being called to the court by the Steward of the Household to the Regent, and twelve other gentlemen. At his meeting with the Regent, he was very gently received by her and all the other noblemen and councilors. And at his first meeting he delivered the Queen's letters, with her recommendations."

The Duchess of Parma, however, in her address, announced that she could not, in consequence, permit the importation of cloth and wool from England until next Easter.

This began the breech with Flanders by England. It was clear that nothing could have prevented such a proceeding. Despite the hostile disposition towards England, Spain continued its imports and exports without disruption. Queen Elizabeth hereby forbade the importation of Low-Country merchandise into her dominions. In the course of the spring, the Flemings began to feel all the hardships which the rashness of their rulers had brought upon them. The magistrates of Antwerp wrote to Cecil on the 27th of May, asking him to use all his influence with the Queen to procure the re-establishment of a free intercourse between the two countries, promising that, for their own part, they would spare no exertion to procure a similar grace at the hands of the Catholic King and the Regent.

Cecil replied with his usual address, "I am solicited to intermeddle in that which I know very well was by some disorders of private merchants, brought to the hand and order of the prince of both parties." He showed them that their request was unreasonable, inasmuch as on the 30th of May, another edict had been uttered by their nation against the English, from whom they now desired that an amicable measure should proceed. "So," he ends, "with some grief of mind, I conclude that the remedy of these evils must grow from whom the occasions of the evils first came."

However, this did not satisfy the parties he addressed, for they repeated their application on the 30th of June, declaring that they could not understand his inability to assist them. To which he replied, that since according to their statement this had been done by princes, and not by private citizens, the restitution of the former state of things must proceed from the princes likewise.

The negotiation of the ambassadors continued throughout the summer, for it is not until the 30th of November, 1564, that we find a *"Copy of accord between the Low-Countries for free intercourse."* By this, it was agreed, that for the adjustment of all existing difficulties between the countries, there should be held in Flanders, an academic meeting to consist respectively of "a Knight of the Garter and a Knight of the Order of the Golden Fleece", one of the "Privy-Council" of either sovereign, and a "civilian". These individuals were to beet at Bruges and in the meantime, all impediments to commerce were to be removed, and free intercourse restored between the countries. But while this negotiation had been proceeding, the English merchant-adventurer who could not afford to be idle, had made a trial effort at the city of Embden, in East-Friesland, a coastal region in the northwest of the German federal state of Lower Saxony, as a market for their commodities, by sending their cloth goods there. Thus the ties, which had seemed for so long, to bind the English to Antwerp, began to dissolve.

Gresham's periods of residence in the Low-Countries were now much shorter than before. In previous years, Antwerp had been his place of abode, and he had only made periodical excursions to London. But now, he made England his home and only visited Antwerp when he was compelled by urgent business to do so. His last journey had been commenced as already stated on new-year's day 1564, in the company of Sir Thomas Cotton. He returned home before the end of January, having probably seen enough during his brief absence to make him anxious to leave a city so unsettled and unsafe.

From letters Gresham wrote after he returned to England it appears instead of returning to his Intwood estate, he went to his lavish estate at Osterley. (Today, Osterley is an affluent district of the historic parish of Islesworth in west London.) It is likely that his newest house in Bishopsgate, "Gresham-house" was still in the process of being built. We do know that it is at Osterley that he and his wife generally lived ever after, dividing their time, as it would seem, between the mansion house in Bishopsgate and their pleasant residence ten miles out of town. There prevails a tradition in Norfolk, that Lady Gresham was the cause of the desertion of Intwood. It is said that she found the place so dull, and so ill adapted to her taste, that in order to disgust her husband with it also, she had a gigantic red brick barn erected immediately facing the back of the house, during one of is periodical journeys to Flanders. Absurd as the story sounds, the structure, which has since been removed, must have presented a very un-picturesque appearance.

The year 1564, would be a tough year for Sir Thomas Gresham in another way, besides the troubles in Antwerp. It is in 1564 that Gresham's only son, Richard, who would have been about 17 years of age, died. Sir Thomas, who had attained rank, wealth, and honors and up to that time had the prospect of reaping the fruit of all his cares destined to follow in his illustrious footsteps, was devastated. Richard Gresham was buried in St. Helen's church, close to his father's house. From the time of his son's death, Sir Thomas appears to have entertained higher views for the disposition of his wealth, and to have cherished the idea of using it for the public's benefit. His bereavement must have been long and severely felt. If one might be allowed to speculate on the subject, it seems in every state of prosperity and seemingly happiness, there are some drawbacks and few men are without some source of enduring anxiety or regret. The death of his son was no doubt something to which Sir Thomas Gresham must have habitually looked back on with immense sorrow. It would also be the thing that would cast the broadest shadow over his declining years.

The events which rendered Flanders a disagreeable place of residence to Gresham, rendered it, as might be expected, no less unpleasant to Gresham's factor, Richard Clough. It was about this time, that he decided it was time to retire and his heart evidently yearned with fondness towards his mother-land of Wales. The lands for which Clough was a suitor, were doubles the same which were granted to him in the course of the year 1564.

He returned to Wales and introduced Flemish building styles into the area with the building of two houses, Bach-y-graig and Plas Clough. He had become so rich that in his home area his name became a synonym for wealth. He became active in astronomy. He was named "Court Master" of the London Merchant Adventurers, now resettled from Antwerp to Hamburg, Germany. He died unexpectedly in Hamburg, sometime between March and July of 1570, while preparing to bring his second wife, Katheryn of Berain, home to the new house he had built for her at Plas Clough on the outskirts of Denbigh, Wales.

Before we leave Richard Clough, this may be a good place to recall his letter to Sir Thomas Gresham written on the 31st December, 1561 from Antwerp, in which he may have planted the seed in Gresham's mind concerning the building of a bourse or Exchange for the merchant-adventurers in London. Now, with the unlikely prospect that Antwerp would ever be the center of trade for England again, Gresham began to formulate the plan to bring about the completion of the idea.

Allusion is made to the founding of the Royal Exchange, in the minutes of the Court of Aldermen, in 1564, though the laying of the first stone would not occur until two years later. In those minutes of the meeting it is stated that in the 4th of January, 1564-5, a proposal was made to the court by Sir Thomas Gresham, (through his servant Anthony Stringer) that a Bourse or Exchange should be built in London at his expense for the accommodation of merchants, provided a site was found on which the edifice might be conveniently erected.

The need of such a building was at that time severely felt in London. Lombard Street was chosen for the purpose. In chapter six, we learned of the origin of Lombard Street and of it being the center of bankers and all money dealings, therefore having the Royal Exchange built in that spot only made sense. The idea for the Bourse had in fact been discussed before but not until the troubles in the Low-Countries, had it began to take on serious consideration. And when Sir Thomas Gresham came forward with the offer to defray the expense of the building of the Exchange, providing a site was found to build upon.

Several parcels of land throughout the areas of Broadstreet, Swan-alley, New-alley, Cornhill, S. Christopher's Parrish, and S. Bartilmew Lane, was bought by the citizens of London at a cost of nearly *£5000.*, subscribed, in small sums by 750 citizens, all whose names are recorded. More than eighty houses were torn down and the ground cleared in order to build the Royal Exchange upon.

Thomas Gresham had passed the years of 1564 and 1565 in England mostly. During which period some slight progress was made towards buying and clearing land, getting it ready for the building of the Bourse.

CHAPTER XVII

When last, we left mention of Mary Queen of Scots, Queen Elizabeth was in search of a suitable husband for her cousin. You may recall that Elizabeth was contemplating her own suitor, Robert Dudley as a match for Mary.

But unbeknownst to Queen Elizabeth, Mary Queen of Scots would soon have designs of her own. His name was Henry Stuart, Lord Darnley.

He was the eldest son of Mathew Stuart, Earl of Lennox and Lady Margaret Douglas, niece of Henry VIII. Being the age of twenty, he was four years Mary's junior. He was brought up Catholic with every expectation of inheriting both the English and Scottish thrones. He learned all the courtly pursuits, being a capable poet, lute player and dancer. He was an excellent horseman, loving the chase and hawking, and was trained in swordplay, shooting, running at the rings, tennis, golf and croquet.

Lord Darnley's mother, Lady Margaret plied Mary, with all the advantages of marrying her son, even suggesting that they could replace Elizabeth and restore a Catholic English crown. However, Mary had no desire to be confrontational with Elizabeth, who would see the marriage as hostile and was still intent on marriage to Don Carlos. In Elizabeth's eyes, if Mary Queen of Scots were debarred for being born outside England, the next in line dynastically were Lady Margaret and her two sons, Darnley and his brother Charles. However, with Lady Margaret remaining Catholic, Henry VIII had already vetoed Lady Margaret under his will, and she was equally unacceptable to the English Parliament. Yet Elizabeth had some sympathy for Lady Margaret and her sons. In February of 1563, she had asked Mary to end their long exile to England and to allow them to return to their Scottish estates.

With Lady Margaret still acting as a center for Catholic intrigue, Elizabeth had kept her under virtual house arrest at Court. Her motive seems to have been to destabilize the Scottish Government, while Mary was continuing to negotiate her marriage to Don Carlos.

Everyone knew what was going on. Lady Margaret worked hard to gain her son's favor with Mary while Elizabeth was still actively promoting Lord Robert Dudley. Elizabeth was frustrated and uncertain how to handle Mary's marriage and, on the 23rd of September 1564, wrote: *"I am at a loss to know how to satisfy her, and have no idea what to say."* William Cecil was aware that marriage to Lord Darnley would make Mary's dynastic claim to succeed Elizabeth unassailable, and it allowed Elizabeth to retain Lord Dudley for herself.

At first, Cecil saw the effeminate Darnley as a temporary diversion for Mary to delay more serious propositions such as Don Carlos, never expecting she would tolerate his bisexual and boorish character for long. Yet he saw Darnley as being much less dangerous than a foreign prince, having personal shortcomings which would destroy Mary's credibility. Darnley was already parading his own dynastic claims to both the Scottish and English thrones. He was a 'political lightweight' insufferably spoilt by his doting parents. If Cecil wanted to overlook Mary and Elizabeth's heir, Darnley was next in line. Besides, he was male, was born in England, and was not debarred under Henry VIII's will. With Lord Dudley still harboring ambitions to marry Elizabeth, he eventually tipped the balance with Cecil to promote Darnley as Mary's consort and together they tried to encourage Elizabeth to agree with them.

Mary soon began to see the advantage of marrying Darnley. The marriage would strengthen her claim to the English thrown should things between her and her cousin Elizabeth turn truly sour.

Darnley arrived in Edinburgh on the 13th of February 1565 and traveled on to Fife, where Mary was hunting. He apparently made a favorable impression on Mary. They went hunting and hawking together. He displayed his veneer of courtly skills as a musician, poet and dancer, charming Mary with his lute playing and enjoying cards and dice with her.

Although Lord Darnley appeared to be effeminate in some ways, Mary found him extremely attractive, perhaps partly due to his tall frame. Standing 6' 3" to Mary's own height of 6'. She loved the fact that as a dancing partner, she didn't tower above him as she did with most men she came in contact.

No one believed the match would prosper. Elizabeth was never likely to approve it. Yet Lord Darnley lost no time in proposing marriage, which Mary just as quickly turned down. As he was Catholic, she needed to 'prepare the ground'.

When the suit to marry Dudley fizzled out, it became inevitable that Mary would marry Darnley and she sent a convoy to England for Elizabeth's consent. This was refused with a claim that she took offense at Darnley's failure to seek her permission himself before leaving England.

During the first week of April, 1565, Darnley became ill with a measles-like rash accompanied by sharp pain in his stomach and in his head. These showed all the symptoms of secondary syphilis, which may have been contracted in England before his arrival. Mary insisted on nursing him herself and any formality between them evaporated. As he slowly recovered any pretense of Royal decorum disappeared. She was overwhelmed with feelings that she probably didn't know she possessed. He was too narcissistic to become infatuated, seeing her only as a trophy. No one had bargained on the Queen falling in love out of unbridled passion.

Meanwhile, in that April of 1565, Sir Thomas Gresham would experience yet another death in the family when his step-mother Isabella Worpfall-Gresham died. Isabella was the second wife and widow of Thomas's father, Sir Richard Gresham. She had appointed her son, Sir Thomas, joint overseer of he will, and among other legacies bequeathed to him a "counterpane" of fine imagery. (A counterpane is a finely made quilt, usually passed on as a family heirloom). This particular heirloom contained images of grasshoppers, together with two carpets, one for his hall and the other for his parlor, embroidered with similar representations of the family crest.

Lady Isabella Gresham, resided in Milk-Street, in the parish of St. Lawrence Jewry, and possessed five other tenements in Lad-Lane, which besides her own dwelling house, she left to the Mercers' Company for charitable purposes. It was her wish that the rent of this property, should be annually distributed among the poor householders of the parish where she lived and the adjoining parishes of St. Mary Aldermanbury and St. Leonard in Foster-Lane. It was further ordained that "such writings as should be made concerning the said good and charitable purpose, or the full effect thereof, should be openly read once every year in the Mercer's Hall to the said commonality, for the intent that the true meaning of Lady Isabella might be better known and performed."

While Sir Thomas Gresham dealt with the arrangement of his step-mother's will, the intrigue of Mary Queen of Scots' marriage plans continued.

Mary ignored Elizabeth and went ahead with marrying Darnley. Before the wedding on the 29th of July, she confirmed that Darnley would henceforth be known as King Henry, but resisted his demand for the Crown Matrimonial.

By September, Mary was pregnant and Darnley spent long periods away from Edinburgh supposedly with his father on hunting expeditions, but in practice plotting to gain Catholic support for him to take the crown. He had delusions of grandeur, as there was no concerted support for him in Scotland, although his efforts on behalf of the Catholic Church were recognized abroad. Darnley invested with the Order of St. Michael by the French ambassador with similar praise coming from the Papacy. Mary was furious and cancelled an understanding that they ruled jointly.

Darnley was spending increasing time in the Edinburgh brothels. Mary was left on her own, and amused herself playing cards with her acting Secretary of State, David Riccio.

The former Secretary, William Maitland who opposed Mary, hatched a plan to tell Darnley that the relationship between Mary and Riccio was improper, although it certainly was not. Some of the Scottish nobles promised Darnley the Crown Matrimonial if he would agree to arrange Riccio's murder and uphold the Protestant religion. Extraordinarily Darnley agreed. Maitland's real motive was to implicate Darnley in the murder and by association, Mary. Darnley hoped to carry out the murder in Mary's presence, in expectation that the shock would cause a miscarriage and her likely death, allowing him to gain the Crown.

On the morning of March 9th, the King, (Darnley) played tennis with Riccio, presumably to avoid any suspicion and in the evening Mary held a small family small family dinner at Holyrood in a small room next to her bedroom. Riccio arrived decked out in a gown of furred damask over a satin doublet and russet velvet hose. He wore a cap, which he failed to remove as he should have done in her presence. Much to the surprise of the guests, the King joined them and sat down next to Mary. He seemed to be in a good mood and was well received. But soon after the King arrived, one of the conspirators, named Ruthven, appeared, wearing a helmet and armor under his cloak. He demanded that Riccio should be handed over, while Riccio cowered for protection behind the Queen. Mary demanded to know Riccio's offence. Ruthven replied; "He hath offended your honor, which I dare not be so bold as to speak of." He also accused Riccio of hindering the King's grant of the Crown Matrimonial and of banishing many of the lords with a plan to forfeit their estates. Mary replied that if Riccio had done wrong, he should stand trial. She asked Darnley if Ruthven was acting on his behalf, but he denied any involvement.

Members of the dinner party tried to seize Ruthven, but he drew a pistol and advanced with his dagger on Riccio, who was still hiding behind Mary in the window recess. Ruthven manhandled the Queen out of the way, telling her that he was acting with the King's consent. At that moment, other conspirators appeared and one of them seized the King's dagger, thrusting it into Riccio so close to the Queen. Now on his knees and clawing at the Queen's skirts, Riccio cried out; "Justice! Justice! Save me, my Lady! I am a dying man! Spare my life!

Darnley leapt at Riccio, grabbing him by the hand that was clinging to Mary's skirt, bending back his fingers until he released his grip on the skirt. Several of the conspirators dragged Riccio out of the room.

Riccio was dragged through the Queen's bedchamber where armed guards were waiting. More than a dozen men, it has been said, savagely stabbed Riccio to death. There were between fifty and sixty stab wounds found on his body

The conspirators left the King's dagger embedded in Riccio's side. Darnley arranged for Riccio's mutilated body to be removed from the bedchamber. It was thrown down the stairs and laid across a wooden chest in the porter's lodge. The porter removed the King's dagger and stripped the body of clothing.

On the following day, Riccio's remains were quietly buried in the Conongate cemetery near the door to Holyrood Abbey. Mary later arranged for his body to be reburied with full Catholic rites in 'a fair tomb' at the Abbey Church at Holyrood.

Despite Riccio's death, none of the plot's objectives were achieved. Darnley did not gain the Crown Matrimonial. Mary did not suffer a miscarriage, but managed to separate the King from his fellow conspirators, and with the help from Earl of Bothwell, escape to Dunbar.

James Hepburn, the Fourth Earl of Bothwell, a committed Protestant himself, rushed to Mary Queen of Scots aid in putting down a rebellion of the conspirators.

Bothwell was Lord Admiral of Scotland, and although he possessed a reputation for bravery, he was also known to be lecherous, brutal and power hungry. But Mary regarded him as her savior and he quickly became her most trusted advisor. It was now Bothwell rather than Riccio who had the Queen's ear. Mary regarded him as her savior and he quickly became her most trusted advisor.

Mary was unable to accuse Darnley of his treasonable involvement without prejudicing the legitimacy of her unborn child, but the remaining conspirators were sent into exile.

They now sought revenge against Darnley for revealing their involvement and signing a declaration before the Privy Council that he had played no part in the murder. His fellow conspirators promptly sent Mary the bond approving the murder, which he had signed. He continued his Catholic plotting with foreign heads of state, hotly denying his part in any wrongdoing....

*****

On the 7th of June, 1566, Sir Thomas Gresham lay the first stone of the foundation, accompanied by several aldermen who each placed a gold piece in the foundation. The earliest notice of this undertaking to be met with in his correspondence, occurs about Easter of 1566, from which it is evident that the original edifice cannot have been entirely of brick. Gresham writes: *"I have written for my factor Clough to come home for the holiday. I will tomorrow give my attendants upon you to know further your honor's pleasure. Most humbly beseeching you as to have in your remembrance to get me permission of the Queen Majesty to go to Norfolk for twenty days, to my things there and to take order of my free-stone for my Bourse."* This letter was written to Sir William Cecil April 10th 1566.

The following brief letter, written four months later, contains Gresham's next allusions to the progress of the edifice. It was addressed to Sir William Cecil from a house which Sir Thomas Gresham had inherited from his father situated at Ringshall in Suffolk. What is discoverable concerning this residence, will be stated after the reader has been made acquainted with the contents of the following letter, – the only one in Gresham's hand-writing where any mention of Ringshall occurs.

"Right honorable Sir,"

"After my most humble commendations, it may like your honor to understand that as of the 13th present, I met with my Lord Keeper at Sir Clement Heitham's house, whereas his Lordship sealed the Queen Majesty's bonds, and so departed towards his house at St. Alban's." (Sir Clement Heitham was an important knight in his generation. He was the most well-known member of a

family which ranked with the best gentry of Suffolk. He was knighted sometime between 1553 and 1556 and obtains frequent notice in Queen Mary's Privy-Council books. He had been appointed to many duties of trust during her reign. His epitaph reads in part, *Sir Clement was endued with great pregnancy of wit and with suitable powers of eloquence. He was a strict Roman Catholic and a most loyal subject. He had been chosen Speaker of the House of Commons by Philip and Mary, during whose reign he had represented several boroughs in parliament and enjoyed the office of Chief Baron of the Exchequer from which he conscientiously retired on Elizabeth's accession.*)

Gresham's letter continues... "*Being within 14 miles of my house of Ringshall (whereas I make all my provision for my timber for the Bourse), I was so bold as to make a start to view the same: where I did receive letters from my servant Richard Clough on the 14th of this present month, which according to my most bound duty, I have thought it good to send your Honor what occurrences passed. Tomorrow I intend to depart for London, whereas I trust to find in a readiness money which I promised to furnish to the Queen Majesty by exchange and to make my entrance into Flanders with all the expedition that I can for the accomplishment of her Highness's instructions.*"

"*Thus, with my most humble commendations to the Earl of Leicester and the Earl of Ormond, I most humbly take m leave of you.*"

"*~ Sent from my house at Ringshall in Suffolk, the 13th day of August, 1566.*"

"*At your Honor's commandment*",

    "*Thomas Gresham*"

The manor house of Ringshall was previously called the manor of St. John of Jerusalem because it was built upon the site of the old Hospital of St. John. It was once a place of some magnitude. It had been granted at the dissolution of the monasteries to Sir Richard Gresham, by Henry VIII and comprised a considerable portion of the parish of Ringshall. The estate descended to Sir Thomas Gresham, who, as we learn from the preceding letter, occasionally made Ringshall his residence. He must have found the manor very convenient since his house was within an hour's ride of Ipswich, where he could at any time take a ship to Flanders.

This, in part, serves to explain how it happened that the treasure and stores he was commissioned to transport to from Antwerp, were shipped sometimes to Ipswich and sometimes to London. The proximity of the Ipswich port to his own residence and the convenience of water-carriage then to the metropolis, rendering it scarcely less eligible as port of destination than London itself.

This letter above, was written when the Bourse was in the earliest stage of building and serves to confirm in a very interesting manner, the prevailing tradition is that the timber used in its construction came from Battisford in Suffolk.

The thickly wooded area of some two-hundred acres separated Battisford from Ringshall. It was upon this ground that the Royal Exchange was framed at five or six saw-pits that were there. Most of the timber for the Exchange came from there. Tradition has it that the frame-work of the Exchange was constructed in the country and then brought to the city of London by water.

No one can have compared the view of the Exchange in London with that of the Bourse at Antwerp, without being struck with the extraordinary resemblance those edifices bore to one another. Men are prone to follow precedent, and imitate an approved model and that would be a sufficient explanation of this coincidence. But it may be better still explained by the fact that it was a Flemish architect who was employed by Sir Thomas Gresham to supervise the progress of his building. It isn't known for certain what the man's Christian name was, but in several letters written by Clough, he refers to the architect's last name as Henrike or Henryke. Clough mentions in one letter on the 4th of August, 1566, that Henrike and his men had arrived and the carpenters also. Clough kept Sir Thomas updated on the progress the builders made in the framing.

*****

On June 19th, 1566, Mary Queen of Scots gave birth to her son, James, in Edinburgh Castle, ending any hope for Darnley to succeed to the Scottish throne. His relationship with Mary continued to deteriorate. By the time Mary gave birth to their son, Darnley had backslid into a life of debauchery, neglecting his royal duties and displaying a sullen resentment towards Mary's relationship with Bothwell. His disappearance from court prompted talk of a possible annulment of the royal marriage. But when the Queen learned he was seriously ill in Glasgow, she travelled to his bedside and later arranged for a horse-litter to carry him back to Edinburgh to convalesce at Kirk o' Field. For months Mary had spoken of her husband with nothing but contempt, and the gesture concern for him was out of character.

Divorce did not seem practical without prejudicing James's legitimacy, but her nobles, without consulting Mary, began to develop a plan to murder Darnley....

CHAPTER XVIII

While the operations were going forward in London, the troubles in the Low Countries reached a crises. A long succession of aggravating causes, both from within and from outside, had at first engendered the discontented and finally confirmed an unruly spirit in the people. The Inquisition had come to enrage all classes of people and drive them almost into a state of rebellion. Once seriously excited, an angry populace is an engine which it is scarcely possible to reduce to a state of quiet without a catastrophe. When in addition to political causes of irritation, the spirit of fanaticism is abroad, the attempt seems nearly hopeless. It was, to take it in its general feature, the struggle of a highly civilized, enlightened and luxurious people, against the oppressive acts of an encroaching and unpopular foreign government, Spain.

When it is considered that the state of things materially affected Sir Thomas Gresham, that they altogether occupied his attention at this period of his life, and that they form the subject of almost every letter which Clough addressed to him - it will not be deemed foreign to the subject, but rather than the reverse, that the history of the period should be here entered into with a little more minuteness.

Eventful as the sixteenth century was in many ways, for nothing was it more remarkable than for the religious crisis which it witnessed in England, in France, in Germany and in the Low Countries. To stem the tide of reformation the Emperor Charles V, had recourse to the publication of rigorous edicts, or degrees issued known in history as the *Placcarts*. These sometimes dealt with civil issues, but more often than not, they were generally were about religion. They had been directed against the Anabaptist and sectarians of every description, not omitting the followers of Calvin and Luther, whom they denounced in common with the other enemies of the church of Rome. But edicts such as these were calculated to inspire terror rather than to enforce obedience. To preserve the peace of the state, it was found necessary to modify the severities which they prescribed, by subsequent enactments of a milder nature. They remained nevertheless, in effect and the people of Flanders preserved a galling sense of the obnoxious precedent, of which, in conformity with the line of policy he had ever pursued towards them, they dreaded, lest King Philip should avail himself to encroach yet further upon their civil and religious liberties.

The recent introduction of the Inquisition into the provinces, more than any other event, had aggravated their natural aversion to the court of Spain and rendered them unsettled and disloyal. Finally, the council of Trent, which had ended in 1563, was felt to have resulted in an additional grievance. It was admitted in the Low Countries two years later with reluctance, for it condemned more severely than ever anything that was not within the pale of the Roman church. It would have been even more unfavorably received, had the people been aware that the kings of France and Spain had formed a secret league to maintain the Roman Catholic faith free from violation in their respective dominions. The Inquisition was of course the instrument by which it was contemplated to achieve the intended triumph.

Such was the state of public feeling in the Low Countries in the year 1566, when the first decided step was taken to resist the tide of oppression which seemed every day to be gaining force.

A small party of gentlemen having assembled at Breda, at the home of a Calvinist named Phillip de Marnix, Lord of St. Aldegonde, bound themselves by oath to sacrifice their lives and fortunes in the defense of the liberties of their country. They signed a pledge proclaiming their intentions and denouncing the

Inquisition in the most emphatic language. This pledge obtained immense circulation and was translated into nearly every language of Europe.

The effects of this confederacy were immediately felt throughout the provinces. The spirit which had animated its members spread over the country like a contagion, enlisting in one common cause, persons of every stature, from noblemen to peasants. In a short space of time, upwards of two thousand signature were obtained to the resolutions adopted at Breda.

Among these were the names of Floris, Baron de Montigni, brother of Philip de Montmorenci, Count Mansfield, Count Hoogestraate, and Louis of Nassau, brother of the Prince of Orange; Henry de Brederode, Viscount of Utrecht; the Counts of Culmebourg, and De Bergh; together with a large proportion of the nobility. Brederode took the lead of the party, for which he was well qualified by his illustrious descent as well as his personal intrepidity.

Regarding the other principal characters in the rebellion against the Inquisition, William of Nassau, Prince of Orange, whose name stands at the head of the nobility of the time, was nominally a minister of the regent and governor of the provinces of Holland and Zealand, but it was well known that his heart was with his confederated fellow-countrymen. At a later period of life, when a fitting season had arrived, he boldly threw off the mask and became the bulwark of Protestantism and the most conspicuous character in the history of the troubles. He had been educated in Lutheran principals and from his early youth had been bred a statesman and a soldier. He possessed a great firmness and resolution, clear liberal views, a commanding intellect and was quite beloved and respected.

Lamoral, Count Egmont, also belonged to the highest grade of nobility and was considered a better soldier than the Prince of Orange, but he was not so distinguished a statesman. He was adored in the provinces of Flanders and

Artois, which he governed and was so popular that when the Duchess of Parma was made regent of the Low Countries, the public voice had already nominated Egmont to fill that exalted station. The prince and he had been on indifferent terms until this period, when each being regarded with suspicion, an identity of feeling as well as of interest drew them together and they became indissoluble friends.

Philip de Montmorenci, an officer whose intrepid valor characterized him as a person of rashness, was admiral of the seas. He had served well his country and in addition to every other cause of disaffection, could not forget the injury which had been done to him when he was called to Spain. The government of the province of Gueldres was taken from him and given to Count Meghem. During his abode at the court of King Philip, however, he had organized a system of intelligence which he subsequently turned to good account and of which the Prince of Orange, in the end, availed himself materially.

The first resolution of the newly organized body was to wait upon the regent in some force and to request an alleviation of their grievances. For this purpose, they assembled at Brussels and on the 5th of April, 1566, having obtained the promise of an audience, made their appearance at court. They walked in two by tow, forming a long line, which was brought up by the Count of Nassau and Brederode, the latter of whom acted as spokesman. He demanded in the name of the people, that the Inquisition should be abolished, the Placcarts suspended and that a general assembly of the states should be held. Nothing decisive could be expected at such an audience, but it served to create an immense sensation throughout the country and occasioned immediate and serious communication between the regent and King Philip. The king listened reluctantly to her highness' remonstrance and at last sent equivocal promises that the existing grievances should be alleviated, but he resolved, in secret, to establish the Inquisition in Flanders by the sword and to punish the most conspicuous of the insurgents as rebels, whenever he should get them under his power.

While the court of Spain was trifling with the regent - delaying to acknowledge her letters or sending such replies as could not with safety, be communicated to the people - the only remaining moment when the catastrophe which ensued might perhaps have been averted, was lost. Seditious (causing people to rebel against authority) meetings were being held throughout the provinces, but nowhere was the same order observed which prevailed at Brussels. At St. Trond especially, where upwards of two thousand armed men assembled, the spirit which had until then, worn the dignified air of calm patriotism, began to look very much like a rousing rebellion. Every day added strangers and bad characters of every description to the ranks of the insurgents, so much so, that in a short span of time the whole country became agitated, to the great alarm of the regent and her counsellors, who, when they discovered that it was too late to restore order, applied to King Philip more pressingly than ever. This had little effect however, as on former occasions.

The hordes of disaffected persons and miscreants of every description which, for a long time, had been congregating in different parts of the Low Countries, had by this time increased to an alarming extent, but, nowhere more than at Antwerp. The materials of which these masses of men were composed, were of the most suspicious kind. Outlaws, vagabonds, paupers, thieves - men without religion and without law, swelled their ranks. By far the most prominent feature I this motley assemblage were the refugee sectarians of Germany and France, who had joined themselves, at first secretly, but by degrees without attempt at concealment, to the disaffected body. It is curious indeed to notice how craftily the German Anabaptists and other fanatics, contrived to engraft themselves, as it were, on the troubles of this period and give a religious character to what should have been a civil, rather than a religious struggle. The preached in the open air in French or in Flemish, propounding doctrines which they barely understood themselves. They often substituted the doctrines with their own impractical theories. How little these dogmatizers had the welfare of the people whom they professed to enlighten at heart, needs hardly saying. Large crowds awaited them wherever they went, while the efforts which the local authorities occasionally made to put them down, only added strength to their cause and prejudiced the lower orders in their favor.

 The insurgents were holding their turbulent meeting at St. Trond during the months of May, June and July of 1566, while the preaching was being carried on with activity throughout the Low Countries. The first consequence of this system of excitement was the spoliation of several religious houses, by a small body of miscreants, in more than one part of the kingdom. But it was not until the month of August, that the fury of the storm was felt and the extent to which fanaticism will hurry a mob of ruffians, perceived by the panic-stricken inhabitants.

 During all these months, Richard Clough never failed to communicate the particulars of every incident that occurred to Sir Thomas Gresham at least once a week and sometimes more often than that. As a contemporary chronicler, Clough's narratives possessed considerable historical interest, while his graphic manner constantly reminds us that the words are those of one who had been an eye-witness of the scenes he describes. The following extracts from two of his letters of the 10th and 22nd of July, 1566, will require no commentary after what has just been stated in illustration of the history of the period.

 "...We have had here, a marvelous stir on Monday night. At about eleven of-the-clock, the news was given out that the town was betrayed, and that there

should be let in at the gates a great number of horsemen and footmen. So that this stir occurred at night, all men in harness, and great watch at the gates, and in the morning, it somewhat ceased. So that, presently, some are in danger, for the coming people are given to understand that a company of them should have betrayed the town. And as this day it is appointed that there shall be preaching and on Friday and Sunday, and so weekly in most parts of the country."

"Last Saturday, a proclamation [was declared] that no man should do to sermon upon pain of hanging. On Sunday morning more than 16,000 persons left the town and went to sermon, all with their weapons in battle array. After the sermon they returned to town and went to the bailiff's house (who had taken one preacher prisoner two or three days before and commanded him to free the prisoner which he refused to do. They proceeded to the prison where they broke into it and freed the prisoner before departing."

"A similar incident happened on Sunday in Hoogstraten." (a municipality located in the Belgian province of Antwerp) "The preacher there, being at his sermon outside of town, when the priests rang an alarm, thinking that meant the country had risen against them, contrary to the meaning of the alarm."

"All this notwithstanding, the Regent it is said, had prepared a number of horsemen and footmen to overrun the people here at the preaching. The Lords of Antwerp realizing this, sent word to the Regent on Saturday, demanding she back off sending forces and if she refused, they would bring utter ruin and destruction upon the town of Antwerp. The Regent did forego the plans and the sermons went on without incident."(* Author's note: The Regent of Brussels was Margaret of Parma, the half-sister of Phillip II of Spain.)

A week later, Clough wrote to Gresham saying; "As for the occurrence here, it is not much other than that the people still go to preaching more or less. Last Thursday I saw a great number of people on their way to sermon, very many of them, the best and wealthiest of the town. On Friday, the provost marshal mustered about 400 men at Macklin, but what he will do with them God knows. Having mustered them, he would likely have sent 200 to Brussels which Brussels refused then entrance and shut the gates against them."

Occurrences such as this must of course alarmed the Regent to no slight degree.

Richard Clough wrote on August 4th, that the Regent pretends to be sick and that she had sent her "jewels and plate" (plate being items of gold such as crowns, cups, scepters etc.) to Cologne, Germany and would have gladly gone herself.

It is his letter of the 21st however that narrates the fearful catastrophe.

August 21, 1566, in Antwerp

"Sir, for that I have not received any letters from your Mastership of late, I have less to write concerning your affairs. All things are in good order here, (God by praised!), but how long it shall remain so, God knows, for we have had here last night quite a stir. All the churches, chapels and houses of religion have been utterly defaced and no kind of things left whole within them, for everything was left broken and destroyed. Being done so with such order and with so few folks, that it is to be marveled at."

"So you will understand how this matter began, yesterday about 5:00 o'clock, the priests, thinking to have song service, as we call it, the company began to sing psalms, the company being merely boys. As they began, Margrave and other Lords came into the church and rebuked them. But all in vain, for as soon as they turned their backs, the boys began again. At about 6:00 o'clock, they broke up the choir and began their book study. While they were at study, the vandals returned and began to break and destroy things in the church. From there, they went to the parish churches and some to the other houses of Religion and it is a wonder that they were able to carry out so much destruction in one night. There is not even a place left to sit in the church."

"As these matters go forward, I hope God sends a good end. But if you do come, as I look for you to within a day or two, you shall see for yourself. I pray to God that all may be well and end well."

Scenes equally disgraceful had been witnessed throughout Zealand, at Flushing, Middleburgh, Ghent, Mechlin, Boubourg and Breda. And in all the principal cities of Brabant, except Louvain and Brussels, where a similar demonstration was expected daily.

Clough maintained that the Protestants were not to be blamed, for as far as he could see, there was not one that was involved. It was vagabonds that followed that were to blame. He did say however that *"some of our nation are blamed, and not without cause, for there are a great many in number in this town that had fled out of England for robbing and such like, and these kept such a stir in the spoils!"*

He reported that all kinds of merchandise was at a stay and that most men of reputation had fled abroad into all other places. *"For all likelihood,' he said, "this matter cannot end well and the town shall be in danger of being spoiled because the vagabonds of the country were drawing near. God send us quietness!"* wrote Clough.

The letter from which these last extracts have been taken, never reached Sir Thomas Gresham, but was forwarded to Cecil by Richard Candelier, the person who superintended Gresham's affairs in Lombard-Street and into whose hands, when Gresham was away, it naturally fell. Sir Thomas, in consequence of the approaching payments at Antwerp and Clough's repeated hints that his presence would be very desirable in that city, had finally taken his departure and so had the opportunity of seeing with his own eyes, the scene so described in detail to him by his correspondent.

Gresham left London on the 23rd of August and the same post which was the bearer of Clough's letter, brought Candelier dispatches from his master written between Dunkirk and Newport. While the commotions which Clough describes were going on in the principal towns of the Low Countries, it is not surprising that all financial operations were, for a while, suspended and as soon as it became necessary to renew any of the Queen's bonds, or negotiate any fresh loans with Antwerp merchants, the presence and personal influence of the Queen's Merchant were found to be indispensable.

Clough had written him word on the 22nd of July that he was unable to conclude satisfactorily with Sir Paul Van Dalle, relative to a certain money transaction, adding, *"If you may be spared at home, I would wish that you come at once, for I do not doubt in the least that Van Dalle will work with you in turn."*

Gresham, when he enclosed this letter to Cecil, showing what a dangerous world awaited him, proposed waiting until the 3rd of August, and offered that as soon as he was furnished with the necessary instructions, he would at that time, cross the seas.

Clough's request that he come to Antwerp must have been an unwelcome summons for Thomas Gresham, for a month had scarcely elapsed since he had lain the foundation-stones of his Bourse. He was busily engaged at the moment in watching the progress of the new structure. Writing on the 13th of August from his house in Ringshall in Suffolk, where he was providing the timber needed for the undertaking, he told Cecil that he intended to depart for London the next day, whereas he trusted to find everything in readiness for the Queen's exchange, so that he could prepare to leave for Flanders.

Gresham reached Antwerp on the 29th of August and on the 1st of September, wrote again to his friend Cecil, telling him that he had never seen so many hungry Irishmen, greedy for money, but that the storm had abated, as if spent by its own fury. But what had chiefly contributed to the restoration of order was a compromise which the Regent had made with the insurgents of St. Trond, on the 23rd of August, the same that had been alluded to by Clough in his letter of the 11th. She had promised that the Inquisition would be suppressed and consented that the preaching should go forward without impediment, on the condition that Mass should be again performed in the churches and that the Roman Catholics should suffer no molestations from the professors of the reformed religion.

In consequence of this arrangement, "Temples" as they were called, began to be erected in Antwerp for the accommodation of the Protestants. Clough wrote on the 29th of September, 1566, *"They have laid and begun the foundation of four new temples, besides the great barn at St. Michaels, which is very handsomely trimmed -for a preaching place."*

King Phillip of Spain had lost control in the troublesome Netherlands. During the course of the next year he would see no other option than to send an army to suppress the rebellion. On the 22nd of August, 1567, Fernando Alvarez de Toledo, the 3rd Duke of Alba, marched into Brussels leading 10,000 troops.

The Duke of Alba took harsh measures and rapidly established a special court to judge anyone who opposed the King. The Duke considered himself the direct representative of Phillip in the Netherlands and frequently bypassed the Regent, Margaret of Parma and making use of her to lure back some of the fugitive nobles, which caused her to resign office in September of 1567.

Most notable of the fugitive nobles mentioned above was the Count of Egmont, head of one of the wealthiest and most powerful families in the Low Countries, and Philip de Montmorency also known as the Count of Horn. He commanded the stately fleet which had conveyed King Phillip II from the Netherlands to Spain, where he remained at the Spanish Court until 1563. The Count of Horn placed himself with the Prince of Orange and Count of Egmont at the head of the party which opposed the Spanish Inquisition by Cardinal Granville and ultimately forced his resignation.

Egmont and Horn were arrested for high treason, condemned and a year later decapitated on the Grand Place in Brussels. Egmont and Horn had been Catholic nobles, loyal to the king of Spain until their deaths. The reason for their execution was that Alba considered they had been treasonous to the king in their tolerance to Protestantism. Their executions, ordered by a Spanish noble, provoked outrage. More than one thousand people were executed in the following months. The large number of executions led the court to be nicknamed the "Blood Court" in the Netherlands, and Alba to be called the "Iron Duke". Rather than pacifying the Netherlands, these measures helped to fuel the unrest. Many conformed to Protestantism.

CHAPTER XIX

Gresham lost no time in bringing his business at Antwerp to an end: writing by the regular post on the 8th of September he announced his intention of immediately returning home, in the following words: *"Likewise I have spoken with the Queen's creditors for the prolonging of the rest of the debts., with whom I have had much ado; but (thanks be to God!) now I am at a point with them. So that I have delivered them the new bonds to consider; and upon the receipt of the old, I do intend (with the leave of God and the Queen's permission) to make my journey homewards with the old bonds; and so to depart this town with as much honor and credit to my sovereign as ever I did in all my life. For, with my sudden departure, I shall give the bourse and all other merchants to understand that I have no more need of money, and that I have contented all the creditors; which is most convenient for me so to do as the time now requires. For that I do see and feel already that here is no more money to be had at any price; by reason I have gone through all the money-men by one practice or other, and especially with all them which I needed to deal with, Schetz, Paules Van Ball, Rellinger, Lixall, the heirs of Lazarus Tucker, and diverse others of whom there was not a penny to be had, by the reason they be so fare ought with their Prince, and very sore indebted in this place, and take up all they can get, themselves, to preserve their credit. So, Sir, I will not further trouble your honor of the great scarcity of money that is here; nor also what trouble I have had to come by this money. But therein refer me to the report of others. Being right glad, in this miserable time, that I have accomplished the things that her highness sent me over for this week."* Gresham added, *"I do intend to bank the Queen Majesty's creditors, both young and old."*

"On the 14th of this month, the Prince of Orange sent a request for me to dine with him. He provided me with great entertainment. He inquired about the health of the Queen Majesty. He discussed with me all the proceedings of this town, and what a dangerous piece of work it was, and how he now agreed with the Protestants. He even read to me the agreement proclamation being a copy of the same document proclaimed at the town-house. (I am enclosing a copy of it with this letter."

"But in all this discourse he said, King Phillip would not be content with our doings. This causes me to think this matter is not yet ended, but likely to come to great mischief; especially if the King of Spain gets the upper hand".

"He also asked me whether England was considering departing this town or not. I assured him I had heard of no such matter."

"Sir, I like nothing here of these proceedings. Therefore your honor would do very well to consider some other realm and place for the making of our business dealings that is now made within our realm. Whereby her Majesty's realm may remain in peace and quietness, which in this time of upheaval, is one of the chief things your honor has to look at."

"Considering what terms this country now stands in, which is ready to cut another's throat for matters of religion. And the Court, (as far as I can perceive) isn't likely to set up the masses and the idols again; for here at Brussels the main church is kept by force, that no man shall do any hurt to the masses nor to the idols."

The Prince of Orange (who was governor of the town of Antwerp) was right in his surmise, that the concessions made by the Regent in order to restore her dominions to a state of quietness, would by no means be approved of at the court of Spain. And he probably had an instinctive apprehension, (equally well founded,) that in case the recent disturbances should be rigorously investigated, his personal safety might be exposed to considerable hazard. In conversing with Sir Thomas Gresham on the subject, his object seems to have been to discover, if possible, what disposition was entertained towards the revolutionary party by Queen Elizabeth and her ministers.

"In all his talk," continues Gresham, *"he said unto me, 'I know this will not content the king.' He drank a toast to the Queen Majesty. I in turn presented a toast to the Princess his wife, which he seemed to like."*

Being covertly coaxed by Gresham, to perhaps drink more than he should, the Prince began in great fury to rant and rave against the Emperor, Maximilian II, whose proclamation prohibited and made it death for any German to bear arms against the King of Spain. This was deeply resented by the Prince of Orange. Though he was usually subtle with his opinion concerning the Emperor, he now expressed contempt at the table, due to the wine laying open the secrets of his heart.

The Prince said that the emperor, and the King, and whosoever was of their opinion, deceived themselves. That not only would the Germans take arms, but so would a great number of other nations bordering upon the empire, including the Danes and the Swedes and others, which both would and could help the confederated Low-Countrymen.

One can imagine the satisfaction felt by Gresham, knowing the collection of information he had obtained from the Prince and his several cups of wine, which he knew would be most welcomed to his friend Cecil, upon his return to England.

Gresham concluded his letter by relating an incident that occurred later.

"Since that evening spent with the Prince of Orange, I met with a man named Giles Hoffman, (who the Queen Majesty owes a good deal of money,) who had great discussion with me about this business. He is a life-long Protestant, and asked me whether I would go to the sermons or not. I said that I would, and in conclusion he asked me if I thought the Queen Majesty and her realm would give aid to their noblemen, as she did in France for the religion's sake. To that, I asked him whether the noblemen had demanded any help of her Majesty. He said he didn't know if they had or not. Then, I answered that I was no counselor, nor never dealt with such great matters."

Although Sir Thomas Gresham prudently avoided offering any opinion on this subject, Elizabeth's favorable disposition towards the Prince of Orange was well known. Not that, as yet, she confessed this openly. It was, on the contrary, her practice to express disapprobation of any attempt on the part of the subject to take up arms against the sovereign, (or, as she phrased it, "the body revolting against its head,") under whatever circumstances.

A still more likely motive for maintaining the appearance of neutrality in these disturbances, was her anxiety to avoid a rupture with the kings of France and Spain, who would have simultaneously become her declared enemies, had she openly assisted the Prince of Orange. But her inclination to favor his party soon after displayed itself on more than one occasion, when, in the cause of Protestantism had, in a measure become identified with the success of his arms.

Once more arrived in London, Gresham seems to have altogether relinquished the management of his affairs in the Low Countries to Clough, whose correspondence about this period is extremely voluminous and circumstantial. Every letter narrates some novel event, or communicates some fresh piece of intelligence illustrative of the spirit and temper of the times, forming altogether a running commentary, as it were, on the history of the period.

*****

As Lord Darnley was convalescing, after contracting smallpox, at the site occupied by the collegiate church of Kirk o' Field, about a ten minute walk from Holyrood Palace, where Mary and the baby were living, his enemies were secretly filling the cellars of the house with gunpowder.

At two o'clock in the morning of February 10th, 1567, Kirk o' Field was blown to pieces by a huge explosion which was said to have been heard throughout Edinburgh. Certainly Mary would have been awakened by the sound of the explosion so close in proximity and more than likely rose from her bed to observe the orange glow of the fire from the direction where her husband slept.

The townspeople of Edinburgh were also awakened by the blast and several citizens quickly dressed and headed out in the direction of Kirk o' Field. They found the building reduced to rubble and still in flames. A quick effort was made to search the rubble for the occupants of the house which included Lord Darnley, however, neither Darnley nor his personal servant were found in the burning embers. Their bodies were soon discovered in the nearby gardens. The night-gown clad body of Lord Darnley as well as his servant showed signs of strangulation and did not appear to have been injured or killed in the explosion.

It was speculated that perhaps something had awoken Darnley and he had attempted to flee the house, with his assistant. What *was* obvious is that both men had been murdered.

It was a murder that would never be solved. While there was and remains to this day no definitive answer to the question of who murdered Lord Darnley, most historians agree that Bothwell with or without Mary's complicity, concocted the plot. To be sure, there was no direct evidence establishing Bothwell as the murderer, but for those associated with the Royal Court, it was only too easy to guess. Bothwell was a ruthless opportunist aiming at nothing less than the Kingship of Scotland.

Mary Queen of Scots observed the standard forty days of mourning for her husband, while rumors spread throughout not just Edinburgh, but all of Scotland, that her mourning was insincere and even that she herself, was part of the murder plot.

On the 24th of April 1567, Bothwell and 800 of his men met Mary in the road between Linlithgow Palace and Edinburgh and Bothwell warned Mary that there was danger waiting for her in Edinburgh. He then insisted that she go with him to Dunbar, to his castle, so that he could protect her. Upon reaching Dunbar at around midnight, while Bothwell and Mary were alone, he suddenly took her in his powerful arms and kissed her. She rebuffed him, which only made him want her more and in the ensuing struggle, he raped her, according to Mary.

She at first was mortified and told Bothwell that he would lose his head for forcing himself on her, but she realized she couldn't leave and was practically a captive of Bothwell. When he repeated his aggressions for her then next night, she found herself not fighting him so much, for she *had* indeed been attracted to Bothwell even before the murder of her husband Lord Darnley.

It isn't known exactly how soon afterward, but soon, Mary agreed to marry Bothwell. On the 12th of May, Mary made Bothwell, Duke of Orkney and then married him on the 15th of May at Holyrood, just over a week after his divorce from Jean Gordon, Countess of Bothwell, was finalized.

Scotland was shocked and outraged. Mary and Bothwell were besieged at Bothwell Castle while on "honeymoon". While the marriage was controversial, some scholars believe that Mary was forced into the marriage and not a willing participant.

Both Mary and Bothwell escaped the castle safely and raised an army of supporters. They fought a battle against the opposition at Carberry Hill. They were defeated and Mary was forced to abdicate on her imprisonment in Loch Leven Castle. She escaped prison one year later with the help of her Catholic supporters. She was defeated again by the Protestant forces, this time at Langside near Glasgow. She tried to flee to France, but her ship was blown ashore in England by high winds. There she sought the protection of her cousin Queen Elizabeth…

CHAPTER XX

At about the same time Mary Queen of Scots and Bothwell were married, Sir Thomas Gresham's factor, Richard Clough was getting married also.

A hiatus during this period occurs in Clough's correspondence. It seems that he had received orders to remain in Antwerp until the stone for the Bourse - which had been promised should arrive by Easter - should be finally shipped to London. According to a letter Gresham wrote to Sir William Cecil on the 16th of April, that he had desired Clough to "*'come over'* after he had dispatched all my provision of my stone for the Bourse, and him that had taken it in hand."

But Clough had a delicate affair of a private nature to attend to in North Wales, which must have rendered all of his other commitments less important to him. For he had be residing in Antwerp as a bachelor in the middle of April, 1567 and by mid-May, he returned from his excursion to Wales - a married man, on a visit with his wife at Gresham-House.

The following letter, announcing the event to the Secretary, was written by Gresham.

"*Right Honorable Sir,*"

"*It may like you to receive letters from my servant, and other of my friends, that my Richard Clough, has returned from Wales, and there, married Sir John Salisburie's son's wife, and is here resident with me. So that I do intend tomorrow to dispatch him overseas for which I will give my attendance to know what the Queen Majesty's pleasure and yours is, for the payment of her Highness's debts due in August....*"

"*At Your Honor's Commandment*
             Thomas Gresham"

Clough chose for his wife, a remarkable woman, Katharine Tudor, also known as Katherine of Berain, the only daughter and heiress of Robert Fychan, Esq. of Berain, by the grand-daughter of King Henry VII.

Clough and his new bride returned to Antwerp, but never before had he returned to the scene of his duties when the prospects of the Low Countries were so gloomy as he did on the present occasion.

Just how deceiving the assurances had been of King Philip's approaching visit to his northern dominions, now became apparent, for although he still said he was coming, the Duke of Alva, with an army of 10,000 men, was ordered to proceed towards Flanders. It took little imagination on the part of the people to understand that whatever the professed object and intentions of this action by King Philip and the Duke of Alva might be, they were themselves in fact no longer a free people, but about to become the subjects of a military deploy invested with unlimited power and attended by an armed force of the nation they hated the most.

Sure of assistance from the Admiral de Coligny, and confident of a strong party in their favor in France among the Huguenots, it had been proposed to intercept Alva's army and prevent him from obtaining entrance into the provinces. But the counter action never took place and the Duke of Alva arrived in Flanders, unwelcomed and unobstructed.

This was the last stroke of Spanish policy served also to disclose the hollowness of King Philip's promises and to show the foulness of his intentions towards the Low Countries. His early efforts to quench the spirit of the people had proved unsuccessful. The expulsion of the troops he had left behind, had come about by the unanimous insistence of the commons. They had compelled the King's favorite minister, Cardinal Granville to withdraw himself. Opposition had been raised to the placards and the inquisition and the people had finally taken up arms to defend their civil and religious liberties.

The flourishing commerce which, since the breaking out of the troubles, had been visibly declining, those industrious and densely populated towns which King Philip's own harsh measures were rendering desolate and unproductive - to say nothing of a once happy country, the most flourishing perhaps in Europe, were now distracted and reduced to misery. It was resolved, to the contrary, to administer violent remedies to every evil of the deceased state. Obedience was henceforward to be enforced by the exercise of military law. Order was to be procured by the capital punishment of the disobedient, and the desertion of towns prevented by a proclamation which forbade anyone to leave the country without the sanction of the court.

How ineffective was this line of policy in restoring the Low Countries to their pristine condition soon became apparent in the destruction of the whole fabric. Indeed, one can scarcely believe that King Philip ever anticipated any other outcome to his work than that which resulted from it. He seems to have acted in a spirit of envy and or of revenge, rather than with a view of the ultimate benefit of his subjects.

Historians all agree that Alva was a monster of cruelty - proud, unrelenting, repulsive, if not brutal in his manners. He was so notorious for these qualities, and so universally detested.

It was in vain that the most faithful of Philip's ministers, at the risk of incurring his lasting displeasure, pointed out the unfitness of Alva for the post which had been assigned to him. The King was inflexible, and Alva set out on his ill-fated journey at the head of the army of 10,000 men.

On the 22nd of August 1567, Alva made his entry into Brussels, accompanied by a large train of followers and others whom the Regent had dispatched from the Capital to meet him.

In a letter Clough addressed to Sir Thomas Gresham he wrote: *"The soldiers that came with Duke de Alva are all placed in towns and villages including Louvain, Leer, Brussels, and Ghent and in diverse other small towns thereabout. At their first entrance into Ghent, they took old castle by force. They proceeded to the new castle and would have it, but the captain told them to leave it, so they departed. Then they went to the Borough master and demanded the keys of the town which he refused to hand over, whereupon they entered his house and took them by force. They demanded the keys to all men's houses so they could go in and out at their pleasure..."*

The Duchess Margaret of Parma, made no secret of her indignation at being superseded when Alva produced his commission from King Philip appointing him 'Captain General' and asking the Duchess to cooperate with him in ordering all the cities in the Netherlands to receive the garrisons which he would send them.

In September of 1567, The Duke of Alva established a new court for the trial of crimes committed during the 'troubles'. It was called the 'Council of Troubles', but will be forever know in history as the 'Blood Council'. It superseded all other institutions.

So well did this new and terrible system perform its work that in less than three months 1,800 of the highest, the noblest and the most virtuous men in the land, including Count Egmont and Admiral Horn, suffered death. The whole country became a 'Charnel House' by definition meaning a place where human skeletal remains were stored - columns and stacks in every street, the doorposts of private houses, the fences in the fields were laden with human carcasses, strangled, burnt and beheaded. Within a few months after the arrival of Alva, the spirit of the nation seemed hopelessly broken.

The Duke of Alva took up his position as Governor-General and among his first steps was the erection of the celebrated citadel of Antwerp, not to protect, but to control the commercial capital of the provinces.

Events marched swiftly. On February 16, 1568, a sentence of the inquisition condemned all the inhabitants of the Netherlands to death as heretics. From this universal doom only a few persons, specially named, were exempt and a proclamation of King Philip, dated ten days later, confirmed this decree of the Inquisition and ordered it to be carried into instant execution, without regard to age, sex or condition.

This is probably the most concise death warrant every framed up to that point in history. Three million people, men, women and children were sentenced to the scaffold.

The Prince of Orange at last threw down the gauntlet and published a reply to the active condemnation which had been pronounced against him in default of appearance before the Blood Council. It would, he said, be both death and degradation to acknowledge the jurisdiction of the infamous 'Council of Blood', and he refused to plead before those he said were not fit to be the valets of his companions and himself.

Preparations were at once made to levy the troops and wage war against Philip's forces in the Netherlands. Then followed the long, ghastly struggle between the armies raised by the Prince of Orange and his brother, Count Louis of Nassau, and those of Alva and the other Governors-General who succeeded him.

At one point, it seemed the Prince of Orange and his forces were about to secure a complete triumph, but the news of the massacre of St. Bartholomew in

Paris, brought depression to the patriotic army and a corresponding spirit to the Spanish armies and the gleam faded. The most extraordinary feature of Alva's civil administration were fiscal decrees, which imposed taxes that destroyed the trade and manufacturers of the country.

There were endless negotiations inspired by the States-General, the German Emperor and the Governments of France and England to secure a settlement of the Netherland's affairs, but these, owing to insincere diplomacy, were ineffective.

*****

The long-spoke-of project of an alliance between Queen Elizabeth and the Archduke Charles of Austria, brother to Maximilian II, the reigning Emperor of Germany, had now become so far matured, that the Earl of Sussex, Thomas Ratcliffe, was ordered to proceed to Vienna in order to negotiate the treaty. Three of his letters written from that capital have appeared in print, but most of his correspondence remains unpublished. One of *these* letters - the first - in consideration of its having been written from Antwerp and above all, because it shows the connection of the Earl with Gresham is presented in substance here.

His lordship, Ratcliffe addressed Queen Elizabeth herself and communicated the circumstances of his arrival and entertainment. He had reached Antwerp on the 3rd of July and proceeded to his lodgings at Sir Thomas Gresham's house where, "Monsieur de Symary, master of the Hostel to the Regent and governor of Macklyn" came and apologized for his poor reception. The Earl informed de Symary that he had letters from the Queen addressed to the Duchess Margaret of Parma - the Regent of Spain where upon that very day,

Count Mansfield, governor of the city of Antwerp came with 3000 soldiers to welcome him and escort him to the Court.

Very honorable was the reception which the Regent gave to the Earl of Sussex. In the course of their brief conference, she pledged herself to do everything in her power to conserve and increase the friendship between the crowns of England and Spain. When the Earl of Sussex recommended (being commanded by the Queen) the "favoring of the causes of the merchants; that so by their means there grew no unkindness. The Regent readily promised compliance, and said Queen Elizabeth and her subjects had for such a long time, found benefit in goodwill and harmony, and she thought that neither Her Majesty, nor her subjects could do as well in trust with any new alliances. Ratcliffe wrote to Queen that the Regent wished him great success in his journey to the Emperor. After that, she ended the formal meeting with the Earl and invited him to dinner where she entertained him for three or four hours. She commended Queen Elizabeth for the 'great gifts" she had heard God bestowed upon her. She also offered her service to Queen Elizabeth any time she required it, because she was happy to show Her Majesty how much affection she felt for her. The Earl assured the Regent that Queen Elizabeth felt likewise in her affection toward the Regent. (whether that was true or not)

The Regent wanted to express to the Earl of Sussex her gratitude for the Queen's concern over the tumults in the Low Countries and sympathy at their termination and begged that she would not believe all she had heard of the severities intended to be practiced by the King of Spain, who she had no doubt, would act with clemency towards his subjects.

Toward the end of the meeting between the Regent and the Earl of Sussex, he tells… *"She said she heard so much of Your Majesty by the Count of Stolburg, as she desired much to see your picture, which with some travel, she* recovered. And for that it was drawn in black, with a hood and a coronet, (which she perceived was not the attire Your Majesty is used to wearing, she desired me, if I had your picture, that she might see it. That I should do her a great pleasure to show her the picture of her, whose person she honored and loved so much."

"I answered, at first, that the pictures commonly made to be sold, did nothing to resemble Your Majesty. But she pressed me until I could not deny having your picture, which she saw, along with the Duchess of Ascot and the Countess of Mansfield and certain other Lords and Ladies. In whose presence, Monsieur de Maldingham affirmed it to be so like you that he was speechless. And that when he last saw Your Majesty, you were wearing the same attire. The Regent, along with the rest, affirmed they saw thereby as much as they had heard of your person and wished they might also see and hear themselves what they had heard by others of your qualities. They said there was only one fault in Your Majesty, which was - with all these gifts of God, to live sole, without a husband."

"When I had taken my leave, she asked the Duke of Ascot and the Countess of Mayfield to accompany me and show me the town."

The Earl of Sussex said that he would be leaving town the next day and should be in Vienna in about twenty days.

In the Earl of Sussex's letter to Queen Elizabeth, he also wrote of the Regent Duchess of Parma's mention of the recent events in Scotland surrounding Mary Queen of Scots.

"...Her Highness (the Regent) had a long talk with me of matters of Scotland and, as she finds it a hard case to have the subjects rise against their Sovereign and take her prisoner, so does she think that if either she (Mary Queen of Scots), were consenting to the death of her husband or consented to *marry him that she knew consented his death, and would not suffer justice to be executed - God will not forbear punishment..."*

The Duchess of Parma would soon after this meeting with the Earl of Sussex, ask from King Philip, her release from the land where she had been sovereign and at last, obtained it from King Philip and took her departure in December for Parma, finally closing her eventful career in the Netherlands.

Mary Queen of Scots, would remain imprisoned in England by her cousin Queen Elizabeth, until such time she could clear herself of the accusations of Lord Darnley's murder. After trying to escape, she was put under close guard and constant watch. During her years in prison, Mary continually planned her liberation. In early 1587, Catholic supporters of Mary attempted to assassinate Queen Elizabeth so Mary could take her rightful seat on the throne and institute Catholicism once again.

Elizabeth believed Mary was part of the plot to assassinate her. That, being the last straw, Elizabeth reluctantly signed a death warrant for Mary's execution. Mary had been in prison for nineteen years before she was executed on the morning of February 8th, 1587. She was beheaded and it took the executioner three attempts to successfully finish the deed. She was later buried at Westminster Abbey by her son James VI of Scotland who was by then, King of England.

*****

Throughout the troubles in the Low Countries and during the years leading up to the tragic events surrounding Mary Queen of Scots, the main character of this narrative, Sir Thomas Gresham, completed his building of the bourse in

London. The new bourse was a long four-storied building with a high double balcony. A bell-tower crowned by Sir Thomas Gresham's family crest - a huge sculptured grasshopper, stood on one side of the main entrance. The bell in this tower summoned merchants to the spot at twelve o'clock noon and six o'clock in the evening. A stately Corinthian column, crested with the Gresham crest stood outside the north entrance overlooking the quadrangle. Each corner of the building and the peak of every dormer window was crowned by a grasshopper. Gresham spared no expense to let everyone know who had designed and built the bourse by displaying his crest everywhere.

Within Gresham's bourse were piazzas supported by marble pillars, and above were 100 small shops. The covered walks were adorned with statues of English kings. A statue of Gresham stood near the north end of the western piazza.

Richard Clough, whose original idea it had been and who had all along been so much concerned in the creation of the Bourse, and who may reasonably be presumed to have watched its progress from a distance with pride and pleasure, did not live to see its completion. He was cut off in the prime of life, and died of a lingering illness at Hamburg, Germany where he and his wife and their two infant children were residing in his official capacity of deputy of the fellowship of merchant-adventurers, sometime between the 11th of March and the 19th of July, 1570.

The bourse was christened "The Royal Exchange" and officially opened on the 23rd of January 1571 by Queen Elizabeth. She arrived from Somerset House through Fleet Street past the north side of the Bourse to Sir Thomas Gresham's house in Bishopsgate Street, and there dined. After the banquet she entered the Bourse on the south side, where she viewed every part. In the upper part there were no less than a hundred small shops.

Many of the shops in the Bourse had remained un-rented and empty until Queen Elizabeth's visit, in 1571. Gresham, anxious to have the Bourse worthy of such a visitor as Her Majesty the Queen, went around twice in one day to all the shopkeepers and offered all who would furnish wares and light up the empty shops brightly with wax candles, rent free on those shops for a whole year. There were milliners' shops at the Bourse, and shops that sold everything from mousetraps, to birdcages, from shoeing-horns, to lanterns. There were also sellers of armor, apothecaries, booksellers, goldsmiths, and glass-sellers.

The result of this was that in two years Gresham was able to raise the rent from 40*s*. a year to four marks, and a short time after to even more.

The new Exchange, was not without its faults though. Like the central part of St. Paul's Cathedral, in London, The Royal Exchange soon became a hangout for idlers. There was a resentment against the Exchange, because on Sundays and holidays great numbers of boys, children, and " young rogues," would meet there, and shout and make such a racket, so that honest citizens could not quietly walk there for their recreation, and the parishioners of nearby St. Bartholomew could not hear the sermons. Certain women were prosecuted for selling "apples and oranges" at the Exchange gate, and amusing themselves in cursing and swearing, to the great annoyance and grief of the inhabitants and passers-by. A tavern-keeper, who had vaults under the Exchange, was fined for allowing drunkenness, and for broiling herrings, sprats (small fish), and bacon, to the vexation of Worshipful Merchants resorting to the Exchange. A complaint was made of the rat-catchers, and sellers of dogs, birds, plants, &c., who hung about the south gate of the Bourse, especially at exchange time. It was also seriously complained of that Shakespeare's noisy neighbors in Southwark, used to parade before the Exchange, generally in business hours, and there make proclamation of their entertainments, which caused tumult and drew together mobs. It was usual on these occasions to have a monkey riding on the bear's back, and several discordant minstrels fiddling, to give the additional publicity to the coming festival.

No person frequenting the Bourse was allowed to wear any weapon, and it was ordered that no one should walk in the Exchange after ten p.m. in summer and nine p.m. in winter.

Unfortunately, Gresham's original building was destroyed ninety-five years later by the 'Great Fire of London' in 1666. A second complex was built on the site and opened in 1669, but that also burned down on the 10th of January, 1838. It had been used by the Lloyd's of London Insurance Market, which was forced to move temporarily to the South Sea House following the fire.

The third Royal Exchange building, which still stands today, which adheres to the original layout consisting of a four-sided structure surrounding a central courtyard where merchants and tradesmen could do business.

In 1982 the Royal Exchange was in disrepair and was refurbished. In 2001, it was once again extensively remodeled, reconstructing the courtyard to include newly created boutiques and restaurants. The Royal Exchange today is a retail center with shops, cafes, and restaurants.

CHAPTER XX1

But our story of Sir Thomas Gresham and the times in which he lived continue…

As we have seen, the times of Gresham and of Queen Elizabeth were often tumultuous with regard to the enemies of Protestantism which prevailed during the first half of her reign and from the consequences of which, this empire was mercifully delivered.

Even the most candid and right-minded historians with differ in their opinion of Queen Elizabeth's conduct as they consider the magnitude of the danger which menaced her crown, on one hand; and the sufferings of those who became her victims, on the other.

It might perhaps be safely assumed, that if the beautiful Queen of Scots had never existed, the question would not be raised, but would have quietly subsided into a matter of historical record. But suffice to say, that however commendable the objective which Elizabeth had in view, the means she employed to rid the country of the enemies which were thought to endanger its safety are unjustifiable. Nor does it in the least diminish her guilt in shedding Mary's blood, by the fact that Mary herself committed follies and was stained with the implications of her part in the crime of murder.

But there were other female sufferers besides the Scottish Queen, whom historians have written less about. Not because they are less entitled to pity, but because they played a less conspicuous part in the active drama of the period.

The house of Grey is no less deserving of our compassion that the house of Mary (Stewart). The daughters of that noble house command in addition our respect and reverence, which are precisely the sentiments we seem to withhold from the Queen of Scots. Perhaps there is something far more touching in the simple narrative of their sufferings, than in the ostentatious history of Queen Mary's misfortunes and death.

The melancholy fate Lady Jane Grey, Lady Catherine Grey and Lady Mary Grey, daughters of Henry Grey, Duke of Suffolk, and Lady Frances Brandon, the grand-daughter of Henry VII, is too well known to require further notice, nor will the student of English history need to be reminded that the Grey sisters were most unhappy in their end. Being the great-grand-daughters of Henry VII, were considered by many to be the rightful heir to the crown of England, and Lady Jane's short and involuntary reign, had rendered her whole family objects of jealousy and suspicion to Queen Elizabeth.

Jane was a first cousin once removed of King Edward VI. In May of 1553, she was married to Lord Guildford Dudley, a younger son of Edward's chief minister John Dudley, Duke of Northumberland. When the 15 year-old king lay dying in June of 1553, he nominated Jane Grey as his successor to the Crown in his will, thereby subverting the claim of his half-sisters Mary and Elizabeth under the Third Succession Act. Jane was imprisoned in the Tower of London when the Privy Council decided to change sides and proclaim Mary as Queen on the 19th of July 1553. Jane was convicted of high treason in November of 1553, which carried a sentence of death. Although initially spared, eventually both Lady Jane and her husband were executed.

After the death of Queen Mary, *her* half-sister Elizabeth came to the throne.

Since Queen Elizabeth was childless, the two surviving Grey sisters were next in line of succession under King Henry VIII's will, and were not permitted to marry without the consent of the Queen. As a penalty for the crime of contracting a marriage with the Edward Seymour, Earl of Hertford, without previously obtaining the Queen's consent, Lady Catherine Grey was committed to the Tower, as well as her husband Edward.

The Lieutenant of the Tower, permitted secret visits between Catherine and Edward. While imprisoned, Catherine gave birth to two sons, Edward, born 1561, and Thomas, born 1563. After the birth of her second child, the enraged Queen Elizabeth ordered Catherine's permanent separation from her husband and sons. Catherine was removed to the care of her uncle, Sir John Grey. She stayed there until November of 1564, when she was transferred to the charge of Sir William Petre for two years. Then she was removed to the care of Sir John Wentworth and after seventeen months there she was taken to Cockfield Hall in Suffolk.

There, Lady Catherine died of consumption fourteen days later on the 26th of January 1568 at the age of twenty-seven.

There was yet another daughter of this devoted house - Lady Mary Grey, the third and youngest sister, whom least of all has been written. Because so little about her has been written, it is this writer's wish to relate her misfortunes at some length. Particularly as it will be seen that her history is intimately connected with that of Sir Thomas Gresham.

She was one of Queen Elizabeth's maids of honor, (not in the marriage sense but as a 'maid' of the Court or as one of Elizabeth's ladies in waiting). She is described by Cecil as the most diminutive lady at Court. Others have said she was deformed with a crooked spine. Historians have suggested she may have suffered from Scoliosis. One would suppose that with this disadvantage of nature and the fate of her two elder sisters, Lady Mary Grey would have taken heed, nor ever thought of matrimony for herself. In her youth, however, she had been betrothed (promised in marriage) to Arthur, Lord Grey of Wilton, and the match having been broken off, forgetful of her birth and station in life, she fixed her affections on a man named Thomas Keys, whom was the 'Gentleman-Porter' of the Queen's household, or more generally called 'The Sergeant-Porter".

Despite the disastrous consequences of her sister Catherine's secret marriage, Mary also now married without the Queen's consent. On the 16th of July, 1565, while the Queen was absent attending the marriage of her kinsman, Sir Henry Knollys and Margaret Cave, Mary secretly married Thomas Keys.

Among the State-Papers of the period, is preserved a document relating to this event, partly in the hand of Sir William Cecil, entitled *"Articles for examination of Lady Mary Grey"*. Annexed to it are her and her husband's answers to several interrogatories to which the unfortunate couple were subjected. It bears the date August the 19th, 1565.

Q: *"What day were you married?"*

A: *"On the day that Mr. Knollys was married."*

Q: *"About what hour?"*

A: *"At about nine o'clock at night."*

Q: *"In what place?"*

A: *"In the Sergeant-Porter's chamber."*

Q: *"How many were present and what were their names?"*

A: *"The Sergeant's brother - Mr. Edward Keys, Mr. Cheney's man, and Martin Causley dwelling at Cambridge were present, besides Mrs. Goldwell, (a servant of the Lady Howard), and the priest, dressed in a short gown, being old, fat and of low stature."*

"The priest had a book of Common Prayer and read the prayers of Matrimony, and the Sergeant gave the lady a little wedding ring."

Among other impertinent questions she was asked were: *"With whom did you speak of this marriage before the same and since? Also, what tokens or gifts have you received of the Sergeant and what gifts have you given?* To which she replied that she never spoke with none before, and that the Sergeant had given her, first, two little rings, next, a ring with four rubies and a diamond, and a chain and little hanging-bottle of mother-of-pearl. Her property and expectations consisted of £80. yearly, paid out of the Exchequer by the hands of one Astell. Upon the death of Mr. Stokes, she and her sister were entitled to 500 marks, saving £40. a year and upon the death of the Duchess of Suffolk, 1000 marks value of land would descend to the two sisters, the Lady Strange and the Lady Montegle.

On the 21st of August, 1565, Sir William Cecil had written to Sir Thomas Smith from Windsor, *"Here is a unhappy chance and monstrous event, the Sergeant-Porter, being the biggest gentleman in this court, hath married secretly the Lady Mary Grey, the least of all the court...the offense is great...they are committed to separate prisons."* Lord William Howard had written to Cecil the day before, somewhat the same sentiments saying, *"A very fond and lewd has fallen out between my Lady Mary and the Sergeant-Porter.* One would suppose from Lord Howard's letter, that he considered the royal prerogative endangered by this marriage - such astonishment does he express at the boldness of the parties concerned.

Mary and her husband never saw each other again. The Queen confined Mary to house arrest with William Hawtrey, at Chequers in Buckinghamshire, where she remained for two years.

William Hawtrey represented an old and respectable family which had become enriched by several prudent alliances. William Hawtrey had been frequently employed on state affairs in Queen Mary's reign. The Privy council sent a letter to Hawtrey on the 29th of August, 1565 signifying to him that the Queen Majesty's pleasure is that he come to the Court and take charge and custody of Lady Mary Grey - to remain at his house without contact with others, requiring only one waiting woman to attend to her and not allowing Lady Grey to leave the premises. For his trouble the Queen Majesty would see that he was 'in reason' satisfied (compensated). On the same day that this order was issued, measures were taken for the apprehension of the minister who had officiated at the marriage ceremony, or as their Lordships were pleased to phrase it, 'the pretend marriage'.

Lady Mary was given in charge to Hawtrey on the 1st of September, with a letter allowing her a groom as well as a gentlewoman and restating that she was not to be allowed to leave. Although this confinement doesn't appear harsh, it was meant to be very severe.

A nicer location, or one better calculated to make the prisoner in love with captivity, could not have been selected than Chequers. The beautiful mansion stood in a shady valley, sheltered by the Chiltern hills and combined all the advantages of an elevated position, with the actual privacy and seclusion of its site. But with a keeper who was inclined to adhere to the letter of his instructions, such a retreat must have lost more than half of its charm.

Lady Mary was probably never allowed to explore the beautiful and romantic surroundings of the estate. It may be, that she was not even permitted the melancholy pleasure or innocent satisfaction of sitting under 'King Stephen's Tree' - a patriarchal elm in the garden at Chequers, but it was no doubt visible to her in her captivity.

Her remembrance is probably to be connected with the interior of the building, with its many rooms and the library with its bay windows which extended nearly the entire length of the building. Lady Mary must have often sat in front of those windows, intent on the books she loved. Or perhaps writing letters to Sir William Cecil relating her woeful conditions and imploring him to use his influence with the Queen, that she might be forgiven and restored to favor. The earliest of these letters was written on the 16th of December when she wrote: *"I did trust to have wholly obtained her Majesty's favor before this time. Which, having once obtained, I trust never to have lost again. But now I perceive that I am so unhappy a creature, as I must yet be without that great and long-desired jewel (freedom), 'till it please God to put in her Majesty's heart to forgive and pardon me of my great heinous crime."*

In such dejected terms, she invariably lamented her fate, at one time calling herself a *"most poor wretch"* and at another, imploring permission to be allowed to see the Queen when she visited the Lord Windsor, at Bradenham, on her return from the University of Oxford.

In a letter in the beginning of 1567, Lady Mary says: *"Good Master Secretary, I have received your message you sent to me by Master Hawtrey, wherein I do perceive you are in doubt whether I do continue in my folly still, or not. Which I assure you, I do as much repent as ever did any. Not only for that I have thereby given occasion to my enemies to rejoice at my fond part, but also for that I have thereby incurred the Queen Majesty's displeasure, which is the greatest grief to me."*

All this time, poor Keys was lying in the dismal Fleet Prison. He complained of the ill effects which close confinement had on his health, and the advantage which he would derive from the freedom to exercise his body. He also stated that he had served at Court for twenty-two years - that is to say, ever since the reign of Henry VIII, and very reasonably urged this as a plea why he should be released and some employment found for him. This was in a letter dated July 25th, 1566 - *"from this miserable place, the Fleet."*

On the 21st of December, Keys again addressed Cecil on the subject of his confinement. A new warden had been appointed to the Fleet Prison who it seems, was guilty of many acts of petty tyranny over his prisoners. He forbade the Sergeant-Porter the use of the Fleet garden and ordered him for nine months to be confined to his cell. The Queen had allowed him to eat meat while in prison, but the warden gave orders that he should have no more while he was incarcerated.

One may be shocked, at the end of two years, to find him still in prison. He addressed a long argumentative letter, full of penitence and pity on the 7th of July, 1567, to Leicester and Cecil where he reveals the painful circumstances that his children were the companions of his captivity. *"...my poor children suffer punishment with me for this my offense."*

We return to Lady Mary Grey, who, according to Cecil's diary, was "exchanged from Mr. Hawtrey to the Duchess of Suffolk's charge,' about the end of July, or during the first week of August, 1567 - having been for the span of two years an "inmate" of Chequers.

The Duchess wrote to Cecil expressing shock at the few pitiful household effects with which Mary arrived at her house in the Minories (a civil parish close to the Tower of London).

"Good Mr. Secretary"

"According to the Queen's commandment, on Friday night last, Mr. Hawtrey brought my Lady Mary to the 'Minories', to me, although I was supposed to go to Greenwich (a borough of London) *and was unable to stay there with her that night. Yesterday, she came hither with me, it would have been sooner if I could. The truth is, I am so unprovided with stuff here myself, as, at Minories I borrow from my Lady Eleanor, and here, my mistress Sheffield. For all the stuff that I had left with me when I came from the other side of the sea, and all that I have since scraped for and gotten together, will not sufficiently furnish our house in Lincolnshire because I have nothing here.*

Meaning now to buy some new things if I could afford it, but with my son's sickness and with that of my maid's recent death, I really have nothing.

I will not lie to you, I was hesitant to declare to Mr. Hawtrey my lack of provisions, and that is, I was praying that my Lady Mary's stuff might arrive. But he told me that before she occupied his place, she came with nothing of her own! Now I see it, and I believe him. I am sorry that I am not as well stored for her as he was. I am compelled to borrow from my friends in the Tower. She has nothing but an old livery feather bed, all torn and full of patches, an old pillow, and an old quilt so torn as the cotton is coming out of it...."

She goes on with the rather long letter explaining what all she would like to have sent to her in order to take proper care of Lady Mary.

Mary would spend the next two years in the care of the Duchess.

In June of 1569, Mary was next sent to live with Sir Thomas Gresham at his house in Bishopsgate and later at his country house at Osterley. Her stay with the Greshams was an unhappy one, however, as Sir Thomas was now half blind and in constant physical pain, and his wife, Anne bitterly resented Mary's presence in the household.

It was during this period of her abode under Gresham's roof, that Queen Elizabeth visited Sir Thomas and had dinner at his residence, on the occasion of naming and grand opening of The Royal Exchange. Having Lady Mary Grey under the same roof must have been awkward to say the least - the haughty Queen, in all her splendor of royalty, confronting the fallen Lady Mary Grey. But, her ill-starred family had one by one perished on the scaffold, or in prison, and she - the last and youngest, had by a single act of imprudence lowered *herself* from the highest rank to the degree of a common subject. She was still, a prisoner, and the Queen's hostility was not to be softened by submission or sympathy.

Just how unwelcome to Sir Thomas Gresham this addition to his family was, appears in every page of his subsequent correspondence. Henceforth he scarcely wrote a letter, either to Sir William Cecil (who was promoted to the title of Lord Burghley in the early part of 1571) or to the Earl of Leicester, without availing himself of the opportunity to urge *"the removing of my Lady Mary Grey."* In August we find him complaining of the burden and again in September he concludes a letter of considerable undertaking with a request *"...that it may please you to do my most humble commendations to my Lord of Leicester and that it may please you both to have my suit of remembrance for my Lady Mary Grey."*

At the end of the year, the following interesting post script is appended to a letter which was written to congratulate Sir William Cecil on his convalescence and return to Court. *"...I have written to my Lord of Leicester to persuade the Queen Majesty the removing of my Lady Mary Grey, who has been with me these 15 months. I pray you to set your good helping hand for the removing of her, for my wife would gladly ride into Norfolk to see her old mother, who is ninety years-old, and a very weak woman, not likely to live long."*

This post script, would suggest that Sir Thomas and Lady Gresham, means no unkindness toward their unfortunate guest, but rather they have other private family matters to attend and having to watch over Lady Mary Grey puts a great amount of pressure on them.

Throughout the years 1570 and 1571, every letter of Gresham contained the same request that Lady Mary Grey might be removed out of his family. The monotony of which these petitions is painfully broken however by a letter dated the 8th of September, from which the following is an extract.

"...*Doctor Smith, (my Lady Mary Grey's physician) as of this day, at 12:00 o'clock noon, brought me word that Mr. Keys, late Sergeant-Porter, is departed.* (died) *which I have broken unto my Lady Mary - whose death she grievously takes. She requested me to write unto you, to be a means to the Queen Majesty so that she may have Her Majesty's permission to keep and bring up his children. And likewise, I desire to know Her Majesty's pleasure, whether I shall allow her to wear black mourning apparel or not."*

"*Trusting that now I shall be presently dispatched* (relieved) *of her, by your good means and my Lord of Leicester's to whom it may please you to do my most humble commendations...."*

Mary's husband, Thomas Keys had been released from Fleet Prison in 1569, and permitted to return to Kent. However, his health had been broken by the conditions of his imprisonment, and he died shortly before September 3rd, 1571.

Mary begged Elizabeth for permission to bring up her husband's orphaned children from his first marriage, but her request was denied.

It seems ludicrous and cannot fail to rouse one's indignation, no matter what one's loyalty may be, to find Elizabeth trifling with the lives of subjects so inoffensive and undeserving of suspicion as the Sergeant-Porter and his high-born lady. One must be also moved by the quaint notice Gresham takes of Lady Mary's sorrow and her natural wish to transfer her widowed affections to the children of the man she had loved. She seems to have indeed "grievously taken" her husband's death. Besides her wish to wear black mourning apparel, which Gresham surely would have allowed the poor woman to wear?

It was not until May of 1572, after Mary had been under strict house arrest for seven years that the Queen relented sufficiently to allow her to live where she pleased. However, for the time being Mary had no friends to take her in, and insufficient income to live independently. She continued to reside as an unwelcome guest with the Gresham's until Sir Thomas suggested that she be sent to live at Beaumanor in Liecestershire with her late mother's second husband, Adrian Stokes who had recently married Anne Carew, the widow of Sir Nicholas Throckmorton. In 1573 Mary left the Gresham household for good, 'with all her books and rubbish', as Sir Thomas put it.

Mary did not stay long at Beaumanor. By February 1573 she was established in a house of her own in London in St. Botolph's. By the end of 1577 she had been rehabilitated to the extent that she was appointed one of the Queen's Maids of Honor. (Yes, you read that right!)

In April of 1578, while the plague was raging in London, Mary became ill and died at the age of 33. In spite of the intrigues involving her sisters, it does not appear that Mary Grey ever made a serious claim to the throne.

CHAPTER XXII

It is unfortunately impossible, more completely than has been attempted in the extracts from letters we have up to now had the privilege to examine, to trace every detail of Sir Thomas Gresham's life. This is especially true during the first five or six years which came after Richard Clough's death.

We see him throughout that period residing principally in Bishopsgate-Street. Lady Mary Grey for three years forms an integral part of the family group.

We know that in October of 1570, when one of his servants became ill with the plague at Osterley, Sir Thomas and Lady Gresham, retired with the household to Mayfield, in Sussex. This place has been for centuries a favorite palace of the Archbishops of Canterbury, and from the magnificent grandeur which yet remains, especially of the spacious hall with its lofty arches, it is not difficult to for an idea of what it must have been in the days of its glory. It surpassed all of Gresham's other residences in splendor, containing furniture, alone which was estimated at £7,550 and it was here that Queen Elizabeth, during her "Kentish" progress in 1573 honored Sir Thomas Gresham with a visit. No particular details of that event are recorded except that on leaving Berling-Place, the seat of the Neville family, Her Majesty progressed to Mayfield on the 2nd and 3rd of August, and was for a few days entertained by its owner, Sir Thomas Gresham.

One of the room is called 'the Queen's Chamber' to this day and is said to be the same room which Queen Elizabeth occupied. Over the mantel-piece in that room is carved the date 1371 and near it, is said to be the crest of the Gresham family, but this is so obliterated as not to be clearly discerned today.

Sir Thomas seems to have come into possession of Mayfield by purchase at an early period of his life. A considerable portion of the palace is still inhabitable, though much of it is in picturesque ruins.

In July of 1572, when Elizabeth was setting out on her summer progress, royal letters were addressed to the Lord Mayor, (Sir Lionel Duckett) desiring him for the better government of the metropolis during her absence and for the maintenance of good order therein, as well as in the suburbs and other places adjoining the city of London out of his jurisdiction, to once every week avail himself of the advice and assistance of the following persons "of great trust, wisdom and experience - the Archbishop of Canterbury, the Bishop of London, Lord Wentworth, Sir Anthony Cook, Sir Thomas Wroth, Sir Owyn Hopton, Sir Thomas Gresham, Dr. Wylson and Thomas Wilbraham."

Such advantageous results were found to ensue from this jurisdiction arrangement that it was afterwards always resorted to on similar occasions. Gresham continued to be one of the commission until within a year of his death.

In 1576, we find Gresham associated with some of the leading men in the state, in an inquiry into the condition of foreign exchanges, and other matters of similar nature. Had the Secretary position of Sir William Cecil been prolonged, we should have had tidings of many of these circumstances from the pen of Sir Thomas Gresham himself. But with his friend Cecil's elevation to title of Lord Burghley in 1571 and to the dignity of Lord-Treasurer in 1572, on the death of the old Marquis of Winchester, a marked change is visible in the State-Papers.

Looking back on Sir Thomas Gresham's life we have seen in the vigor of manhood and when more intent on commercial pursuits, he had devoted a portion of his wealth, as we have seen, to the erection of a Bourse for the convenience of others engaged in the same occupations as himself, for carrying on the commerce of the world. Since the commencement of that undertaking, ten years had now elapsed. The founder of the Royal Exchange had lost an intelligent friend, Sir Richard Clough, from whose suggestions for the need of a Bourse in London, had arisen that edifice. And to whose active co-operation he was in no slight degree indebted for its ultimate and successful completion. Gresham had also lived to witness the most flourishing community in Europe, Antwerp, ruined and reduced to misery by the arbitrary actions of a single individual. Events such as these, may have somewhat cooled his passion for those pursuits which, when he was a young man, the example of his father and uncles had in the strongest manner recommended to his attention, and in the calmer moments which he now often passed - periods of infirmity and confinement, or seasons of relaxation from business, which he had no children to pass on to, he must more than once have had occasion to speculate with the eye of a practical philosopher on the changing circumstances of his past existence.

He had lived during four of the most remarkable reigns which have ever succeeded each other in the annals of English history. His individual experience had taught him how low a value is to be set on the common objects which men propose to themselves in the higher as well as the lower walks of ambition.

Yet such was the happiness of his moral constitution that, the pictures of the past which his memory brought before him, neither soured his temper on the one hand, nor filled him with visionary views on the other. The experience of a long life had evidently brought him to this simple conclusion: that the cultivation of the gifts which a state has in its power to bestow on its youthful members, are sound learning and religious principles.

To the accomplishment of this object, as far as it seemed attainable by his individual exertions, he now nobly resolved to devote the fortune which he had acquired in service to his country.

It was perhaps towards the close of the year 1574, or the beginning of 1575, that Sir Thomas Gresham had sufficiently matured his plan openly to announce his intentions of founding a college in London, for the gratuitous instruction of all who chose to come and attend the lectures.

Not that the project originated at this period, for it is evident that the same, or one very similar, had been for a long time entertained by him. It seems he had once been understood to promise that he would present £500. to the university of Cambridge, where he had been educated, either in support of some ancient foundation, or towards the erection of a new college. Of this, his Alma Mater did not fail to remind him. The letter which he received from Mr. Richard Bridgewater, the public orator, is still in existence. It is dated March 14th, 1574-75 and was followed on the 25th of the same month by another letter, of which the object seems rather to have been to combat any intention Sir Thomas Gresham might have formed of displaying his generosity in London or at Oxford.

London seems to have been regarded by Cambridge officials with peculiar jealousy. The foundation of a college in that city would, Cambridge officials believed, prove prejudicial to the interests of both universities. They urged as their claim to preference before Oxford, that Gresham had himself received his education within the walls of Cambridge. Simultaneously with this second letter, the university addressed the Lady Burghley (whose husband was their Chancellor) requesting her intercession with Sir Thomas Gresham, insinuating that it was at the lady's instance, that Gresham had originally promised to endow a college, which they mention as now about to be erected in London, with a yearly revenue of more than £600.

To the instrumentality attributed to Lady Burghley, little credit is attached, for it rests on no better authority than a few complimentary letters which weigh little as historical documents.

It seems probable indeed, that in erecting Gresham-House, its founder had in view the purpose to which it was ultimately to be applied. Pressing as were the solicitations with which the university of Cambridge assailed Sir Thomas Gresham, he was not to be diverted from his purpose.

Doubtless his reason for remaining firm was that at Cambridge there were public schools already in abundance. While in London, there existed nothing which deserved that name.

In the following July Gresham accordingly framed his will and made every necessary arrangement for the permanent prosperity of a college, which might be justly called the epitome of a university. He ordained that Lady Gresham should enjoy his mansion-house, as well as the rents arising from the Royal Exchange, during her life, in case she survived him. But from the period of her death, both those properties were to be vested in the hands of the corporation of London and the Mercers' Company.

These public bodies were jointly to nominate seven professors, who should lecture successively, one on every day of the week on the seven sciences of divinity, astronomy, music, geometry, law, medicine, and rhetoric. The salaries of the lecturers were amply defrayed by the profits arising from the Royal Exchange and were fixed at £50. per annum. That was more liberal compensation than Henry VIII had appointed for the professors of divinity at Oxford and Cambridge and equivalent to more than 4 or £500. at the present day.

In this enumeration of the seven sciences, it will be observed that Sir Thomas Gresham has assigned to music a very distinguished place. With divinity being first - the most important and the most sublime subject on which man can exercise his faculties - stands foremost; next, astronomy, as the study which introduces him to a knowledge of the heavenly bodies, and most admirable of his "Maker's" works, naturally follows divinity and occupies the second place: but immediately after these and before the mention of geometry, law, medicine and rhetoric - which are to be considered *human sciences* - music is introduced, as of a nature so beautiful, that it may reasonably be debated whether it partakes more of heaven than of earth.

It cannot be concluded from this circumstance that Gresham was himself great lover of music, be that as it may, it is deserving to note that although at Oxford and Cambridge music shares in academic honors with divinity, law, medicine, etc., Gresham College presents the only instance in England of an endowed lectureship for the promotion of that divine art.

But a more important inference may be deduced from the following enumeration of the seven sciences which Gresham appointed to be taught in his college. In an age when the best and wisest men (women were not yet students), were divided on the subject of religion, that the sound handling of the science of divinity should have been the principal object of his concern, is not remarkable. But it may surprise anyone who is familiar with the state of learning in England in the 16th century that astronomy should stand next in the catalogue. Or that it should be there at all.

When we find the principal noblemen of that age paying attention to what *astrologers* say and only valuing the study of the stars as they seemed capable of revealing the destinies of man, we are surprised to see that, at least to Sir Thomas Gresham, astronomy was not confounded with what some today would call the foolish art, which resembles it so closely in name. By associating it with divinity and the serious sciences, he showed himself to be aware of its importance. He was probably able to see that it was capable of being more useful than his contemporaries general believed.

When Gresham founded his lectureship, only Copernicus had written on the subject of astronomy. The science was specifically not included at neither Oxford nor at Cambridge and may be said to have been unknown in England.

With these preliminaries being settled, Sir Thomas Gresham further ordained in his will that the professors should all be 'unmarried men', and that suites of apartments should be allotted to them at Gresham-House. He felt the large garden which surrounded it, and the quiet and retirement of the place would be highly conducive to their comfort and favorable to the pursuits of the scientific persons who would, in the future, make it their residence.

For now, we will leave the subject of Gresham College and may return to it in subsequent pages, but we have seen enough to notice the tone and temperament of the mind of Sir Thomas Gresham as he grew into an old man. We can see the speculations which engaged his thoughts during his declining years.

The charitable bequests which he made at the same time, must also be reserved for a subsequent page, but it should no longer be concealed, that immediately behind his mansion, in the parish of St. Peter-the-Poor, he had constructed eight alms houses for the poor, of which he provided liberally in his will.

...In witness whereof, I, the said Sir Thomas Gresham, have written this will all with my own hand; and to each of the eight leaves, have subscribed my name; and to the label fixed there unto all the eight leaves, have set my seal with the grasshopper..."

"The 5th day of July, in the seventeenth year of the rein of our sovereign lady Queen Elizabeth; and in the year of our Lord God, one thousand, five hundred, and seventy-five."

It has been seen several times that Sir Thomas Gresham made it a frequent practice to retire from the London metropolis to one of his numerous residences in the country.

Take Ringshall near Battisford, in Suffolk for example, we have no description of it but we know that Gresham resided there and in 1566, he made provision for the timber for his Bourse to be acquired from the adjoining woods. In a similar manner, we have noticed Gresham's journey to Mayfield and saw in his letters from that interesting seat, though no chronicler has left us a description of the gaieties which prevailed there when Queen Elizabeth paused at Sir Thomas's house during her summer progress in 1573. Of Westacre, and many other of his residences, nothing is known whatsoever. Perhaps his favorite place of abode was Osterley in Middlesex, still yet, concerning his house there, few particulars are recorded.

It has been mentioned that there occurs an entry in the register of burials at Heston, in which the parish Osterley-House stood. This refers to Gresham's residence in that area in the year 1562. In the spring of 1564, it will be remembered that we had more than one letter written and sent from that old manor-house, which Gresham had demolished and re-built on a grander scale. It is here, Gresham is again to be found in April 1565. Lady Cecil had been ill, and Sir Thomas Gresham addressed her husband saying, *"As I am right sorry that my Lady, your wife, is ill, so I trust, upon her getting well, I shall see you here. which will be no small comfort unto me. Upon Sunday, God willing, I will give my attendance upon you."* And he thanks his friend for his *"warrant for the purchase of Fawknor's fields"* near Osterley. - *"I would have waited upon your honor myself with these letter's"* says Gresham. In the following month of May, *"I have here, Sir Henry Neville another of my kinfolk, but God willing, upon Wednesday, I will give my attendance upon you."* Sir Henry Neville, whom Gresham mentions here, was the husband of his favorite niece and heir-apparent, Elizabeth - the only child of his elder brother, Sir John, who died in 1560.

Lady Elizabeth Neville died in London, November 6th, 1573, at Gresham-House. Her body was taken to her husband's house at Billingbere and interred at the church of St. Lawrence, in Waltham.

In March and April 1566, we have letters from Osterley again, so it seems to have been a favorite spring residence with Sir Thomas Gresham. Unfortunately we have no drawings or paintings of the house as it must have appeared in Gresham's time, but we know from descriptions that it was a *"fair and stately manor of brick"* and it had an extensive park, which is still abundantly supplied with wood and water that it was formerly *"garnished with many fair-size ponds which afforded not only fish and fowl, swans and other water-fowl, but also great use for mills such as paper mills, oil mills, and corn mills."*

These mills, of which a few slight traces are yet discoverable were erected in Osterley Park as early as 1565.

About this time, in fact, Sir Thomas Gresham seems to have become much attached to Osterley for in 1567, we find him wanting to purchase "Heston" the manor house wherein Osterley stands with diverse other parcels of property. He said, *"This place was more for quietness sake and to be Lord of the soils, than for any profit he should attain from it."* It took several months and a letter to Cecil to please remind the Queen Majesty of his desire to purchase it. He finally acquired the property in May of 1570.

Having given the history of Gresham's connection with Osterley as far as we are able, and brought our narrative down to the period which we had reached our digression, it only remains to notice Queen Elizabeth's well-known visit there in 1576 at which time it would appear that Osterley-House was within a year of being completed. With what splendor tis wealthy owner entertained the Queen from whom he had publicly received so many flattering marks of distinction through a long series of years, must be left to the reader's imagination. All we know for certain is, that one of the entertainments with which he sought to render her stay agreeable was a play by his old friend Thomas Churchyard.

If, to enjoy the favor of one's Queen Majesty, to possess the respect and gratitude of one's fellow citizens and to live in the affections of one's poorer neighbors, can produce happiness, then Sir Thomas Gresham, at this period in his life, must have been a happy man.

However, in surveying any one of his mansions, the lack of children must have perpetually awakened in Gresham's heart the melancholy reflection of regret.

With the exception of an occasional guest, Gresham - House was inhabited only by Sir Thomas and the Lady Gresham and a large staff of servants. At one time, Gresham's very limited family circle had been increased by the addition of a son and a daughter. The son, Richard, you may recall had died in 1564 while still in his teen years. The daughter was still alive, but she was not related to Lady Gresham, though she bore her name. Anne Gresham was a natural daughter of Sir Thomas, whose mother is said to have been a native of Bruges, the capital and largest city of the province of West Flanders in the region of Belgium. But nothing more is known with certainty concerning her birth. Towards his daughter, Gresham made the only reparation in his power, by bestowing upon her all the advantage of a careful education, and an ample dower. She married into a family of high distinction. Her husband was Sir Nathaniel Bacon, second son of Sir Nicholas, the Lord Keeper, by his first wife, Jane, daughter of William Fernely. Sir Thomas Gresham had married this lady's elder sister, so that would mean his daughter Anne married someone who could be considered her cousin.

Sir Thomas Gresham was not destined long to enjoy the repose which age brings with it, and to which a life of energy and action had well entitled him. He appears to have been occasioned by a fit of apoplexy, as he returned from an afternoon meeting of the merchants on Saturday, the 21st of November, 1579. Between six and seven o'clock in the evening, coming from the Exchange to his house in Bishopsgate-Street, he suddenly fell down in his kitchen and being helped up, was found speechless and in a matter of minutes, died.

So, at the age of sixty, after having served the government for nearly thirty years with unbroken honor and integrity, died Sir Thomas Gresham, - one of the most illustrious names of which the annals of London can boast. He found credit of the crown in foreign parts reduced to the lowest ebb, but raised it by his prudent management, and left it higher than that of any other power, at a time, by the skill with which he contrived to control the exchange with foreign countries. He may be considered to have laid the foundation of England's commercial greatness, thereby making the balance of trade preponderate in its favor. He is considered 'the great patriarch of commerce and commercial finance.' He elevated the character of the English merchant and was one of the first to dignify the pursuits of trade by showing that they are far from being incompatible with a taste for learning. In the latest actions of his life, he in a manner, restored to the English government the fortune he had acquired in its service, by numerous acts of public endowments and private charities. He was a true patriot.

His remains were interred on the 15th of December, 1579 in the Church of St. Helen's, beneath a tomb which he had constructed for himself during his life time. His body was followed in procession to the grave by two hundred of London's poorer men and women, clothed in black gowns. His funeral was conducted in a style of splendor rarely paralleled in the annals of private life. The expenses for the ceremony are said to have amounted to no less than £800. ($314,506.00 U.S. dollars today, 2017), being more than double the sum that was spent on funeral services of another famous nobleman, Sir John Thynne.

The costly yet unambitious altar-shaped tomb of Sir Thomas Gresham, may be seen in the eastern corner of St. Helen's Church today. The rest of the monument is of alabaster, richly wrought and sculptured on every side with the armorial bearings of Gresham.

The reader has by this time been made sufficiently well acquainted with Sir Thomas Gresham, through his actions and correspondence, to render anything beyond a general summary of his character here is unnecessary. Notwithstanding this. it may be asserted that his letters prove him to have been an extraordinary man. Acute in counsel - prompt in judgment - and energetic in action, beloved in private life and honored in his public station.

His negotiations with foreign merchants were always successful, even in the most difficult time. He was on terms of intimacy or of friendship with most of the leading noblemen of his time. From ever sovereign under whom he served, he received marks of personal favor.

It seems to be scarcely a matter of conjecture, that from his youth upwards Sir Thomas Gresham, in his conversation and conduct, gave indications of abilities of the highest order, or he would not have attracted the notice of

Northumberland while he was yet a young man. Nor would he have maintained through his life the confidence and friendship of Sir William Cecil. Neither would Queen Elizabeth, who was in general, quite sparing of her favors, have so repeatedly bestowed upon him marks of her appreciation. The Queen had indeed ample reason to be proud of her merchant, for while among the constellation of great names which adorn her legacy that of Sir Thomas Gresham shines with no common brilliancy as a patriot and encourager of learning. He was also mainly instrumental in upholding the dignity of her crown by his practical knowledge of business.

Like a hidden spring, Gresham's influence on the financial mechanism of Queen Elizabeth's policy can neither be readily detected, nor perhaps sufficiently appreciated by us today, but it could not fail to be well known by her. Who is to say how far the subsequent safety of the country is to be ascribed to his exertions? Or, who can calculate the limits which are to be set to his influence over England's prosperity?

His two celebrated foundations are, needless to say, lasting monuments to his generosity and public spirit. His humanity and benevolence are obvious in the almshouses he endowed, and the hospitals he enriched. One shouldn't be surprised to find that he contributed large sums to private charities. It should be recorded to his honor that on his strong moral principles, his name is unblemished. This is no slight praise for one who had both enemies and rivals to contend with, and who lived in an age when men did not hesitate to express their opinions of one another.

It is a mark of good-nature, worthy of notice, that Gresham was ever ready to employ his influence with the great, in favor of his less fortunate relations, friends and neighbors.

So much has been written within these pages of the troubles in the Low-Countries that it would be remiss not to tie up the ends to those events and leave the reader in wonder.

History records an event of great importance, the establishment of the memorable union of the seven provinces which placed the affairs of the Low Countries for the first time since the commencement of the troubles in 1566 on a solid basis. To trace all the intervening steps by which this consummation of the efforts of the Prince of Orange had effected, would lead us too far, and at this stage in our historical narrative, would be untimely. But, the narrative is full of interest for further study.

The troubles continued under every change of government, and at Ghent especially the most fatal discord prevailed. But with a view to cementing together his fellow countrymen by stronger ties than they had up to then acknowledged, the Prince of Orange had the determination in the beginning of 1579, to bring about that memorable alliance between the seven northern provinces, known in history by the name of the Union of Utrecht, which brought a cessation of the troubles, and first distinctly emancipated the Low Countries from the tyranny of Spain. This event Gresham lived to witness. It is not a little remarkable, that he who had known the Low Countries in their glory and watched them through every successive stage of misfortune, degradation and decay, should have lived just long enough to behold the reestablishment of order within them and something resembling the reviving of prosperity.

The Lady Anne Gresham survived her husband by seventeen years, living at Osterley in the summer and passing winter months at the mansion house in Bishopsgate-Street. She died at Osterley House on the 23rd of November, 1596. Lady Gresham was survived by many members of her family by her former husband, William Reade, from whom she was widowed before marrying Sir

Thomas Gresham. Her son, Sir William Reade, would live to a great age, being upwards of eighty-three years old before his death. Her grandson, Sir Thomas Reade, who married Mildred Cecil, the second daughter of our old friend Thomas Cecil, Earl of Exeter, died at Osterley without children, on the 3rd of July, 1595, and was buried in Sir Thomas Gresham's vault. The Lady Gertruda Reade, wife of Sir William Reade mentioned above, died on the 24th of October, 1605 and was also buried in Sir Thomas Gresham's vault.

Lady Anne Gresham's remains were interred in St. Helen's Church also in the same vault with Sir Thomas.

Sir Thomas Gresham was the younger son of a private merchant, whose honors were those of a well-spent life. He was the maker of his own fortunes and died while the brightest wits of the Elizabethan age were yet in their cradles.

APPENDIX A:

THE LAST WILL & TESTAMENT
OF
SIR THOMAS GRESHAM

THIS is the last *WILL* written, and Disposition of me, Sir *THOMAS GRESHAM*, of the City of London, Knight, concerning all my Manors, Lands, Tenements and Hereditaments, mentioned and contayned in one Indenture Quadrupartite, made between me the said Sir *THOMAS GRESHAM*, and Dame *ANNE* my Wife, on the one Partie and Philip Scuddamore, Gent. and Thomas Celey, on the other Partie. Dated the Twentieth Day of May, in the Seventeenth Year of the Reign of Our Sovereign Lady Queen *ELIZABETH*.

1

First, Concerning the Buildings in London, called the Royal-Exchange, and all Pawns and Shops, Cellars, Vaults, Messuages, Tenements, and other whatsoever myne Hereditaments, Parcell or Adjoyning to the said Royal Exchange ; I Will and Dispose, that after Expiration and Determination of the particular Uses, Estates and Interest for Life, and Intayle thereof, limited in the said Indenture, bearing Date the Twentieth of May : I Will and Dispose, that one Moiety thereof shall remain, and the Use thereof shall be unto the Major and Commonalty and Citizens of London, by whatsoever especial Name or Addition the same Corporation is made or known, and to their Successors for Term of Fifty Years then next ensuing, upon Trust or Confidence, and to the Intent that they do perform the Payments and other Intents in these Presents hereafter Limited, thereof by them to be done and performed. And the

APPENDIX

other Moiety of the said Buildings called the Royal-Exchange, Pawns, Shops, Cellars, Vaults, Messuages, Tenements and other mine Hereditaments, with the Appurtenances thereto adjoyning, shall remain, and the Use thereof shall be to the Wardens and Commonalties of the Mysterie of the Mercers of the City of London: (viz.) To the Corporate Body and Corporation of the Company of Mercers in London, by whatsoever especial Name or Addition the same Corporation is made or known, and to their Successors, for Term of Fifty Years next ensuing, upon Trust and Confidence, and to the Intent that they do perform the Payments and sufficiently Learned, to read the said Lectures : The same Stipends and Sallaries, and every of them, to be paid at two usuals Terms in the Year, Yearly, (that is to say) At the Feast of the Annunciation of St. Mary, the Virgin, and St. Michael the Archangel, by even Portions to be paid.

2

And farther, That the said Mayor and Commonaltie and Citizens of the said City, and their Successors, from henceforth, so long as they and their Successors shall by any means have, hold, or enjoy the said Moiety before in these Presents to them disposed, shall give and distribute the Sum of Fifty Three Pounds Six Shillings and Eight Pence, of Lawful Money of England, Yearly, in Manner and Form following, (viz.) Unto Eight Almes-Folks, whom the said Mayor and Commonalty and Cityzens, or their Successors, shall appoint to inhabit my Eight Almes-Houses in the said Parish of St. Peter's the Poor, to every of them the said Almes-Folks, the Summe of Six Pounds, Shillings and Four Pence, to be paid at Four usual Terms in the Year Yearly, (that is to say) at the Feast of St Michael the Archangel, the Navity of our LORD GOD, the

APPENDIX

Annunciation of the Virgin Mary, and Nativity of St. John Baptist, by even Portions.

3

And as Concerning the other Moietie, before in this my present last Will disposed to the said Wardens and Commonaltie of the Corporation of the Mercers : I Will and Dispose, that after such Time as the same Moietie, according to the Intent and Meaning of these Presents, shall come to the said Wardens and Corporation of the Mercers ; and from thenceforth, so long as they or their Successors shall by any Means or Title have, hold and enjoy the same, and that they and their Successors every Year, Yearly shall give and pay and distribute to and for the Finding, Sustentation and Maintenance of Three Persons, by them the said Wardens and Commonaltie, and their Successors from Time to Time, to be chosen and appointed, meete to read the Lectures of Law, Physick and Rhetorick, within myne now Dwelling-House, in the Parish of St. Helen's in Bishopsgate-Street, and St. Peter's the Poore in the said City of London, (the Moiety whereof hereafter in this my present last Will, is by me appointed and disposed unto the said Corporation of Mercers) the Summe of One Hundred and Fifty Pounds of Lawful Money of England, in Manner and Form following, (viz.) to every of the said Readers, for the Time being the Summe of Fifty Pounds, for their Sallaries and Stipends, meete for Three sufficiently Learned to read the said Lectures at two usual Feasts in the Year, (that is to say) at the Feast of the Annunciation of the Blessed Virgin Mary, and of St. Michael the Archangel, by even Portions to be paid : And that the said Wardens and Corporation of the Mercers, and their Successors, from henceforth, and so long as they and their Successors shall by any Means have,

APPENDIX

hold or enjoy the said Moiety, before in these Presents to them disposed, shall Yearly Bestow and Expend One Hundred Pounds of Lawful Money of England, in Manner and Form following, (that is to say) severally at Fower several Terms in the Year in and about the Expences and Charges of a Feast or Dynner, for the whole Company of the same Corporation, to be had and made in the Mercers-Hall in the said City of London, at and in every their Quarter-Day, the Summe of Twenty Five Pounds. And that farther, the said Wardens and Corporation of the Mercers, and their Successors, from thenceforth, and so long as they and their Successors shall by any Means have, hold or enjoy the said Moiety, before in these Presents to them Disposed, shall every Year Give and Distribute to the Relief of the poor Persons and Prisoners in the Hospitals, Prisons and Places, called or known by the Names of the Hospitals of Christ or Christ Church, late the Grey-Fryars, in London; the Hospital of St. Bartholomew's, near Smithfield, in London ; the Spittall of Bethlem, near Bishopsgate-Street ; the Hospital for the Poor in Southwark ; and the Counter now kept in the Poultry, and wheresoever the same Prison hereafter shall be kept, Fifty Pounds of Lawful Money of England, in Money or other Provisions and Necessaries for them, (viz.)To every of the said Five Hospitals, Prisons or Places, Ten Pounds, at Four most of usual Feasts or Terms of Payment of Rent within the said City of London accustomed, or within Eight and Twenty Days next after, by even Portions.

4

And as touching my Eight Alms-houses, situate in the Parish of St. Peter's the Poor, at the Backside of the said Mansion-House, in the said City of London; I Will and Dispose, That after the Expiration and Determination of the

APPENDIX

particular Uses, Estates and Interests for Life, and Entail thereof, limited in the said Indenture Quadrupartite, dated the Twentieth of May, That the same Eight Alms-Houses shall remain, and the Use thereof shall be unto the said Mayor and Commonaltie and Citizens of the said City of London, and their Successors, for and during the Term of Fifty Year, from thence next following, fully to be compleat and ended, upon Trust and Confidence, and to the Intent that they do perform the Payments and other Intents, in these Presents hereafter Limited, thereof by them to be done. And my Trust, and Confidence, Will, Intent, and Meaning is, That they the said Mayor and Commonaltie and Citizens and their Successors, after such Time as the same Almes-Houses shall, by Virtue of this my present last Will, come unto them the said Mayor and Commonaltie and Citizens, or to their Successors, and from Time to Time, so long as they or their Successors shall have, hold or enjoy the same by any Title or Means, shall place or putt Eight poor and impotent Persons into the said Eight Alms-Houses, (viz.) into every one of the said Alms-Houses one Person, and shall from Time to Time, suffer the said Eight Persons that shall be so by them or their Successors there placed and putt, to have, occupy and enjoy the same, without any Fine, or other Thing yielded therefore; and shall also pay unto every of the said Persons that so shall be by them placed and put into the said Alms-Houses, the Summe of Six Pounds Thirteen Shillings and Four Pence, of Lawful Money of England, in Manner and Form before in these Presents expressed.

5

And as concerning my said Mansion-House, with the Gardens, Stables, and all and singular other the Appurtenances in the said Parish of St. Helen's in Bishopsgate-Street, and St. Peter's the Poor, in the City

APPENDIX

of London ; I Will and Dispose, That after the End, Determination or Expiration of the particular Estates, Uses, Interests, and Intailes thereof, limited by the said Indenture Quadrupartite, dated the said Twentieth Day of May : The same my said Mansion-House, Gardens, Stables, and other the Appurtenances, shall remain, and the Use thereof shall be to the Mayor, Commonaltie and Citizens of the said City of London, by whatsoever Name or Addition the same is made or known, and to their Successors. And also to the Wardens and Commonaltie of the Mysterie of the Mercers of the City of London, (viz.) To the corporate Body, and Corporation of the Mercers of London, by whatsoever Name or Addition the same Corporation is made or known, to have and to hold, in Common, for and during the Term of Fifty Years from thence next following, fully to be compleat and ended, upon Trust and Confidence, That they observe, Perform, and keep my Will, Intent Meaning, hereafter in these Presents expressed. And my Will, Intent and Meaning is, That the said Mayor and Commonalty and Citizens and their Successors ; and that the said Wardens and Commonaltie of the Mercery, and their Successors, after such Time as the said Mansion-House, Garden, and other the Appurtenances, shall, by Virtue of these Presents, come unto them, and from thenceforth, so long as they and their Successors or any of them, shall have, hold or enjoy the same, by any Title or Means, shall permit card suffer Seven Persons, by them from Time to Time to be elected and appointed, in Manner and form aforesaid, meete and sufficiently Learned to read the said Seven Lectures ; To have the Occupation of all my said Mansion-House, Gardens, and of all other the Appurtenances, for them and every of them, there to inhabit, study, and daily to read the said several Lectures. And my Will is, That none shall be chosen to read any of the said Lectures so long as he shall be

APPENDIX

Married, nor be suffered to read any of the said Lectures after that he shall be Married; neither shall receive any Fee or Stipend appointed for the Reading of the said Lectures.

6

And moreover, I Will and Dispose, that if the said Mayor and Commonaltie, (viz.) the Chief Corporation of the said City : And the said Wardens and Commonaltie of the Mercers, (viz.) the Corporation of the Mercers of the City of aforesaid, before the End of the said Fifty Years, to them in Form aforesaid lymited; shall procure, and obtain; sufficient and lawful Dispensations and Licences, Warrant and Authority, had and obtained, shall have and enjoy the said Royal Exchange, Messuages, Shops, Pawns, Vaults, Houses, and all other the Premisses with the Appurtenances for ever ; severally by such Moieties, Rates, and other Proportions, and in such Manner and Form as before in these Presents is lymited. Upon Trust and Confidence, and to the Intent that they severally for ever shall doe, maintain and perform the Payments, Charges, and other Intents and Meanings thereof before lymited and expressed according to the Intent and true Meaning of these Presents. And that I do require and Charge the said Corporations and chief Governors thereof, with circumspect Diligence, and without long Delay, to procure and see to be done and obtained, as they will answer the same before Almighty God; (for if they or any of them should neglect the obtaining of such Licences or Warrant, which I trust cannot be difficult, nor so chargeable, but that the Overplus of my Rents and Profit of the Premisses herein before to them disposed, will soon recompence the same ; because to soe good Purpose in the Common-wealth, no Prince nor Council, in any Age, will deny or defeat the same. And if

APPENDIX

conveniently by my Will or other Convenience I might assure it, I would not leave it to be done after my Death, then the same shall revert to my right Heirs, whereas I do mean the same to the Common-Weale, and then the default thereof shall be to the Reproach and Condemnation of the said Corporations afore God.) And farther, in Consideration that such Charges of Wardship, Livery and Primier Seizen, as by my Death shall fortune to be done to the Queen's Majesty, of or for all my Lands, Tenements, and Hereditaments, according to the Laws, and Statutes of this Realm shall be paid and born by Sir Henry Nevil, Knight, and by the Heirs Males, which he hath begotton on the Body of Elizabeth his late wife, deceased, Daughter of my Brother Sir John Gresham, Knight, deceased, while she lived my Cousin and Heir. apparent, their Heirs Males, Executors or Assigns. I do Will and Dispose, as concerning my Mannors of Mayefylld and Wardhurst, with the Appurtenances, and all my Lands, Tenements and Hereditaments in the County of Sussex or elsewere, used or reputed or belonging to the said Mannor or Mannors of Mayefylld and Wardhurst, that after the Expiration of the particular Uses, Estates and Interest for Life and Intayle thereof, limited in the said Indenture, the same shall remain, and the Use thereof shall be unto my Cousin, Sir Henry Nevil, and to the Heirs Males of Dame Elizabeth, his Wife, my Niece : And if my said Cousin, Sir Henry Nevil, Knight or the Heirs Males, begotten by my said Niece, shall not within certain Time after my Death, bear or cause to be born the Charges of Wardship, Livery or Primier Seizen, according to the Intent and Meaning of these Presents, That then such Gift, Limitation and Disposition as I have herein made to my said Cousin Nevil, and the Heirs Males of my Niece's Body, shall be utterly void to all Intents and Purposes, as if they and every of

APPENDIX

them had not been mentioned in these, Presents. And then I Will and Dispose, that the same Premises at Mayefylld and Wardhurst aforesaid, or to the same belonging, shall remain, and the Use thereof shall be in such Sort as the Residue hereafter limited shall be.

7

And as concerning all the Residue of all and singular my Mannors, Lands, Tenements and Hereditaments, whatsoever they be, after the Expiration and Determination of the particular Uses, Estates and Interest, for Years, Life, or Intayle thereof, lymited in the said Indenture, and in these Presents : I do Will and Dispose, That the same shall remain, and that the Use thereof shall be unto my said faithful, loving Wife, Dame Anne Gresham, and to hers Heirs and Assigns for ever; and she to use and dispose of the same at her Pleasure, as she shall think meete and convenient ; Requiring, amongst all other Things, That all my Debts, Legacies, and other Duties whatsoever, by me Due, given, lymited or bequeathed to any Person, or witheld from any Person, shall be fully performed, satisfyed and paid and recompenced, as the Case in Law, Right, Equity or Conscience shall require. In which Behalf I do wholly put my Trust in her, and have no Doubt but she will accomplish the same accordingly; and all other Things as shall be requisite or expedient, for both our Honesties, Fames and good Report in this Transitory World, and to the Profit of the Common-Weale, and Relief of the careful and true Poor, according to the Pleasure and Will of Almighty God : To whom be all Honour and Glory, for Ever and Ever. Amen.
In Witness whereof, I the said Sir THOMAS GRESHAM, have written, this WILL all with my own Hand; and to each of the Eight Leaves have subscribed My Name, and to a Labell fixt thereunto all the Eight Leaves, have set to my Seal

APPENDIX

with the Grasshopper, the Fifth Day of July, in the Seventeenth Year of the Reign of our Sovereign Lady Queen ELIZABETH, and in the Year of our LORD GOD, One Thousand Five Hundred Seventy Five, by me, THOMAS GRESHAM

Witnesses to this last Will and Testament, of the said Sir THOMAS GRESHAM, the Persons whose names be subscribed.

P. Scudamor.
Thomas Billingford
Henry Nevil.

APPENDIX B:

GRESHAM'S LAW

In economics, Gresham's law is a monetary principle stating that "bad money drives out good". For example, if there are two forms of commodity money in circulation, which are accepted by law as having similar face value, the more valuable commodity will disappear from circulation.

The law was named in 1860 by Henry Dunning Macleod, after Sir Thomas Gresham (1519–1579), who was an English financier during the Tudor dynasty.

Good money is money that shows little difference between its nominal value (the face value of the coin) and its commodity value (the value of the metal of which it is made, often precious metals, nickel, or copper).

In the absence of legal-tender laws, metal coin money will freely exchange at somewhat above bullion market value. This may be observed in bullion coins such as the Canadian Gold Maple Leaf, the South African Krugerrand, the American Gold Eagle, or even the silver Maria Theresa Thaler (Austria). Coins of this type are of a known purity and are in a convenient form to handle. People prefer trading in coins rather than in anonymous hunks of precious metal, so they attribute more value to the coins of equal weight. The price spread between face value and commodity value is called Seigniorage. Because some coins do not circulate, remaining in the possession of coin collectors, this can increase demand for coinage.

APPENDIX

On the other hand, bad money is money that has a commodity value considerably lower than its face value and is in circulation along with good money, where both forms are required to be accepted at equal value as legal tender.

In Gresham's day, bad money included any coin that had been debased. Debasement was often done by the issuing body, where less than the officially specified amount of precious metal was contained in an issue of coinage, usually by alloying it with a base metal. The public could also debase coins, usually by clipping or scraping off small portions of the precious metal, also known as "stemming" (ridged edges on coins were intended to make clipping evident). Other examples of bad money include counterfeit coins made from base metal. Today all circulating coins are made from base metals, known as fiat money.

Gresham's law states that any circulating currency consisting of both "good" and "bad" money (both forms required to be accepted at equal value under legal tender law) quickly becomes dominated by the "bad" money. (For a formal model see Bernholz and Gersbach 1992). This is because people spending money will hand over the "bad" coins rather than the "good" ones, keeping the "good" ones for themselves. Legal tender laws act as a form of price control. In such a case, the artificially overvalued money is preferred in exchange, because people prefer to save rather than exchange the artificially demoted one (which they actually value higher).

APPENDIX

Consider a customer purchasing an item which costs five pence, who possesses several silver sixpence coins. Some of these coins are more debased, while others are less so – but legally, they are all mandated to be of equal value. The customer would prefer to retain the better coins, and so offers the shopkeeper the most debased one. In turn, the shopkeeper must give one penny in change, and has every reason to give the most debased penny. Thus, the coins that circulate in the transaction will tend to be of the most debased sort available to the parties.

If "good" coins have a face value below that of their metallic content, individuals may be motivated to melt them down and sell the metal for its higher intrinsic value, even if such destruction is illegal. As an example, consider the 1965 United States half dollar coins, which contained 40% silver. In previous years, these coins were 90% silver. With the release of the 1965 half dollar, which was legally required to be accepted at the same value as the earlier 90% halves, the older 90% silver coinage quickly disappeared from circulation, while the newer debased coins remained in use. As the value of the dollar (Federal Reserve notes) continued to decline, resulting in the value of the silver content exceeding the face value of the coins, many of the older half dollars were melted down. Beginning in 1971, the U.S. government gave up on including any silver in the half dollars, as even the metal value of the 40% silver coins began to exceed their face value.

A similar situation occurred in 2007, in the United States with the rising price of copper, zinc, and nickel, which led the U.S. government to ban the melting or mass exportation of one-cent and five-cent coins.

APPENDIX

In addition to being melted down for its bullion value, money that is considered to be "good" tends to leave an economy through international trade. International traders are not bound by legal tender laws as citizens of the issuing country are, so they will offer higher value for good coins than bad ones. The good coins may leave their country of origin to become part of international trade, escaping that country's legal tender laws and leaving the "bad" money behind. This occurred in Britain during the period of the gold standard.

The law was named after Sir Thomas Gresham, a sixteenth-century financial agent of the English Crown in the city of Antwerp, to explain to Queen Elizabeth I what was happening to the English shilling. Her father, Henry VIII, had replaced 40 percent of the silver in the coin with base metals, to increase the government's income without raising taxes. Astute English merchants and even ordinary subjects would save the good shillings from pure silver and circulate the bad ones; hence, the bad money would be used whenever possible, and the good coinage would be saved and disappear from circulation.

Gresham was not the first to state the law which took his name. The phenomenon had been noted much earlier, in the 14th century, by Nicole Oresme. In the year that Gresham was born, 1519, it was described by Nicolaus Copernicus in a treatise called *Monetae cudendae ratio*: "bad (debased) coinage drives good (un-debased) coinage out of circulation." Copernicus was aware of the practice of exchanging bad coins for good ones and melting down the latter or sending them abroad, and he seems to have drawn up some notes on this subject while he was at Olsztyn in 1519. He made them the basis of a report

APPENDIX

which he presented to the Prussian Diet held in 1522, attending the session with his friend Tiedemann Giese to represent his chapter. Copernicus's *Monetae cudendae ratio* was an enlarged, Latin version of that report, setting forth a general theory of money for the 1528 diet. He also formulated a version of the quantity theory of money.

According to the economist George Selgin in his paper "Gresham's Law":

As for Gresham himself, he observed "that good and bad coin cannot circulate together" in a letter written to Queen Elizabeth on the occasion of her accession in 1558. The statement was part of Gresham's explanation for the "unexampled state of badness" England's coinage had been left in following the "Great Debasements" of Henry VIII and Edward VI, which reduced the metallic value of English silver coins to a small fraction of what it had been at the time of Henry VII. It was owing to these debasements, Gresham observed to the Queen, that "all your fine gold was conveyed out of this your realm."

Gresham made his observations of good and bad money while in the service of Queen Elizabeth, with respect only to the observed poor quality of British coinage. The earlier monarchs, Henry VIII and Edward VI, had forced the people to accept debased coinage by means of their legal tender laws. Gresham also made his comparison of good and bad money where the precious metal in the money was the same metal, but of different weight. He did not compare silver to gold, or gold to paper.

APPENDIX C.

GRESHAM COLLEGE
Highlights from Founding to Present Day

Gresham College lectures have been taking place since Elizabethan times. From spies and break-ins through to Dickens and a flood of gin, here are some of the highlights from over 400 years of free public lectures.

1597

Gresham College was founded:

Gresham College was founded in the former mansion of Sir Thomas Gresham, located where Tower 42 now stands on Bishopsgate.

It was the first university in England besides Oxford and Cambridge, making it London's oldest higher education institution still in existence today.

APPENDIX

1597

Professor of Music Smashes Down Walls

One of the original conditions of being a Gresham Professor was that they lodge at the College. John Bull, the famous English composer, friend of Queen Elizabeth I and the first Gresham Professor of Music, took this condition of employment quite seriously.

Fearful of losing his Professorship even before his first lecture, due to the fact his rooms were still occupied by Sir Thomas Gresham's step-son William Reade, Professor Bull forced entry to the rooms by engaging a mason to help him break down a wall.

Naturally this rather annoyed Reade, who then took legal action against Bull.

Ten years later, John Bull was forced to leave his post as Gresham Professor of Music, after he fathered a child with an unmarried woman. However, it is unclear whether he lost his job for this, or for the fact that he then married her, since marriage was forbidden to Gresham Professors at that time.

APPENDIX

1657

Sir Christopher Wren becomes a Gresham Professor:

Christopher Wren was appointed the 9th Professor of Astronomy at Gresham College in 1657. Later to become the architect of modern London after the Great Fire, one of England's greatest ever scientists. Sir Christopher was only 25 when he began his Gresham lectures, which he delivered for the next three years.

APPENDIX

1665

Robert Hooke appointed Gresham Professor:

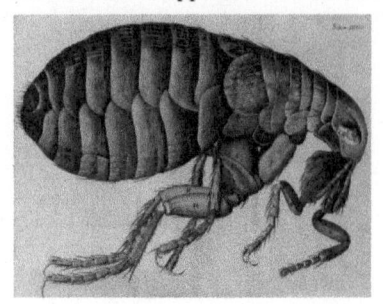

One of England's greatest scientists and inventors, Robert Hooke, was appointed Gresham Professor of Geometry in 1665. This was also the year in which he published his revolutionary and best-known work. *Micrographia,* the first book to illustrate insects, plants, etc. as seen through a microscope. Samuel Pepys – a member of Parliament, described the book as "the most ingenious book I ever read in my life."

Hooke remained at Gresham College until his death in 1703, when he was unfortunately outlived by his great rival, Isaac Newton. It is reputed that Newton is responsible for there being no known surviving portrait of Hooke.

APPENDIX

1666

Samuel Pepys watches an experiment in blood transfusion:

One of the first blood transfusions was carried out at Gresham College. This was recorded in Samuel Pepys' diary in typical brilliant style.

"At the meeting at Gresham College tonight there was a pretty experiment of the blood of one dog let out, till he died, into the body of another on one side, while all his own run out on the other side. The first dog died upon the place, and the other very well, and likely to do well."

"This did give occasion to my pretty wishes, as of the blood of a Quaker to be let into an Archbishop, and such like; but, as Dr. Croone says, may, if it takes – be of mighty use to man's health, for the amending of bad blood by borrowing from a better body."

This was in one of the meetings of the Royal Society, which operated within Gresham College during this period.

APPENDIX

1666

The Great Fire

The Great Fire of London burnt down most of the city, but spared Gresham College.

However since the Royal Exchange had been destroyed by the fire, King James I decreed that the traders and merchants would meet to do business at Gresham College. Therefore, overnight the College changed from a sleepy home of academia into being a heaving place of commerce with over 3000 traders crowding into the College.

APPENDIX

1710

The Royal Society move out of Gresham College:

Having been founded at the College in 1660 and spending the subsequent 50 years operating within Gresham College, The Royal Society finally moved to their own place in 1710, located on Crane Street, not far where Gresham College is based today.

The Royal Society started from groups of physicians and natural philosophers. The society's core members are scientists and engineers from the United Kingdom and the Commonwealth selected based on having made a substantial contribution to the improvement of natural knowledge, including mathematics, engineering, science and medical science. Members are elected for life. Sir Isaac Newton was one of the earliest members of the Royal Society, elected in 1672.

Among the present-day scientists, Stephen Hawking is a member, elected in 1974.

APPENDIX

1821

Latin – the language of Professors

Gresham College ceased in 1821, to require lectures be delivered in Latin by its Professors. The requirement to offer lectures in English *and* Latin had been in place since the founding of Gresham College in 1597. Then, it was an assurance of the accessibility and usefulness of the lectures. Sir Thomas Gresham had wanted his College to be a place of international learning and so he wanted visiting scholars from all over the world to be able to meet and learn at Gresham. Two-hundred and twenty-four years later, Latin was no longer the way to achieve this, but the accessibility mission continues to this day.

APPENDIX

1842

The "New" Gresham College is opened.

Gresham College gets a new home, on the corner of Gresham Street and Basinghall Street. The building is still standing, although today it is used for other purposes. The hall and many of its original furnishings are still as they were.

APPENDIX

1891

10.000 Pennies scattered on the lecture hall floor.

Karl Pearson, perhaps the most important mathematician of modern statistics, was a Gresham Professor of Geometry between 1891 and 1893. His lectures on "The Geometry of Statistics and The Laws of Chance" were very popular, drawing audiences of as many as 300 students.

It is, however, likely that the College's administration didn't think him quite so wonderful, due to the props he would sometimes use. Reports tell us that in some lectures he used dice, roulette wheels and 10,000 pennies scattered on floor!

APPENDIX

1942

Party in the Blitz

The College ceased to offer lectures during the bombing of London throughout WWII. The College premises did not sit idle though, having been used briefly by the Air Raid Disasters Department, it was subsequently used as a venue for dances and concerts. In the summer of 1942 around 27,000 people paid to attend concerts in the hallowed halls.

APPENDIX

1991

The College Moves Into Barnard's Inn Hall

The College finds a new permanent home in the 14th Century hall off High Holborn.

Barnard's Inn was established as an Inn of Chancery in 1454, where it acted as a school for law students. The hall as it is today dates from the 15th Century with 16th Century linen fold wood paneling. The roof timbers include the only surviving crown posts in Greater London, as the Great Fire of London stopped just meters away from the hall on Fetter Lane.

APPENDIX

1993

The First Female Professor

Heather Couper became the first ever female Professor at Gresham College in 1993. She was appointed Gresham Professor of Astronomy...after only 396 years of the College's existence!

APPENDIX

1997

400 Years of Gresham!

Having been founded in 1597, the College celebrated its quad-centennial in 1997 with a book on the College's history. Written by Richard Chartres (Bishop of London and Emeritus Gresham Professor of Divinity) and David Vermont (former Chairman of the Gresham College Council), the book is as interesting as this history would suggest.

Please contact the College if you are interested in obtaining a copy of the book.

APPENDIX

2000

Film

The first ever lecture to be filmed at Gresham College took place on Monday, the 14th of February, 2000. The lecture was titled: "Governance and the City" delivered by Professor Daniel Hodson.

APPENDIX

2017

Lectures Continue on a variety of subjects:

May 16, 2017 - Professor Vernon Bogdanor delivers a lecture on 'Queen Elizabeth II'. 6pm, Museum of London

Bibliography:

Calendar of State Papers Foreign: Henry VIII
Calendar of State Papers Foreign: Mary I
Calendar of State Papers Foreign: Edward VI
Calendar of State Papers Foreign: Elizabeth, Vols. 1-13
British History Online:
The Life and Times of Sir Thomas Gresham by J.W. Burgon (London, 1839, new edition 1968)
Sir Thomas Gresham (1518–1579) by F. R. Salter (Parsons, London, 1925)
Baynes, T.S., ed. (1875–1889). "Sir Thomas Gresham". *Encyclopedia Britannica (9th ed.)*. New York: Charles Scribner's Sons.
Welch, Charles (1890). "Gresham, Thomas". In Stephen, Leslie; Lee, Sidney. *Dictionary of National Biography*. **23**. London: Smith, Elder & Co.
Blanchard, Ian. "Gresham, Sir Thomas (c.1518–1579)". *Oxford Dictionary of National Biography (online ed.)*. Oxford University Press. doi:10.1093/ref:odnb/11505.

Adrian Stokes, 232
Alexander Blyth, 6
Alice Blyth, 6
Alva, 206, 207, 208, 209, 210
Amy Dudley, 144
Anna of Saxony, 96
Anne Boleyn, 10, 70
Anne Carew,, 232
Antonio Bonvisi, 115
Antwerp, 18, 20, 21, 22, 23, 32, 33, 35, 36, 37, 39, 40, 41, 47, 54, 55, 56, 57, 58, 60, 63, 64, 68, 69, 71, 75, 76, 77, 79, 83, 84, 89, 90, 92, 93, 101, 103, 105, 106, 107, 108, 109, 110, 112, 113, 117, 118, 135, 137, 138, 140, 141, 142, 155, 158, 159, 160, 164, 165, 166, 167, 169, 170, 171, 182, 189, 191, 192, 193, 194, 195, 197, 198, 205, 206, 209, 210, 237
Archbishop of Canterbury, 236
Arthur, Lord Grey of Wilton, 222
assassination, 96
Audrey Lynne, 10
Balthasar Gerard, 96
Bishopsgate, 53, 113, 114, 169, 214, 229, 235, 245, 248, 253, 255
Blood Court, 196
Bothwell, 179, 183, 202, 203, 205
Bourse, 71, 105, 110, 171, 172, 180, 181, 182, 194, 205, 214, 215, 216, 236, 242
Brussels, 14, 46, 48, 56, 84, 91, 92, 165, 167, 188, 189, 191, 192, 193, 195, 196, 198, 208
Cambridge, 13, 30, 223, 238, 239, 240, 241
Candelier, 158

Candiller, 54, 67, 70
Cardinal Wolsey, 10
Carlos, 95, 151, 153, 173, 174
Catholic, 30, 34, 35, 46, 49, 61, 74, 85, 115, 136, 168, 173, 174, 175, 177, 179, 181, 186, 196, 203, 213
Catholic Church, 115
Cecil, 34, 54, 56, 58, 60, 63, 64, 65, 66, 68, 69, 73, 74, 75, 81, 82, 83, 87, 103, 104, 105, 106, 109, 114, 117, 118, 119, 120, 121, 122, 123, 124, 125, 135, 149, 150, 151, 156, 157, 158, 159, 163, 166, 167, 168, 174, 193, 194, 195, 199, 222, 224, 227, 228, 236, 242, 243
Chamberlain, 9, 163
Charles V, 14, 18, 22, 43, 185
Clough, 64, 75, 76, 77, 90, 94, 95, 107, 108, 111, 112, 155, 165, 170, 180, 182, 185, 190, 191, 193, 194, 195, 200, 205, 206, 208
Council of Trent, 103, 136
Count Mansfeld, 64, 74, 75, 76, 78, 139
Count Meghem, 188
Darnley, 61, 173, 174, 175, 176, 177, 178, 179, 183, 201, 202, 213
Duke Augustus, 102
Duke of Alba, 195
Duke of Farrara, 141
Duke of Guise, 136, 137, 138, 139, 143, 155
Duke of Holst, 102
Duke of Savoy, 46, 138, 140
Duke of Saxony, 103
Earl of Arundel, 30

Earl of Pembroke, 30
Earl of Warwick, 16, 17, 86, 152
Edward Courtenay, 43
Edward III, 7
Edward VI, 5, 15, 16, 20, 25, 27, 28, 36, 69, 85, 86, 115, 220, 261
Egmont, 187, 196
Elizabeth, 5, 9, 10, 28, 29, 34, 36, 41, 43, 44, 45, 46, 48, 49, 52, 54, 56, 58, 60, 61, 63, 65, 69, 70, 73, 74, 75, 77, 81, 82, 84, 87, 107, 113, 117, 119, 121, 122, 137, 139, 140, 143, 144, 147, 149, 150, 151, 152, 153, 156, 159, 163, 164, 166, 167, 173, 174, 175, 176, 181, 199, 200, 203, 210, 211, 212, 213, 214, 215, 219, 220, 221, 222, 229, 231, 235, 236, 242, 243, 244, 247, 257, 261
Elizabeth I, 5, 34, 36, 41, 70, 121
Emmanuel Philibert, 46
Flanders, 7, 10, 20, 33, 39, 40, 41, 46, 54, 55, 56, 57, 68, 84, 87, 103, 107, 113, 135, 136, 141, 142, 155, 156, 157, 166, 167, 168, 169, 170, 181, 182, 186, 187, 189, 195, 206, 244
Francis Dereham, 9
Fugger family, 22
Gérard, 96, 97, 98, 99, 100
Gresham, 5, 6, 7, 9, 10, 11, 13, 14, 15, 20, 23, 24, 30, 34, 36, 37, 38, 39, 51, 53, 56, 63, 64, 65, 66, 68, 69, 70, 74, 75, 77, 79, 82, 83, 84, 87, 106, 112, 113, 114, 117, 120, 125, 158, 159, 164, 166, 169, 170, 171, 180, 193, 197, 214, 232, 235, 237, 238, 240, 241, 242, 243, 244, 246

Alice, 5
James, 5
John, 5
Lady, 5
Thomas, 5
Gresham-House, 113, 114, 205, 239, 241, 243
Guildford
Jane, 15
Hans Keck, 75, 79
Henry Carey, 70
Henry Stuart, Lord Darnley, 173
Henry VIII, 5, 6, 8, 9, 10, 14, 15, 16, 17, 21, 29, 36, 69, 85, 115, 144, 173, 174, 181, 221, 227, 239, 261
Horn, 196, 208
Hospital of St. John, 181
Hugh Latimer, 35
Inquisition, 104, 136, 185, 186, 187, 188, 195, 196, 209
Intwood, 16, 156, 158, 164, 169
Intwood-Hall, 16
Isabella Worpfall, 11, 176
Isabella Worpfall-Gresham, 176
James Gresham, 5
James Hepburn, 179
James Hepburn, the Fourth Earl of Bothwell, 179
Jane Grey, 15, 28, 29, 43, 220
Jane Seymour, 16
Jarman Sewell, 114, 115
Jasper Schetz, 21
Jean Gordon, Countess of Bothwell, 203
Jean Scheyfve,, 27
John Bellenden, 73
John Bradford, 35
John Dudley, 13, 15, 17, 86, 144, 220

John Gresham, 5, 6, 7, 8, 16, 24, 84, 114
John Hooper, 35
John Lingard, 49
John Rogers, 35
Keck, 75
King Edward, 15, 16, 21, 22, 24, 27, 35, 69, 75, 85, 112, 161, 163, 220
King Francis II, 73
King James V, 58
King of Denmark, 102
King of Spain, 46, 58, 96, 103, 135, 139, 140, 141, 143, 198, 199, 211
King of Sweden, 102, 104, 106
King Phillip, 195, 196, 198
King Philp, 96
Kirk o' Field, 183, 201
Knollys, 103, 223
Lady Catherine Grey, 220, 221
Lady Dormer, 56
Lady Frances Brandon, 220
Lady Gresham, 107, 169, 239, 244
Lady Isabella Gresham, 8
Lady Margaret Douglas, 173
Lady Mary Grey, 220, 222, 223, 224, 225, 228, 229, 230, 231, 235
Landjuweel, 89, 90, 93
Leicester, 122, 181, 227, 230, 231
London, 6, 7, 8, 9, 10, 13, 15, 18, 20, 29, 30, 38, 39, 40, 41, 44, 46, 51, 52, 53, 54, 56, 57, 70, 75, 77, 79, 83, 84, 87, 89, 94, 101, 107, 109, 110, 112, 113, 115, 156, 157, 158, 159, 166, 169, 170, 171, 172, 181, 182, 185, 194, 200, 205, 214, 215, 216, 221, 228, 232, 236, 237, 238, 239, 242, 243, 245, 246, 251, 252, 253, 254, 255, 261
Lord Abergavenny, 43
Lord Chancellor of England, 115
Louis of Nassau, 187, 209
Low Countries, 10, 19, 41, 53, 56, 66, 95, 96, 125, 136, 155, 185, 186, 188, 189, 190, 194, 196, 200, 206, 207, 211, 213, 248
Low-Countries, 6, 168, 169, 171, 248
Margaret Cave, 223
Margaret of Parma, 96, 191, 195, 208, 210
Margaret Tudor, 61
Mary Boleyn, 70
Mary I, 5, 42, 70, 261
Mary of Guise, 58, 60, 61, 73, 74
Mary Queen of Scots, 73, 150, 173, 176, 179, 183, 202, 205, 212, 213
Mercers' Company, 6, 7, 176, 239
Merchant-Adventurers, 79
Monsieur D'Essé, 59
Nathanial Bacon, 15
Nicholas Wotton, 73
Northumberland, 13, 15, 17, 22, 28, 29, 30, 34, 46, 47, 144, 152, 158, 220, 247
Osterley, 114, 169, 229, 235, 242, 243, 244, 248
Oxford, 226, 238, 239, 240, 241, 261
Philip, 43, 45, 46, 47, 48, 49, 56, 57, 58, 76, 78, 92, 96, 99, 100, 102, 114, 135, 136, 137, 151, 152, 156, 166, 181, 186, 187, 188, 189, 196, 206, 207, 208, 209, 213, 251
Phillip de Marnix, 186

Pope, 83, 94, 95, 111, 140
Pope Pius IV, 94, 95
Prince of Condé, 136, 137, 138, 139, 141, 142
Prince of Mantua,, 138
Prince of Orange, 95, 96, 97, 100, 102, 187, 188, 196, 198, 199, 200, 209, 248
Privy Council, 29, 30, 143, 144, 149, 151, 179, 221
Protestant Reformation, 115
Queen Catherine Howard, 9
Queen Elizabeth, 60, 69, 117, 119, 163, 219, 222, 244, 247
Queen Mary, 9, 34, 36, 39, 42, 43, 45, 69, 85, 112, 114, 115, 144, 152, 161, 180, 220, 221, 224
Queen of Scots, 46, 58, 61, 150, 151, 152, 219, 220
Queen's Majesty, 31, 55, 65, 69, 70, 71, 75, 76
Ratcliffe, 210, 211
Reginald Pole, 43, 47, 48
Riccio, 177, 178, 179
Richard Clough, 41, 42, 75, 89, 90, 94, 100, 102, 107, 112, 155, 167, 170, 171, 181, 190, 192, 205, 214, 235, 237
Richard Gresham, 6, 170, 176
Richard II, 7
Ringshall, 180, 181, 182, 194, 242
Robert Dudley, 64, 81, 138, 143, 144, 146, 149, 151, 152, 158, 173, 174
Roman Catholic Church, 74, 136
Royal Exchange, 6, 171, 172, 182, 214, 215, 216, 217, 229, 237, 239, 251, 256

Scotland, 15, 58, 59, 60, 69, 73, 74, 81, 85, 119, 151, 152, 153, 177, 179, 202, 203, 212, 213
Secretary Paget, 14
Seymour, 14, 16, 85, 221
Shakespeare, 115, 216
Sir Edward Guildford, 15
Sir Francis Bacon, 15
Sir John Robsart, 144
Sir Robert Southwell, 43
Sir Thomas Chamberlain, 100, 105, 161
Sir Thomas Cotton, 165, 169
Sir Thomas Gresham, 5, 6, 11, 42, 75, 86, 89, 112, 113, 114, 117, 170, 180, 182, 214, 235, 236, 238, 239, 241, 242, 245, 247
Sir Thomas More,, 115
Sir Thomas Parry, 56, 63, 64, 66, 69, 78, 82, 117
Sir William Cecil, 56, 57, 60, 65, 66, 69, 75, 83, 101, 105, 112, 117, 120, 137, 143, 144, 163, 180, 205, 223, 224, 226, 230, 236, 247
Sir William Dansell, 19, 31
Sir William Paston, 5
Smith, 122, 161, 163, 224, 231, 261
Somerset, 16, 17, 18, 59, 84, 85, 86, 122, 214
The Regent, 14, 167, 191, 211, 212
Thomas Blount, 145
Thomas Cranmer, 28, 35
Thomas Culpepper, 9
Thomas Keys, 222, 223, 231
Thomas Sackville, 82
Thomas Wriothesley, 17
Thomas Wyatt, 43
Throckmorton, 55, 119, 123, 149, 161, 163, 232

Tower of London, 10, 45
William Ferneley, 15
William Fernely, 245
William Harvey, 56
William Hawtrey, 224
William Lynne, 10, 13
William Maitland, 73, 152, 177

William Paget, 30
William Paulet, 48, 68, 81, 122
William Rastell, 115
William Read, 15
William Roper, 115
William the Silent, 95, 96, 98
Worshipful Merchants, 216

Printed in July 2019
by Rotomail Italia S.p.A., Vignate (MI) - Italy